POLICING THE VICTORIAN COMMUNITY

£4.50

POLICING THE VICTORIAN COMMUNITY

The formation of English provincial police forces, 1856-80

Carolyn Steedman

ROUTLEDGE DIRECT EDITIONS

ROUTLEDGE & KEGAN PAUL
London, Boston, Melbourne and Henley

First published in 1984
by Routledge & Kegan Paul Plc
39 Store Street, London WC1E 7DD,
9 Park Street, Boston, Mass. 02108, USA,
296 Beaconsfield Parade, Middle Park,
Melbourne, 3206, Australia, and
Broadway House, Newtown Road
Henley-on-Thames, Oxon RG9 1EN
Printed in Great Britain by
Hartnoll Print, Bodmin, Cornwall

Library of Congress Cataloging in Publication Data

Steedman, Carolyn.
   Policing the Victorian community.

   (Routledge direct editions)
   Bibliography: p.
   Includes index.
   1. Police--England--History--19th century.
2. England--Politics and government. 3. County
government--England--History--19th century.
4. Boroughs--England--History--19th century. 5. Labor
and laboring classes--England--History--19th century.
I. Title.
HV8195.A5E537 1983.   363.2'0942   83-4467
ISBN 0-7100-9575-9

CONTENTS

Preface   vii
Acknowledgments   ix
Abbreviations   xi
Introduction   1

PART ONE GOVERNMENT AND POLICING   11
1 Government and policing   13
     i   Legislation   13
    ii   Towards 1856: models and theories   17
   iii   Towards 1856: soldiers and policemen   21
    iv   The County and Borough Police Act   25
     v   The Home Office and the provinces   27
    vi   Policemen as soldiers: the Murphy Riots   32
   vii   The Government Inspectors of Constabulary   38
  viii   Borough versus county   41
    ix   The pattern of county policing   47
     x   The structure of county control   50
    xi   The rise and fall of an administrative police   53
   xii   The police and the vagrant poor   56
  xiii   Ratepaying as theory   59

PART TWO MEN AND POLICEMEN   65
2 Making a county force   69
3 Origins   80
4 Becoming policeman   92
5 A policeman's life   106
6 An entirely new situation   116
7 Security: the campaign for police pension rights   124
8 Identity   131
     i   Policemen as working men: on strike   132
    ii   The trade of policeman   137
   iii   Good and faithful servants   143
9 Possibilities: the example of the licencing laws   148
10 Conclusion   157
   Notes   165
   Bibliography and sources   201
   Index   211

PREFACE

The original research on which this book is based was prompted by a
silence on the part of mid-nineteenth-century commentators on the
questions of police and policing in provincial England. This nineteenth-century absence of comment was echoed in the few police histories that were available twelve years ago, which dealt in almost
exclusively Metropolitan terms.

Yet it was clear that the analytic silence of the mid-Victorian
years masked theories of control and management that were used in
the governmental circles of provincial communities in the years
after 1856, the date of the first compulsory police act. It has
been pointed out that much modern sociological investigation of
the police 'assumes that we "know" what the police, as an institution, really is'. This casual assumption of knowledge allows
'common-sense' definitions to take the place of theoretical understanding, (1) and these modern, everyday definitions have often,
in their turn, been transported back to the mid-nineteenth century
as a device of historical interpretation. (2)

It became obvious very early during the course of the research on
which this book is based that the ideology that informed the government and control of mid-nineteenth-century provincial communities
could not often be revealed by the use of modern definitions of
police and policing, whether they were of the common-sense or analytic variety. A complicated set of theories underlay the management of provincial police forces between 1856 and 1880. As the
roots of those theories lay in various contemporary perceptions
of a governmental and social context, then they had to be interpreted in the light of that context.

This book attempts to deal with the particularity of that perception; and so it becomes not so much an account that tells of the
police (though it certainly does that) as of the way in which a
society, at many levels, and from many class perspectives, understood itself to operate, and of the way in which theories of ownership, servitude, obligation, and the reciprocality of social relations manifested themselves in different communities.

In pursuit of a mid-nineteenth-century particularity, this books
deals, among other questions, with the division of labour in police
hierarchies, the emergence of Victorian policing as both a craft

and a profession, and with the way in which notions of professionalism were used by certain policemen to argue against what would,
in modern terms, be called accountability. The class background
of mid-nineteenth-century police recruits and the contradictory
nature of their class position is seen as fundamental to the questions of who controlled the police in the provincial communities
of Victorian England. All these questions, as far as they concern modern police forces, have received a great deal of attention
since the research on which this book is based was completed. (3)
Had recent sociological investigations been available ten years ago
then my archive research could have been directed somewhat differently — and much more easily. Particularly, the question of
who controls a working-class police in a class society could have
been pursued more sharply and directly.

However, the final historical narrative would have remained much
the same. This seems particularly clear over the question of
'policing'. A complex and sophisticated definition of policing has
emerged from recent sociological inquiry, an account of the way in
which societies might be regulated through the manipulation of ideas
and images as much as through coercion. (4) Had this kind of
definition been available in 1970, I would have had a label for what
I was searching, and a sharper understanding of what magistrates
and watch committee members were up to as they manipulated the
metaphors of soldiers and servants in sending their policemen upon
the streets. In fact, the mid-nineteenth-century theory and practice of policing that emerges from these pages is the historical
groundwork of more recent definitions.

Most of the archive research on which this book is based was
undertaken when I was a post-graduate student at Cambridge between
1969 and 1972. An earlier account is deposited in Cambridge University Library. (5) Recently, some use has been made of this
earlier work in Victor Bailey (ed.), 'Policing and Punishment in
Nineteenth Century Britain'. (6) I am pleased that it has proved
helpful in this way, but I would like to make it clear that more
recent archive research on my part, and reconsideration of my
original material, would now lead me to oppose some of the conclusion that my earlier findings are used to support. Particularly,
I do not now consider that 'no radical alteration in the general
structure of policing took place following the County and Borough
Police Act of 1856'. (7) In fact, 19 & 20 Vict. c.69 had a profound effect on the local administration of local law, and the
policing that upheld it.

ACKNOWLEDGMENTS

This book has been some time in the making, and those who have helped
me with their comment and advice over the years may well have forgotten doing so. I should like to express my gratitude to the following people: Henry Parris, Peter Hennock, John Vincent, Geoffrey Best,
Mr D. T. Brett, the Librarian of the Police College at Bramshill,
Mr F. B. Stitt, the Archivist of the County of Staffordshire, Gill
Sutherland, Raphael Samuel, Philip Donnellan, whose BBC television
production 'Gone for a Soldier', broadcast in March 1980 led me to
John Pearman's Memoirs; and Karen Clarke. More recently, the advice
of Stephen Yeo, Rodney Mace and Maureen Cain has been invaluable.
Peter and Betty Pearman of Silver Springs, Maryland generously provided me with hospitality, access to John Pearman's Memoirs, family
letters and memories, during January 1981. I am extremely grateful
for their help.

This book is based to a large extent on original work undertaken
between 1969 and 1972, an account of which is deposited in Cambridge
University Library under the name of Pilling and the title 'The
Police in the English Local Community, 1856-1880'. This early
research was funded by a Social Science Research Council grant, held
at Newnham College, Cambridge. I am grateful for the financial support of the SSRC, and of the Fellows of Newnham College.

ABBREVIATIONS

HMIC	Her Majesty's Inspector of Constabulary
HO	Home Office
PP	Parliamentary Paper
PMAA	Police Mutual Assurance Association
QS	Quarter Sessions
RIC	Royal Irish Constabulary

In this book all chief officers of police in counties are called 'chief constables', and all those in boroughs 'head constables', though the title in boroughs was often 'superintendent', 'chief superintendent', or 'chief constable'.

INTRODUCTION

This book deals with the creation of English police forces as part
of a system of local government in the years between 1856 and
1880. The police history that has been produced for a century now
by policemen and ex-officials of the Home Office (1) has had a
profound effect not only on policemen's understanding of their role
in past and present communities, but also on the administrative
historians who have produced a police history for academic consumption. This book is intended as a corrective to those accounts
that see the formation of police forces as the product of the
application of an urban — specifically a Metropolitan — model in
the provinces. (2) In fact, provincial watch committees and rural
magistrates developed coherent theories of local government and
policing during this period. It was their understanding of social
discipline and community order that provided the background to the
development of mid-nineteenth-century police forces. The first part
of this book deals with this background. But within this context
it was the working-class men who became provincial policemen, who
out of their understanding of these administrative circumstances,
shaped recognisably modern police forces. The second part of this
book deals with this development, and those men.

The policemen who have written the greater part of police history have understood something of the importance of the relationship between local policemen and local government in the mid-
Victorian years. The inspectors and superintendents who were
commissioned in 1956 to write local force histories to celebrate
a century of compulsory policing knew that the history of 'the men'
was important. (3) They searched for something more than changes
in uniform, the altered silhouette of helmets and the introduction
of bicycles and fingerprinting in order to measure a changing
relationship between policemen and local government. They were
unable though, to find this relationship, because the policeman
they had in mind was the patient, neutral, respectable <u>officer</u>
whose conscious creation was one of the developments of the years
1856 to 1880. The model constructed in those years does not fit
the thousands of working-class men who joined Victorian police
forces, and who left, never having in fact become policemen in this
sense. Nineteenth-century police forces consistently present this

contrast between an extraordinarily stable officer class, and a
fluctuating, impermanent lower rank. Town councils debated the
problem, inspectors of constabulary annually devised explanations
for it in their reports to the Home Office, and any administrative
history that ignores the rapid turnover of the lower ranks in all
mid-Victorian police forces cannot explain how modern police forces
were brought into being.

   Though it was the class of permanent policemen, officers for the
main part, who agitated for pension rights, who turned local police
Friendly Societies into a nation wide assurance association, who
took the initiative in all national organisation and who bought
their right to middle class sympathy by a consistent presentation
of themselves as a 'very patient, long-suffering set of men', it
was that much larger group of constables who made up the fluctuating lower ranks that was used as a tool of social policy by local
governments. Police hierarchies in the mid-nineteenth century
reflected rigidly the social hierarchy of their time. Police
officers were recruited as officers, drawn from the ranks of
failed farmers, former land agents, bailiffs and clerks. (4)   The
men under them, unimportant working-class men, were recruited and
maintained as such by local police hierarchy and local government.
What was bought when a rural labourer signed a police recruitment
form was not just his willingness to work for low wages, but his
understanding and acceptance of a set of social relationships.
This understanding was sought out, and paid for, by rural police
authorities and urban watch committees alike.

   In both counties and boroughs the largest group of policemen
was drawn from a rural labouring background, and men with the social
assumptions dictated by that experience were deliberately recruited
in cities as well as in the countryside. Indeed, it was not only
in the excellent deference of its working men-become-policemen that
county police management was seen, in a reversal of much nineteenth-
century administrative precedent, as a model for urban law-keeping
and social discipline. The County and Borough Police Act of 1856
(19 & 20 Vict. c.69), which compelled all local authorities to set
up police forces, defined the traditional rural area of judicial
administration — the petty sessional division — as the essential
unit of rural police distribution and deployment. In thus revers-
ing the tendency of previous permissive police legislation of the
1830s and 1840s to supercede this judicial unit, and by putting
the individual magistrate at the apex of the local police division,
the power of rural justices, acting both individually and cor-
porately in quarter sessions, was actually strengthened in the
years after 1856. This aspect of the day-to-day police activity
in county police divisions therefore contradicts the picture
presented by much administrative history, of the slow, but inexorable, dominance of central government over local in police
matters. (5) The formation of a compulsory police in 1857, and
legal changes embodied in the County and Borough Police Act of
1856, which allowed local government to use policemen for
a wide range of administrative functions within local communities,
actually increased the local powers of local governments.

   This provincial experience was well understood at the Home
Office, though an assertion of the rights of all local government

was scarcely created by or applied to Home Office policy. Indeed, the traditional picture of the inspectors of constabulary carrying Home Office principles of regulation and neutrality to the boroughs, still holds good. (6) Yet the great majority of parliamentary staff at the Home Office in these years had personal experience of provincial government and administration, in their capacity as local magistrates. This experience was overwhelmingly rural in nature, and a consistent preference on the part of Home Office staff for referring matters back to the local interpreters of the law — the justices — has to be seen as a coherent and positive policy directed towards maintaining the autonomy of certain aspects of county government. In police matters, then, in the mid-nineteenth century, there was a widespread approval for the structure and relationships of rural society, expressed in the policy of recruiting rural workers as policemen, and in the governmental attitudes mentioned above. The prescriptive pattern for nineteenth-century policing was rural, not urban.

County policing was seen as a model for urban areas in yet another, more important, way. Most English police history has expounded so successfully the virtues of an unarmed, exclusively civilian force, that the models and theories of control and order that shaped county police management in the mid-nineteenth century, many of which were in fact military, have remained undiscovered. The immediate background to the first compulsory police legislation of 1856 was the Crimean War, and the threat to domestic order that was expected to follow peace and the return of the Crimean regiments. But informing that immediate cause (dealt with here in section (iii) of Chapter 1),was a much deeper belief that the primary justification for a local constabulary lay in its ability to face local insurrection, and put it down. Borough police forces were for the main part unable to act in this way in the face of riot, for the number of police in an area was based on the number of people living there, and very few cities were big enough to employ enough policemen to make them an effective local army. A study of the Murphy Riots of the late 1860s, dealt with in some detail in the first part of this book, shows how county police forces were seen as, and used as, a kind of army by local government and local ratepayers in the mid-Victorian years. The reaction of central government to this particular series of disturbances shows how the ability of a local police force to act in the case of riot came to be seen as a measure of its efficiency, and how the lack of such an ability caused borough police management to be seen as inferior and inadequate.

But behind the picture of the local county constabulary armed, ranked in formation, making a charge in English cities in the 1860s, lay an earlier image of the army as a way of ordering life, of men and masters united in defence of property and social order. This is why the most ready name that mid-nineteenth century magistrates, town councillors and ratepayers alike had for a policeman was 'servant'. The idea of a local militia was a potent one for property owners, for it suggested a return to a rural age of grace, when a village labourer who had become a militia man — a servant uniformed and armed — was united in common purpose with his masters. The quasi-military ideals that shaped much mid-Victorian development

of police forces can throw some light on the different uses made of
social theories by different classes of people in the mid-nineteenth
century. It is likely that the village labourer signing the police
recruitment form saw what he was doing as something like what his
fathers had done before: taking the King's shilling. And there was
also available another, popular idea of armies that differed at
many points from the official theories of control and order. That
popular idea drew on the images of Army of God and New Model Army,
and would seem to have offered the possibility of the radicalisation
of social relations. Some permanent mid-Victorian policemen saw
the possibility of those armies becoming contemporary and concrete
in a local force's offer of promotion through the ranks by faith
and good works. Most of these men were to be disappointed, as the
second half of this book shows.

Many temporary policemen did not of course, have such high expectations of their local forces and, like Harold Cheetham, a Stockport
brickmaker and one time president of his union, entered their local
army of right in order to tide themselves over a period of unemployment. Harold Cheetham was questioned in 1868 by a select
committee inquiring into trade outrage during his presidency of
the Stockport Brickmakers' Union four years before. He was asked
by a committee member whether in 1864 he had carried a staff '. . .
like a policeman's staff?' — 'Yes, something similar.' — 'You have
been a policeman, have you not? . . . And you know how to use a
staff? — 'I do not know that I ever used one often.' (7)   If
working-class men were to be admitted to the official community
of law, order and government, even in the minor capacity of paid
servant and policeman, then the skills they had learned officially
might become personal skills, and be perceived as threatening, as
were Harold Cheetham's. But for those working-class men who
stayed to become permanent policemen, the image of the police as a
kind of army was not just a matter of drilling and learning how to
make a baton charge. The army that altered and improved class
relations, that provided an escape from the real hierarchy of social
relations by offering men the chance to rise through the ranks,
offered some policemen a consistent reference point for an understanding of their daily life. (8)

It is another version of this belief in the power of an institution to alter and improve social and class relations that has dictated much of the police history that has been written in the past
fifty years. This particular version of the belief has a long
history, unsupported for the main part by documentary evidence.
Shored up and reiterated in the body of work produced by the police
historian Charles Reith in the 1930s and 1940s, it finds its roots
in the early nineteenth century, during the Peninsula War, when
Sir John Moore, commander of the 51st Regiment, drew up a plan
for internal army reform that had a profound influence on some
of the officers serving under him. What caught the imagination of
later policemen — and those who have written their history — was
that in 'Military Training' and 'Moral Training' (documents unfortunately lost), Moore outlined a method for achieving moral
improvement within the ranks through a prescribed attitude of
officers to men. The duties and obligations of each part of the
military hierarchy towards the other parts were laid down and made

plain. Charles Rowan, one of the first two Commissioners of Metropolitan police to be appointed in 1829, had served with Moore, and
in his first instructions to the officers of the Metropolitan police
to be 'firm and just and at the same time kind and conciliatory'
to the constables under them, Charles Reith, a journalist writing in
the 1940s and 1950s, saw the ideal-type of instruction delivered
to the ideal-type of police force. (9) Reith's six volumes of
police history, written between 1938 and 1956, saw the Metropolitan
force as the Platonic model of which provincial police forces were
but the pale reflection, and indeed, presented provincial police
history as the history of the adoption of the model by borough and
county during the rest of the nineteenth century. (10)

This 'highly conservative teleology' (11) is read by modern
policemen and has helped shape some recent history written by them.
Reith's books, and more recent accounts of the police and their
history, (12) are testimony to the endurance of a particular social
belief, different versions of which were held both by sons of the
nineteenth-century landed gentry become chief constables, and
ploughmen become policemen: that the relationships of men within
institutions can, and ought to, set a pattern for wider social
relationships. Reith believed that the relations between officers
and men promoted in Commissioner Rowan's instructions served as
'a vision of what should and could be the relationship between
policemen and public'. (13) Reith's history is easy enough to
dismiss — it rests on very scanty evidence — but it is important
because it echoes the beliefs of Victorian chief constables and
police officers who, in taking some working-class men and making
them into policemen, saw the possibility of disciplining much
broader sections of working-class communities in the way they had
disciplined their constables. Part of the means envisaged was the
laying down of ordered, hierarchic relationships, which often drew
consciously on the metaphors of a 'naturally' ordered rural community and in which masters and men knew the obligations of their
place.

Out of the governmental and administrative circumstances mentioned above, English police forces made themselves. Yet what
was it that was made? An American journalist docking at Liverpool
in 1859, and setting eyes on an English policeman for the first
time, was only surprised at how familiar he looked: 'the exact
likeness of the conventional policeman of the stage'. (14) Unless
a history of English police forces can examine their making, then
we end up like that journalist, only surprised at how familiar the
constable of the 1860s looks to modern eyes. The nineteenth-century
policeman's handbook told him what he ought to be: neutral, passive,
a mere symbol for the citizen's own self-discipline. Constitutional
textbooks of the late nineteenth century said, as does most police
history written by policemen, that this is what he was. (15)
'Neutrality' is not used here in the modern sense of politically
uncommitted. Police legislation of the 1850s certainly provided
for the disenfranchisement of policemen not already disqualified
from voting by their lack of status as ratepayers; but it is the
argument of this book that a local police was highly political and
understood to be so, in that it functioned as part of a local system
of control and management, specifically, in this period, as the

defensive arm of local property-owners, and as the administrative
agency of local magistrates and watch committees. Neutrality, in
mid-nineteenth-century terms, was a kind of institutionalised un-
importance, and its working can most clearly be seen in the contemporary definition and use of the term 'discretion', a term which,
to this day, is used to define a relationship between police and
public.

The first instructions issued to the Metropolitan police by their
first Commissioners did actually employ the term 'discretion'; (16)
and these rules and regulations were reprinted to guide provincial
police forces hundreds of times over the next fifty years. (17)
'Discretion', according to these sources, was the institutional
virtue of being able to make intelligent decisions on the spot; it
was presented as a restricted decision-making ability, and it in
fact allowed a hierarchy to cope with workers who were not constantly supervised by their superiors. But it was heavily qualified as
a virtue, hedged around with reminders of the structure of the
force, and the particular claims of the 'respectable' when a constable came face to face with them. Some of the effects of this
restricted sphere of judgment are discussed later in this book,
over the question of the Game Laws, in particular the Night Poaching
Prevention Act of 1862. (18)

The notion of police neutrality had some of its roots in a common observation that mid-nineteenth century policemen actually did
very little in the public eye, except walk around, and watch.
Action against the respectable was proscribed; but so was a great
deal of action against working-class people, not least because
unsupervised action could put isolated men in physical danger. It
may be as well that Metropolitan policemen had more need of a formula like discretion than did provincial forces (reiteration of the
word in dozens of handbooks is, after all, no reliable guide to
local interpretations of it), for Metropolitan policemen possessed,
through various police acts of the 1830s and 1840s, a much greater
ability to act without reference to a hierarchy. In the provinces,
on the other hand, it is clear that no policeman could act individually, and that only limited action was possible without reference
being made to a superior officer.

This neutrality, this passivity, was not just a formula. Nineteenth-century police forces were made out of precise social circumstances, out of the theory and practice of provincial local government, and out of class relations. Policemen took an active and
conscious part in this making: neutrality and passivity were not
simply forced upon them; they were equally the creations of men
caught in impossible circumstances.

1856 saw the first compulsory police legislation, in the County
and Borough Police Act (19 & 20 Vict. c.69). There had been partial
permissive legislation directed at the counties before this, and the
establishment of paid police forces in boroughs had been made compulsory under the Municipal Corporations Act of 1835 (5 & 6 Will. IV
c.88). Within the space of six months — the winter and early spring
of 1856-7 — every community in England (19) became subject to a
system of surveillance, some of them for the first time. At first,
the lack of provincial reaction to this innovation is surprising,
though it can be partly explained by the piecemeal existence of

forces since 1835, and a quarter-century's experience of the Metropolitan police. But the silence, the lack of reaction, continued.
Between 1856 and 1880 only ten questions concerning the provincial
police were asked in the House of Commons. I have found only one
reference to a provincial policeman — in Francis Kilvert's diary
for the early 1870s. Between Dickens's dealings with Metropolitan
police officers and detectives in the 1840s, and Flora Thompson's
memories of village life in the 1880s, there is, as far as I know,
nothing. (20) There is also a lack of visual evidence of policemen
from these years. Contemporary engravings show occasionally the
waiting silhouette concealed in the shadows, (21) but the more common, and less revealing, image is the iconography of the popular
press, as for example in 'Police News': the wooden-faced constable
grasps the collar of the apprehended in his left hand, his baton
is raised menacingly in his right, face and figure frozen in the
immobility of eternal battle.

This lack of middle-class and literate awareness of policemen
rested partly on what a policeman was seen to be, and that perception rested in its turn on what he had been before he turned
policeman: ex-craft shoemakers and rural labourers were poor and
unimportant men, only fools dressed in blue. It had much to do also
with an understanding of local government that made the policeman
part of a pre-existing hierarchy that could be explained in ways
that did not necessitate any special discussion of his position.
Indeed, urban ratepayers saw their police forces unproblematically
and precisely as servants, paid to protect property and keep the
streets clean. The notion of the policeman's neutrality had some
of its roots in an understanding of the invisibility of paid
servants.

It has been suggested that:
the modern uniformed police constituted a recognition that co-
ercive social control could not remain in the hands of non-
specialists; a recognition that the maintenance of social inte-
gration required an organisational deployment of coercion which
defined all citizens worthy of protection; a recognition that the
maintenance of order required 'the substitution of law for politics and the substitution of the daily efforts of police for the
occasional and overactive use of military force . . . . (22)
All these factors constitute a description of changes that took
place in the years under discussion here. Yet, at the same time,
mid-nineteenth-century local administrators went to great lengths
to recruit the social virtues rather than professional practice to
local forces; the daily organisational distribution and routine work
of provincial police forces precisely defined some citizens — or at
least their property — are less worthy of attention than that of the
local ratepayers. It is a central argument of this book that a
well-understood local political system manifested itself in the distribution of forces; and it is argued here that the use of the army
(and various militias and volunteer forces) in the years between
1950 and 1880, though certainly less frequent than it had been in
the 1830s and 1840s, was seen within the localities as part of the
same system of control and management as the police was.

Modern knowledge of the British police reflects an organisation
that has been increasingly centralised over the past century.
Local studies may reveal the extent to which community norms and

consensual definitions of policing dictate modern policemen's understanding of their jobs; (23) but this understanding of position
and role is quite distinct from the situation in the provincial
England of the 1860s and 1870s where such an understanding had a
structural base in local rate law and the local control of administrative law.

Legal commentators of the 1880s, looking back over the years of
silence on the question of the police, suggested to their readers
that something new had come into being in the last half-century. (24)
For, as one of them put it, whilst the idea of 'policing', that is,
of ordering and regulating societies in certain ways, particularly
through the gathering of information and the device of registration,
was an old one, the idea of 'the police', a body of men permanently
maintained to prevent and detect crime on a nation-wide scale, was
quite new. (25) But outside the pages of the textbooks, at the level
where ratepayers handed over sums of money in the expectation that
local policemen would act as paid servants of local property, the
national aspects of 'the police' were far less important than the
local 'policing' functions that they were asked to perform. The
appointment of policemen to act as poor law relieving officers,
inspectors of nuisances, market commissioners, impounders of stray
cattle, and inspectors of weights and measures, all made them more
complete servants of property within the local financial structure
of local forces.

In this way, communities were defined locally, and regulated
locally. They were legally and financially defined as groups of
property-owners who paid sums of money, in the form of rates, to a
local authority which undertook to protect their property. They
were regulated locally, through local bye-laws and the appointment
of policemen to such administrative roles as inspector of nuisances
and inspector of common lodging houses in the mid-Victorian years,
and the range of such work increased dramatically after 1856.

This developing local control of social life through law locally
administered was a measure of the change that one advocate of
bureaucratic centralism underwent in the years between 1830 and
1850. Edwin Chadwick, who in 1829 was an exponent of the centralised control of local police forces, was in 1853 advocating
local supervision of local forces. He had learned something in
those twenty years from the resistance of local magistrates to
several permissive rural police acts: the consultation of local
'feeling' was necessary for the efficient operation of local forces,
and that feeling was located firmly in the pockets of local ratepayers, and in their desire to exercise close control over the
spending of their money. (26)

A real change had taken place in this system of local government
by the 1880s. In the previous quarter-century, policemen had been
minutely supervised by local magistrates and watch committees
through their ability to impose upon the police a wide range of
administrative tasks. As 1880 approached, more and more central
legislation came to define local police forces as agencies of central government without any mediation by magistrate or watch committee. Local police forces became, in administrative terms, an
agency of central government, and a recognisably modern police.

This book is concerned with provincial police forces and with provincial police government. It has frequently been suggested that the Metropolitan police force constituted the model for provincial forces. In fact, the governmental structure of the Metropolitan force was quite different from that of county and borough, the Home Secretary being responsible to Parliament for its operation. It had a range of laws to operate with that were unknown to provincial forces, and its personnel were drawn from great distances, strangers to the city, (27) not part of the local economy and the map of public and personal disaster that furnished recruits to county and borough forces. The Metropolitan situation and the Metropolitan policeman were, for the main part, quite irrelevant to the policing of provincial communities, and are dealt with in this book only where it is important to question their use as a model for forces outside London in the years after 1856.

This book draws together and questions together the nature of local government in the mid-Victorian years and the structure of life within local communities. Nevertheless, it is divided into two parts (either of which could be read independently of the other). The first part presents the administrative and governmental background to the development of modern police forces. This first part, 'Government and Policing', is intended as an extended introduction to the longer second part, 'Men and policemen', which deals with those who were both the subjects and agents of this change. In some county record offices there lies in the constabulary registers the most minutely detailed account of part of some working-class men's life. To see the mid-nineteenth-century policeman as worker, subject to local economic change, the constabulary records of two Midlands counties have been used. To discover what those workers understood of their situation, to see their wives and children, to trace the use by them of an institutional ideology to make a set of social beliefs, the policeman's newspaper, the 'Police Service Advertiser' (later the 'Police Guardian') has been consulted. In the 1860s permanent professional policemen began to enter deferentially the reflecting, literate world that writes cumbersomely phrased letters and bad poetry, and they knew that their newspaper was the only place where many of them could — anonymously — speak. The other policemen, the ones who didn't stay, are harder to find outside the pages of the constabulary record books. However, they made pay claims, sometimes they went on strike, and their brief existence as policemen was reported by inspectors of constabulary, by borough head constables to their watch committees, and in the local press.

Working-class men — the ones who did stay — made themselves into policemen. To say this is to suggest that it took more than discipline imposed from above to turn a ploughman into a policeman. It is to acknowledge something of what those men constructed for themselves out of circumstances of restriction. If policing, like partial enfranchisement, trade union legislation and compulsory mass education, the licensing laws and sanitary legislation, is to be pointed to as a way in which working-class life came to be regulated and, in some instances, contracted to the state in the second half of the nineteenth century, then the development of police forces must be seen separately from the efforts that sought to order, discipline and cleanse working-class communities. For it

was working-class men who walked the streets and the hostile country
roads to discipline the kinds of community from which they had made
an earlier journey. The development of a modern system of police
demanded obeisance and conscious identification with their masters
from some working-class men. To make that identification involved
a harder journey than that from village workshop to the recruiting
sergeant's desk, and some men have left evidence of the conscious
struggle by which they became policemen. Their testimony may serve
to illuminate a wider arena of nineteenth-century social and political life, in which more people than policemen took part in systems
of government and belief that were fundamentally opposed to their
own interests.

Part one
GOVERNMENT AND POLICING

GOVERNMENT AND POLICING

Local government in the mid-nineteenth century was a highly visible
government. The meaning of local administration of law and statute
was plain to see: the policeman appointed as poor law relieving
officer moving vagrants towards the tramp ward; the vagrant ward
housed in the same building as the police station and the magistrates' court in some cities; the common lodging house inspected
not by an officer of local government, but by the superintendent
of local police. We need to be able to understand something of
what people on the tramp through Cambridge, issued with a ticket
to the vagrant ward by the desk sergeant at the central police
office, understood of the relationship between local government
and the ordering of life within local communities.

The first part of this book is designed to show what the legislative and governmental basis for that understanding was. It is
divided into several sections, dealing with the provincial theories
of finance and community control, the contrasts made between rural
and urban social relations, and the work done by policemen within
the localities that helped form distinctly modern police forces.
Policemen's capacities were defined by reaction to contemporary
events as much as by legislation, and police action during the
Murphy Riots of the late 1860s is singled out as an important
example of this process. However, it is with the legislative background to the formation of provincial police forces that this chapter begins.

(i) LEGISLATION

Part of a mid-nineteenth-century perception of police forces and
an understanding of the role they played in local communities was
dictated by successive legislative enactments of the early nin-
teenth century, and the types of policemen and means of government
they created. This definition of police and policing fell into
several clear statutory stages, a first one being marked off by
the Municipal Corporations Act of 1835 (5 & 6 Will. IV c.88) and
the compulsory policing clauses it contained. (1)

The pre-1835 period provided a double pattern: that of the parish

constable and of the constable employed under local act. The former, his powers for the preservation of community order deriving
from common law, was appointed by the vestry and directed by the
magistrates. His powers were local, in law, and in fact: it took
time, money and effort to get him away from his neighbourhood in
pursuit of an offender. The constable appointed under a local act
had his duties prescribed: he operated for the good ordering of a
certain place. Much the same was true of the constables appointed
by the unreformed municipal corporations. If they were not inheri-
tors of immemorable tradition appointed by the court leet and
functioning as parish constables, then they were appoihted by an
independent body acting in the same area as the corporation with
powers under local act. (2) The legislative provision for town
police was extended by the Municipal Corporations Act of 1835, which
directed that the reformed corporations appoint a sufficient number
of constables, and frame rules for their operation. (3)

Under the Municipal Corporations Act, local improvement boards
were enjoined to hand their powers to maintain and direct bodies of
police over to the reformed corporations, though they did retain
responsibility for policing local areas, that is to say, for paving
and lighting streets, suppressing nuisances, and so on. Within a
few years several large improvement boards had voluntarily handed
such policing powers over to the municipal corporations, and in
these circumstances a body of police again undertook a policing
role. (4) But in general, the reform of local government in the
1830s left a significant legacy for local administrators: how ever
directed, whoever controlled them, whether they lit and extinguished
lamps, or inspected reported nuisances or not, a body of police was
seen as retaining very strong links with the much older concept of
policing, and understood as being maintained for a general good
ordering of a specific place.

The act of 1835 did not affect the parish constables in the counties. Neither for that matter did the permissive Rural Police Act
of 1839 (2 & 3 Vict. c.93) which enabled magistrates in quarter
sessions to establish paid police forces. There were 38 English
administrative counties, and by the early 1850s 18 had established
constabularies, 7 had done so in some districts, and 13 had opted
for injecting new life into the parish constable by using two permissive police acts, one of 1842 (5 & 6 Vict. c.109) and one of 1850
(13 & 14 Vict. c.20). (5) The former provided for the payment of
parish constables, attempted to improve their image by restricting
appointment to men assessed to the poor or county rate at £4 a year,
and outlined the ideal of efficient, division-wide organisation. (6)
But it was the vestry that implemented the act, a constable's field
of operation still extended no further than the boundaries of his
own parish, and he was paid, not out of the general county rate,
but out of the poor rate, by the overseers. Traditional financial
and administrative boundaries were in fact maintained under these
acts.

Under the first of these two acts, that of 1842, there was provision for justices to appoint and to pay (out of the county rate)
a superintending constable. This provision was extended by the
amending act of 1850. A superintendent could be appointed for
each petty sessional division of a county, and he was put in charge

of all parish constables and lock-ups. But his powers extended no further than the division boundaries and even paying parish constables could not provide for a superintendent's control of them. 'Parish constables are little better than so much live lumber,' said one magistrate in a county that had tried the system, 'and have rather thwarted the active superintendent than otherwise.'(7)

Twenty years before this, the Lighting and Watching Act of 1833 (3 & 4 Will. IV c.90) had attempted to deal with the difficulties inherent in organising parish constables. This act gave the power of appointing paid watchmen to an inspector chosen by the vestry. It is impossible to find out how far this act was used, and when and where, (7) but where its use is encountered it was obviously seen as a way for magistrates to avoid establishing a rural police after 1839. In eagerly petitioning quarter sessions for its application, they argued how cheap it was, and incidentally demonstrated its uselessness, for magistrates had no powers to protect property under it, and watchmen could not even serve warrants. (9) As a piece of legislation it did not, as one police historian has argued, mark 'a reaction to the parish as a traditional unit of policing'. (10)   It is true that it could apply to the ubiquitous 'place' as well as to the parish, and that the inspector appointed under it could unite with his colleagues from other parishes. But the financial basis for organisation remained the parish, the rating authority the vestry. It makes better sense to read this act in the light of existing improvement measures, or as a precursor of the Town Police Clauses Act of 1847. It was with this last measure that the edges between 'policing' and 'police' became statutorily blurred.

The Town Police Clauses Act (10 & 11 Vict. c.89) was designed to provide a pro forma for local acts. With ratepayer sanction commissioners were to appont a superintendent and a number of constables. These were to be properly sworn police officers of the crown. Commissioners had the power to make bye-laws and to fine for a whole range of nuisance offences. (11)   Any local authority could take the Police Clauses Act upon itself — boards of guardians, vestries, municipal corporations. But in county areas magistrates had long recognised that, theoretically at least, parish constables were better routine executors of the law than policemen appointed in this new way, with their powers severely curtailed by local bye-laws.

Traditional deployment of the parish constable cut across the neat lines of legislative development. So, to a much greater and less examined extent, did the local executive agencies of the administrative state. The Local Government Act of 1858 (21 & 22 Vict. c.98) superseded the Lighting and Watching Act and the Town Police Clauses Act, and was in this way a confirmation of local act. Boards of health became policing authorities. Municipal corporations, improvement boards, and boards of guardians were constituted boards of health under the Public Health Act of 1848 (11 & 12 Vict. c.63) and the Local Government Act of 1858 and it is therefore not surprising to find police forces performing policing functions — the inspection of lodging houses, the surveying of cellar dwellings — in the second half of the nineteenth century. (12)   When they acted in this way policemen were performing an administrative function, the job that a local government inspector would otherwise

have done. Policemen were obliged to do this work because for most
urban authorities they were the most convenient and cheap executive
force to hand. The cleaning of the streets, responsibility for
lighting, the suppression of street begging and many other policing
functions like these were devolved on to local police forces by
local bye-laws and local acts. The distinctive feature of the
social discipline experienced by local communities in the mid-
nineteenth century was this devolution on to police forces of those
powers of surveillance inherent in the policing functions of local
authorities. In this way, as will be seen later, the discipline
and punishment of people living in those communities was provided
for by much more than the definition of crime and the operation of
the criminal law.

       With such a history of legal provision, and under such adminis-
trative circumstances, lack of reaction to the County and Borough
Police Act of 1856 (19 & 20 Vict. c.69) — and what some historians
have called its lack of impact — is partly explained. The new act
in fact gave a clear legal prescription for the kind of policing
described above: it empowered magistrates to make a local police
force perform duties other than peace-keeping ones. In the early
months of 1857 there was a rush of quarter sessions orders to
appoint policemen as assistant poor law relieving officers and
inspectors of weights and measures. The parish constable had
always had a responsibility for nuisances that affected the well-
being of the community, though this responsibility had often been
unused. But there were specific administrative circumstances to
greet the Police Act of 1856 which allowed the extension of policing within local communities to become widespread and stabilised.

       The establishment of any one county force after 1856 meant that
it covered a multiplicity of administrative areas. Cheshire constabulary, to take one extreme, covered an area in which there
were twenty-six places that administered central sanitary provision
under the Local Government Act of 1858 (21 & 22 Vict. c.98). For
the police to operate this act (and in Cheshire they did) meant the
inspection of common lodging houses and the control of nuisances.
Even a rural county like Dorset presented its police with twelve
such areas. (13)   A borough police might be more used to performing this kind of policing function, but many corporations also
became boards of health for the first time in 1858, and so the
range of borough policing was extended and consolidated in the
years after 1856. (14)

       Recently, it has been noted that one county police force ex-
tended its dealings with 'normal' crime in the years after 1856,
rather than concentrating, as it had previously done, on repressing
disorder. (15) If this conclusion is to be extended to other areas
and a longer period of time, then it has to be recognised that a
large amount of police activity was concerned not only with the
anomalies that the criminal law defined, but also with the area
of public impropriety outlined by administrative law.

(ii)   TOWARDS 1856: MODELS AND THEORIES

The legislative background outlined above is an inadequate way of
assessing how the police were understood in the years after 1856.
But it does indicate two unifying approaches: a way of accounting
for police presence in nineteenth-century terms, and a delineation
of the financial and administrative context of the locality.   The
principles paraded in Parliament and the furore of municipal
agitation against Palmerston's police bills of 1854 and 1856 all
passed into quiet acceptance in the winter of 1856-7.   The 'new'
police of 1857 was not new; the stages of growth indicated in the
last section had provided for the mobility of personnel and the
dissemination of different ideas of what a policeman was.
    There has been some argument about the transference of a Metro-
politan model of police to the provinces, and discussion has centred
on the number of men lent to the provinces by the Metropolitan
police commissioners in the years after 1829 (when the Metropolitan
force was established).   This number was undoubtedly small, (16)
but there is evidence of a high mobility among the officer class
of English police forces in the 1840s and 1850s, and for the practical purposes of earning more and improving status, not much distinction was made by these men between county, borough and superintending constable systems.   A number of men did leave the Metropolitan force, not on loan, but having handed in their resignation
in order to become provincial policemen.
    But it took more than a railway journey and a man's new job to
transfer a model, especially when it is unclear what that model
was seen to be.   Charles Reith, using the casual evidence of many
nineteenth-century policemen, argued that the model embodied the
great principle of 'prevention' — the prevention of crime.   According to his argument 'prevention' was an ideal inculcated into the
Metropolitan officers in the formative years of the force.   Promotion through the ranks, a <u>prescribed</u> attitude of officers to men,
'firm and just, kind and conciliatory', was the bedrock of 'prevention'.   This principle, so the argument goes, provided a vision
of what 'should be the relationship between policeman and public';
prevention of crime being successfully induced by a similar 'defined
behaviour on the part of administrators and servants of law'. (17)
    But nineteenth-century policemen seem never to have seen pre-
vention as other than the physical presence of enough policemen
to delay or deter an unspecified number of anti-social events, and
nineteenth-century police forces never truly represented this kind
of separate social order in which men of merit might rise, but
rather reflected rigidly the social hierarchy of the outside world.
The Metropolitan officer travelling to become a provincial policeman
may have taken with him a method of working, and ideas about distribution and organisation of personnel, but these were specifically
rejected by a coherent theory of local government that thought
detection the best form of protection.
    A good deal was known in the provinces about the Metropolitan
force, and its system of organisation was frequently presented as
contrast and counterpoint to rural needs and organisation.   The
magistrate who opined that under a system of regular patrols London
policemen 'tired themselves to very little effect,' expressed a

common rural viewpoint. A paid constabulary on the Metropolitan
model would give rise to a great deal of 'unnecessary lounging',
and such men would be 'forever watching and suspecting'. Gentlemen such as this Kentish magistrate did not believe in the existence of crime until it was committed. What they saw in the Metropolitan system was an organisation by which all 'interest' in crime
was removed to the hands of an arbitrary authority, Commissioners
of Police, responsible to no man. (18)

These objections to a preventative police in the years after
1839 demonstrated the real meaning of support for a detective
police: it was cheaper. Magistrates proposed small-scale systems
of police to complement existing forces in London and the boroughs.
The Superintending Constable Acts of 1842 and 1850 (5 & 6 Vict.
c.109; 13 & 14 Vict. c.20) were used in precisely this way. There
was support too from unlikely quarters for the view that an urban
police was not appropriate for rural needs. When Metropolitan
Police Commissioner Rowan (the man who had supposedly drawn up the
great 'preventative' blueprint in his original instructions to the
Metropolitan police) was asked to advise county magistrates on
police presence, he said that 'a rural police was rather to prevent
crime by detecting offenders rather than to prevent it by their
actual presence in every village.' (19)

The assumption that a police force was best used to remedy isolated acts of social anomaly was common in these years. At Caistor
in Lincolnshire, after a series of offences against property, ratepayers petitioned local magistrates for protection. A London police
officer was appointed under the Special Constables Act (5 & 6 Will.
IV c.43) for three months. At the end of this time the magistrates
refused to reappoint him on grounds of expense. 'The following day
after [he went away] they [the depredations] began again.' (20)   The
Select Committee on Police of 1853 heard many stories like this.
Essex farmers who petitioned quarter sessions for application of
the Rural Police Act of 1839 in areas of incendiarism were, a year
later, earnestly praying that 'the police force be not increased
nor continued'. (21) Bearing this common response in mind, the
principles behind the rejection of the permissive act of 1839 in
twenty English counties need to be more closely examined. It was
in the rejection of central statute that county magistrates clearly
revealed the governmental theories with which they worked.

Men who in Parliament condemned the Rural Police Act as 'un-
English' and 'unjust,' made more revealing statements at home, in
quarter sessions. A magistrate and county member warned his brother
magistrates in Kent of the erosion of magisterial sway embodied in
the act of 1839: 'The system would go far to complete that principle
of centralisation . . . (would) interfere with the administration of
the law by the unpaid magistracy . . . is bound to be followed by a
paid magistracy.' The measure was calculated to 'sever all the ties
that unite the community'; an ancient system of parochial constables
ought to be preserved 'for the moral effect of enlisting the mass of
the people in the execution of the law (was) . . . of the highest
importance.' These objections were in no sense prescriptive. They
depended for their force upon the reiteration of a belief in an
established social order: the ties that united the community were
specified as those between 'landlord and tenant' and 'master and
servant'. (22)

Objections to the Rural Police Act can be classified in several ways. First was the rejection of centralisation, which was not an objection to London, nor to Home Office rule, never even viewed as a remote possibility, but was rather an objection to country centralisation, the removal of autonomy from petty sessions to quarter sessions, from individual justices to that body of magistrates easily swayed by the lord lieutenant and the larger landowners. The petty sessional division was not just a geographical and administrative area. It was part of the financial map of the county, and its moral and emotional geography was well understood. A move away from the autonomy of the judicial division, a type of regional centralisation was, in the long run, to be one of the clearest results of the County and Borough Police Act of 1856. In the early 1840s, this result was foreseen, and feared. (23)

A corollary to this objection was a positive rejection of the idea of preventative policing, locally defined as 'watching and suspecting', which cost too much money, demanded too many men, and which would result in an alien peace, imposed upon communities, rather than arising from an ordered set of social relations. The model was the locality, the focal point the petty sessional division. A section of the Kentish magistry was able to make its theory of police known to central government in the years between 1839 and 1856. Five measures, all designed to inject life into the parish constable, were presented to Parliament in these years. They all originated in Kent. (24) The first, drafted by a Kentish magistrate in 1841, proposed that constables should be subject to certain requirements of age, physical fitness and literacy. Expenses incurred by them were to be paid on an order issued by the magistrate in petty sessions on the overseers of the parish in which the crime to be paid for had been committed. There was to be a superintendent of constables in each petty sessional division, paid not out of the county rate, but out of the poor rate of the different parishes. This superintendent was to be appointed by the magistrates in petty sessions. (25)

This was substantially the measure that became law in 1850 with the second of the Superintending Constable Acts (13 & 14 Vict. c.20). In the county where this measure originated, opposition to the Rural Police Act of 1839 grew in strength during the 1840s. Kent had only managed to evade it by three votes in quarter sessions in 1840. When its adoption was again proposed in 1849, it was rejected by thirty votes. (26) The Superintending Constable Act of 1850, on the other hand, was supported precisely because, through the agency of the superintendent, it provided for increased control by the magistrate over the parish constable. Counties like Buckinghamshire and Kent which adopted it as an alternative to a rural police had watched with some alarm the severance of police from magistracy that accompanied the acceptance of the act of 1839 in some areas. (27)

The theory of police that Kentish magistrates managed to get embodied in central statute was a reflection of its particular geographical circumstances. In a maritime county, under a general fear of invasion, the rhetoric that called for 'enlisting the mass of the people in the execution of the law' had a particular meaning. Throughout this period, and after 1856, it was assumed that a body

of parish constables, and later a county police, would provide the
basis of a volunteer defensive force under the direction of the
magistrates. The first chief constable appointed in Kent after
1856 was elected to office because he presented the magistrates in
quarter quarter sessions with a plan that proposed using the new
police as a basis for drilling and arming the county's labourers,
thereby placing 'the county at an advantage' were fears of invasion
to become real. (28)

In fact changing administrative circumstances were to allow local
magistrates to retain considerable autonomy long after the compulsory Police Act of 1856. The Criminal Justice Act of 1855 (18
& 19 Vict. c.126), for example, supported this autonomy by allowing
many larcenies, formerly tried at quarter sessions, to be tried by
justices in petty sessions. (29) It will be argued that demise in
the authority of the individual petty sessional magistrate over
police matters is only really to be seen when a corporate theory
of police work had grown up among policemen themselves. As a background to this development, the superintending constable system is
important, because it represented an intelligible theory of control
that originated in the provinces. It also brought the claims of a
professional police face to face with magisterial autonomy as 1856
drew near.

Superintending constables occupied a particular position in what
was already a reasonably well-understood police hierarchy. Magistrates knew that with the money they offered these men (salaries
ranged throughout the country from £65 to £125 per year) they were
buying experience and expertise. By 1852 the thirteen counties
that used this police system employed an aggregate of 118 superintending constables. Men who joined a county in this way had
usually been inspectors in the forces they had left, and the most
common experience among the total number was previous work in the
Essex constabulary. These professional policemen, though universally condemnative of the system they had to work under, were willing to take jobs in counties like Buckinghamshire and Kent because
the position of superintending constable was recognised as a step
towards the head constableship of a borough force, and because the
system offered faster promotion than a rural police force did. (30)
When the superintending system was abandoned after 1856, promotional
opportunities for officers declined.

Subjection to the orders of a magistrate in petty sessions was
a severe restriction to this sort of professional policeman. In
Kent, the superintendent was not allowed to leave the sessional
division without the written consent of a local justice, and he had
to visit every parish in that division at least once a month. However, the inherent defects of the system took some time to become
apparent. In 1853, whilst the Select Committee on Police was
taking evidence, and the Kentish system was being roundly condemned
by one of its former officers, an incident that revealed precisely
the strains the system was under occurred in Kent. One of the
magistrates resident in the Tonbridge division instructed his
superintendent to apply to his fellow officer in Ashford division
for aid in a local riot. One Ashford magistrate refused to let the
man cross the division boundaries, and the Tonbridge justices had
to call on the Metropolitan police. (31)

Six months later the chairman of quarter sessions proposed that the superintending constables should be chosen by a constabulary committee of quarter sessions on the grounds that such a body would be more likely to choose its policemen wisely. Protestations — 'it will be taking the power from the great body of magistrates of appointing their own officer' — were ignored and the motion was carried. (32) In Kent at least, the move towards county centralisation was on.

Borough police forces received far less attention than the counties did from the select committee on police of 1853, but what attention there was was very critical indeed. Very small boroughs were especially singled out for adverse comment, and in the final report of the committee it was suggested that they be compulsorily co-joined with surrounding county forces. It was suggested as well that larger boroughs be placed under a management similar to that of rural police forces. (33) These proposals were based on two criticisms, first of borough police government by watch committees, and second of the inability of any borough force (except perhaps those of Liverpool and Manchester) to deal with a riot situation. This latter criticism was especially made by professional policemen.

Legally, the watch committee of a borough council occupied the position of a chief constable of a county force, and the borough head constable was merely the chief officer of a body of police. County chief constables had a statutory autonomy and were free to create forces in their own image, but a borough force operated within the framework of local bye-law and legally its head constable was only an employee of the watch committee. (34) Borough ratepayers held the reins with a greater consciousness of control than county rate payers, for in the municipalities the rating authority was an elected one. The relationship between money and borough police management was presented to the select committee on police by several witnesses. (35)

By the mid-1850s, then, both magisterial and watch committee control of existing police forces were under attack. Criticism rested on a want of uniformity, on the exposure of a patchwork system of policed, semi-policed and unpoliced counties, of borough forces ranging in their size and their ability to discipline a community. It was on such a platform of criticism that the police bills of 1854 and 1856 were introduced. (36) But by the mid-1850s there was another, more pressing, reason for introducing a compulsory police.

(iii)   TOWARDS 1856: SOLDIERS AND POLICEMEN

An interpretation of English police history that has concentrated on its civil nature in contrast with continental systems has ignored the precise nature of the military ideal that helped form the 'new' police after 1856. The notion of the police as a kind of soldiery was inherent in several existing arrangements that influenced the creation of provincial police forces before 1856. One of these was the Essex constabulary (set up under the permissive Rural Police Act of 1839), another was systems of internal defence such as the militia, and the third was the Royal Irish Constabulary.

When John Bunch Bonnemaison MacHardy, chief constable of Essex, gave his evidence to the Commons select committee on police in 1853, he knew that his county force was already seen as a model and a training ground. Twenty years later the chief constable of the North Riding remembered how

when the Act (of 1856) became compulsory on counties there was a great call for experienced policemen to assist in the formation of our forces. I availed myself of Admiral MacHardy's kindness and he let me have by their wish three officers . . . from his force. (37)

The germ of MacHardy's theory of police lay in his long propagation of a plan that he was never in fact allowed to put into practice, though part of it was implemented in Essex and some other English counties. MacHardy saw in the organisation of the Essex constabulary the basis for a wider protective force, that is, a volunteer defensive force which, co-operating with the coast guards, would make calling out the militia during times of crisis or invasion unnecessary. Edwin Chadwick, who had given evidence to select committees before on the number and type of police needed for the effective policing of society, liked MacHardy's ideas, and his approving discussion of them before the committee of 1853 marked a general change in his attitude to ratepayer control, and a greater willingness to allow a locality to manage its own police. (38) As the map of interest and finance on which local police forces operated becomes plainer, it is important to note that the idea of national and general defence was, in a coastal county like Essex, seen as a matter for control by local paymasters. Those who propagated the idea of a locally raised defensive force centred on a local constabulary were able to draw on an old contrast between an ancient 'constitutional force' — a local militia — which might act as a 'bastion against the standing army of the crown.' (39)

MacHardy was not alone in seeing county constabularies as types of defensive militia: we have seen, for instance, the preoccupations of the Kentish magistracy translated into statute in 1850. County police forces were habitually listed with the army and the militia when the state of national defence was reckoned in the 1850s, and in 1853, three years before the introduction of compulsory policing, MacHardy reckoned that the existing county constabularies could provide a defensive force of 14,000 men 'which could in cases of emergency be augmented and armed'. (40) Was this military vision reflected in the organisation and distribution of the Essex constabulary? Actual working arrangements in the county followed those of the Metropolitan police force. The county was separated into divisions, 'the divisions into detachments, and those . . . into guards or beats.' No army officer would have had any trouble in recognising this conventional military arrangement, but men like MacHardy were eager to dispel the notion that they might use the highly militaristic Irish Constabulary as a pattern for distribution of personnel.

Reactions to the Royal Irish Constabulary had been contradictory for twenty years past. On the one hand it was lauded as the most theoretically perfect police system in the world, and in the same breath condemned as despotic in practice. This condemnation usually came from English magistrates who looked with alarm at the regional centralisation it embodied and the severely curtailed powers of local magistrates that it involved. (41) But its police methods (horse patrol around a central station which housed strategically dispersed detachments of police) were certainly used before 1856 in several English counties. But local circumstances worked against the strict application of a model. The chief constable of Hampshire (who had worked in Ireland) might have wanted to 'ingraft the discipline of the Irish Constabulary upon . . . (police) duty in this country', and he very much wanted to train his men in the use of arms, but he still operated his force on the English model — that of Essex. (42) Indeed, when the operation of the post-1839 county forces is considered, little distinction can be made between Irish Constabulary and military experience on the part of officers. Both led to an analysis of police questions in terms of defence against internal and external enemies, and the burden of analysis rested on the question of arming the police.

The question of organised and armed defence became more pressing in the mid-1850s. In 1856 the boroughs were reminded by the Home Secretary that due to the demand for soldiers in the Crimea, the practice of posting small detachments of troops in various parts of the country was soon to be discontinued. (43) The use that the boroughs had made of the army during local disturbance over the past thirty years was taken by conventional wisdom at the Home Office to be a reliable measure of their police forces' inability to cope during ordinary circumstance. The distinction between the counties and the boroughs that had been so thoroughly publicised by the select committee of 1853 was reiterated: boroughs could not keep their own peace, and existing local county forces often had to play the role of a soldiery for them. To many county chief constables, the entire justification for the existence of a rural police was its ability to face a riot and, armed — not always with cutlasses but certainly with batons and the military discipline bestowed by drilling — put down that riot.

Disturbances and riots in Blackburn and Wigan in 1853 had received a good deal of national publicity, (44) and in many ways a numerically inadequate police force in those towns was seen as the cause of disturbance, with ratepayer 'interest' at the root of numerical parsimony. The campaign for a uniform and professional police gained support because of these northern riots, and they both reflected and intensified a contemporary belief that it was the urban situation, not the rural, that demanded a better police system. The theory that towns and boroughs were in themselves areas of social anomaly and nurseries of crime was given frequent airing before the select committee of 1853. (45) Though the attack on poorly policed boroughs concentrated almost entirely on the small number of policemen that they employed, there were depths of moral and governmental irresponsibility revealed to their critics in this simple exercise of counting: what boroughs refused to do was make a police presence strong in proportion 'to a known discipline and numbers of a town population'. (46) They appeared, in contrast with the counties, to abnegate their responsibility to police and govern according to local knowledge.

Compared with the boroughs, county forces were seen more particularly as a sort of peace-keeping force and this perception was

given a specificity by the current debate on national defence. When
the institution of a compulsory police was debated, Britain was at
war: 'the one great reason . . . for the establishment of a uniform
system of police . . . was in order that there might be a uniformity of protection when those who would have to protect us from the
enemy were withdrawn.' (47)

The County and Borough Police Act of 1856 (19 & 20 Vict. c.69),
the first police measure to provide wholesale, general policing
of England and Wales was not just an extension of previous permissive police legislation. Its timing, and many of the provisions it
contained, were dictated by a situation of war, and a contemporary
invasion panic. (48) Its major innovation as a piece of legislation, that is, a contribution to local authorities out of central
funds for the support of a local police, had been argued out in
the context of the debate over the militia bills in the early 1850s.
Revival of the militia was a traditional domestic reaction to a war
situation, the recreation of 'an army for home defence rooted in
the counties, with the gentry raising and offering their depen-
dents.' (49) But the Militia Acts of the 1850s (16 & 17 Vict.
c.134; 17 & 18 Vict. c.13; 18 & 19 Vict. c.1) introduced new governmental ideas into this traditional deployment: 'We look upon it
[the Militia] as a national force and . . . consider that the
expense ought to be born by the public funds, and not by burthens
on the local properties.' (50) The debate over the contemporary
revival of 'the old constitutional force' dwelt on efficiency, the
proper deployment of professional men, and on systematic training
of recruits. More important than this, though, was the reiteration
of ideas about the virtues of a militia's local connections: 'A
local militia conveys the idea of a force not only raised . . . but
[also] called upon to act only in its own immediate locality.' (51)
All these factors were to be absorbed into a consistent theory of
police operations after 1856. The policeman of the post-1856 period
was thus prepared for, not only by the piecmeal legislation of
twenty years past and the 'policing' context of local government
administration, but by a new provincial show: 'After the lapse of
many years the spectacle of domestic soldiering . . . is now once
more exhibited . . . Every county town swarms with its hundreds
of lads.' (52) The social source of this defensive force — the
labourers of 'the smaller agricultural counties' (53) — were to
provide the most consistent source for policemen in the years to
come.

There was of course no statutory connection between a militia
and a police. But through the chronology of events, central government found a new way of discussing and understanding the uses of
police forces, and the pressure of new events brought old arguments
to the fore:

If the money which is now to be wasted on the proposed militia
men had been applied to the establishment of a general constabulary, armed and trained on the Irish model, it would have done far
more towards increasing our security in the event of war . . . .
(54)

At many levels of observation it was impossible to ignore the connections between the new police of 1857, and the memory and theory
of a domestic army.

War <u>was</u> the event in 1855, and what was happening in the Crimea
was at the basis of all debate on the proposed police during 1855
and 1856. Trepidation was expressed at the idea of 'a footloose
army' returning home: 'Peace brought disastrous results in 1816
. . . it was incumbent, with another peace at hand . . . to legis-
late promptly for prevention of crime.' (55) But more potent than
this kind of memory was the questioning of institutions that the
Crimean War forced upon governmental consciousness. The emotional
impact of the war was its revelation of domestic and institutional
inadequacies. Vast, unpoliced stretches of rural England rose like
undefended territory with lines of communication broken, before
the eyes of a ratepaying public.

The footloose, unemployed soldier was joined in the respectable
imagination by the 'whitewashed criminal thrown back upon his own
haunts'. (56) With the Penal Servitude Act of 1853 (16 & 17 Vict.
c.99) transportation began to be phased out. This act, which 'freed
a convict to roam the countryside' on a ticket-of-leave provided
the image of an organised race of criminals 'hold[ing] the country
in military occupation . . . [having] their Headquarters, their lines
of communication, their reports, their pickets, their sentries
. . . .' In 1855 and 1856 no one other concern that might justify
a compulsory police act was referred to so often as the ticket-of-
leave system.   .

(iv) THE COUNTY AND BOROUGH POLICE ACT

The vagrant criminal, fleeing from policed areas to counties without
police forces provided an image of fear for the respectable classes
of the 1850s, and frequently, this largely imaginary figure was given
a firmer outline by politicians. In presenting the County and
Borough Police Bill to Parliament, George Grey skilfully used
memories of a five-year-old crime to give weight to the theory of
vagrant crime. In 1850, unpoliced West Surrey, lying as it did
between the two policed areas of the Metropolis and Hampshire, had
provided a haven for a 'notorious' gang of housebreakers. Eventually a 'horrible' and memorable crime was committed by this gang. The
conventional wisdom of 1850 had seen the local magistracy, in their
former refusal to use the Rural Police Act of 1839 and establish
a paid constabulary, as entirely to blame — 'Mexican magistrates
could have done no worse.' 'It concerns the supreme government of
this country to see that no district is left . . . with an inefficient police because two or three of its local paymasters feel a
disinclination to entertain the charge.' (57) In 1850 this attack
on magisterial ability found its contemporary context in the debate
on the County Rate Expenditure Bills, which threw a great deal of
doubt on the ability of unelected county magistrates to spend wisely the money entrusted to them by ratepayers. (58) This debate gave
very wide publicity to alternative methods of managing county police
forces. Among many other proposals was the suggestion that rate-
payer-elected financial boards should have the appointment of chief
constables, and one lesson that George Grey (Home Secretary at this
time) learned was of the dislike felt by the rural magistracy towards the idea of government by boards. Yet it was a commonly held

solution, and one much favoured by vocal, professional police
officers. (59)   Palmerston's Police Bill of 1854 was an attempt to
institute a compulsory police on these lines — one reason for its
failure. (60)   Yet much responsible provincial opinion condemned
George Grey's much milder measure of 1856 precisely because it left
magisterial autonomy intact.   In Kent, for example, it was attacked
in the liberal press on the grounds that it 'conferred too much
power on the magistrates'. (61)

Both county and borough police management were then under attack
in the 1850s, and the general charge laid against both was parsimony and refusal to recognise the needs of smaller ratepayers.
Nevertheless, there was seen to be one important distinction between
county and borough that transcended any common criticism.   The
interests of 'local paymasters' — of county magistrates — were seen
as an obvious drag on the uniformity of the police.   The only answer
to the threat of vagrant crime (which however erroneous as historical
fact, was a powerful contemporary social theory) was seen to be the
establishment by all counties of an efficient police.   Parsimony on
the part of rural justices resulted in a lack of uniformity in
policing matters, and that was a national concern.   But charges
against boroughs in the management of their police rested not just
on selfishness and corruption, but also far more fundamentally on
the inherent smallness and geographical isolation of the town.   What
they actually were on the map of control — conglomerations of property and people surrounded by countryside — means that they could
not be seen in the same light as county forces.   The geographical
cohesion of the latter could make a unity that would not only promote internal good order, but also provide defensive protection
against a wider world.

The County and Borough Police Act of 1856 (19 & 20 Vict. c.69)
introduced new police theories and methods of working that are apt
to be overlooked if it is seen simply as an extension of the act
of 1839.   It outlined a realistic professionalism, not only in the
appointment of government inspectors to inqure into the state and
efficiency of local forces on an annual basis, but also in the
clauses that dealt with the physical provision for police operations — police stations, charge rooms, cells.   The lack of places
to secure people who had been apprehended had meant a severe cur-
tailment of police activity in many areas in the past, (62) and the
new government inspectors were to pursue with tenacity for the next
ten years the question of building lock-ups.   By this new act, a
career body was delineated and superannuation funds were established.   This career body was isolated from the electoral system,
(63) and policemen were forbidden to work for fee, or take any
other employment.

There were provisions under the act to divide counties into areas
that corresponded with policing needs rather than the traditional
areas of local government; but, as has already been indicated, the
tension between petty session and quarter session was to provide
a real area of conflict for years to come.   The very small boroughs
(those with populations of 5,000 or under) were left out of the
structure of inspection and grant-in-aid altogether.   It was hoped
that these small forces would amalgamate ('consolidate' was the contemporary term) with the surrounding county force.   The larger

boroughs were only included within the structure because of the huge
and successful campaign they had waged against the compulsory consolidation clauses in the police bills of 1854 and 1856. (64)
Channels of bureaucratic communication were laid down: annual criminal statistics were to be returned to the Home Office along with
the government inspector's report. Criminal statistics had been
demanded under the Municipal Corporations Act of 1835 (5 & 6 Will.
IV c.88), but it was only after 1856 that they were forwarded to
the Home Office with any regularity.

The bureaucratic innovation of the act of 1856 was a payment out
of central funds to local authorities; this was designed to reim-
burse a quarter of their expenditure on police pay and clothing.
This provision for central funding was the most overt distinction
between Palmerston's police bill of 1854 and the measure which became law in 1856. By the end of 1856 a situation of war had outlined policing as a national problem with a national solution.
George Grey, who was one of the co-authors of the act of 1856, saw
this central payment to local police authorities as part of a wholesale national system for dealing with social anomaly, like 'reform-
atory schools . . . part of the regular machine for the maintenance
of law and order . . . to be maintained . . . by funds contributed
by all, like our prisons, penitentiaries and workhouses.' (65) In
1856 'national force' had none of its later connotations. It meant
only the abandonment of totally free choice in the provinces, and
suggested that policemen might act beyond the area defined by a rate
levied to pay for their services.

The boroughs had fought the police bills hard, their campaign
causing the abandonment of Palmerston's bill of 1854 and the removal
of the compulsory consolidation clauses from Grey's measure of 1856.
But innovation in police matters did not come from the boroughs,
neither at this time, nor during the next twenty years. A coherent
view of rural government had influenced police legislation for two
decades past, and in the 1850s central government was able to re-
spond to a provincial vision of the rural police as a kind of
soldiery. So, before local government of local police forces in
the 1860s and 1870s is considered, central government, and its precise theoretical and practical relations to the provinces, needs
considering.

(v)   THE HOME OFFICE AND THE PROVINCES

The Home Office did not, as has been suggested, lack a policy towards provincial police forces in the 1860s. (66) Its activity,
and the assumptions that underlay it, were based on its relationship with, and interpretation of, provincial government. Central
control did develop, as has been argued, and the agency of the
inspectors was important for this control. But if less emphasis
is laid on the relationship between Home Office and inspectors (for
that was clearly and statutorily defined) and if more is placed on
the relationship between Home Office and local government (and this
was not at all defined), then a new picture does emerge.

In the years after 1856 Home Office activity was important where
it either supported or contradicted the widely held theory that

police forces were matters of local authority. Home Office officials were most eloquent on the bureaucratic organisation of forces.
They would rule and direct on matters of pay and clothing, on the
physical provision for police effectiveness — the number of lock-
ups and police stations a policing authority needed. There was a
great deal of routine administrative contact over questions like
these, and the Home Office was not at all a remote authority. (67)
The Permanent Under Secretary at the Home Office and his staff were
also concerned with constitutional questions, with the legal question of the policeman's accountability at law, and, in the early
days under Sir George Grey's aegis, stating some fundamental
principles of police impartiality to several surprised boroughs.
(68) In fact, by 1856 the Home Office was working with some fairly
well-established theories of police management: it had after all
been a police authority since 1829 when the Metropolitan force was
established. A fundamental principle, such as the impartiality of
the wage-paid policeman, was not a creation of the act of 1856;
but the act did provide a governmental framework whereby such a
principle might be transmitted.
    A fair amount of correspondence with the Home Office involved com-
plaints from a ratepaying public about local police activity. Such
letters became less frequent as the 1860s passed. (69) The usual
method of dealing with them was to send a copy of the letter and,
if there was one, the incriminating newspaper cutting forwarded by the irate ratepayer to the mayor of the borough and await
explanation. (70) It was usually a borough public that made this
kind of complaint, and the clear relationship of money paid out as
rates, and police services bought, made ratepayers turn to the Home
Office as a kind of police authority. (71) The Home Office was not
entirely unwilling to act in this capacity, though matters were
rarely pursued to a conclusion. To a watch committee under local
attack, time could be gained by appealing to the supposed final
authority of the Home Office. But even county authorities, after
1856, betrayed a good deal of confusion as to how much weight to
give to its opinion. The position was never elucidated by the
department, and whilst in the counties Home Office opinion might,
in the years immediately after 1856, take the form of upholding the
chief constable's statutory position, emphasising his independence
of the local magistrates, the fact that the head constable of a
borough had no legal identity at all dictated an even more varying
response to municipal authorities and municipal ratepayers seeking
advice.
    There is some evidence that the Home Office would have pursued
borough police questions further than it did, had it had the power
to do so. Yet most complaints about borough police reflected an
administrative structure that made investigation impossible. When,
as usual, the Home Office deflected ratepayers' complaints back to
the watch committee, it simply strengthened local perception of
that body as a kind of judiciary. (72)
    But Home Office response was not random, and there are positive
distinctions to be made between questions that its staff would deal
with, and those that it considered to be outside its ken. 'The
Home Office', says Henry Parris, 'often displayed (an) indifference
to local authorities seeking advice.' (73) But the familiar

formulae — 'a matter for the direction of the magistrates' — 'the justices in quarter sessions must certainly be answerable' — involved a positive acceptance of the autonomy of local police authorities. (74) In cases of police management that were not specifically covered by the act of 1856, the Home Office gave the final decision to local interpreters of the law.

Twentieth-century accounts of central/local relations on police matters have ignored the wide range of discretion that the Home Office left the provinces. Its refusal to deal with the consolidation question, for example, was not an abnegation of responsibility, but a clear refusal to interfere in the financial and legal structure of local government. Part of the same conviction was the department's willingness to give advice once the consolidation was a local fait accompli. (75) Support of local autonomy can be seen even where the Home Office had some statutory obligation to supervise a relationship, such as the one between chief constable and rural magistrates. This is especially clear in the Home Office reaction to the military ambitions of some newly appointed county chief constables in the years between 1857 and 1862. The volunteer fervour was at its height in these years, fears of French invasion being rampant in maritime counties, and a new domestic army, in the form of locally recruited Volunteer detachments was being created in many English counties. Many newly elected chief constables had presented their interviewing committees with plans to use the 'new' police as a foundation for a Volunteer force, as had Captain Ruxton, the new chief constable of Kent. By 1859 magistrates in that county were growing alarmed at his single-minded turning of policemen into soldiers, and they applied to the Home Office for advice. At the beginning of a long correspondence with Whitehall, Captain Ruxton was tactfully reminded of the statutory limits to his power. Six months later he was told sharply by the Home Office to abide by the act of 1856. (76) In 1873 the then Home Secretary gave public voice to a view long held at the Home Office: that chief constables were a dangerous set of men, and that their danger lay in the statutory autonomy of their position, which disturbed the structure of relationships between Home Office and county magistracy. (77)

One factor that is often forgotten in a discussion of the relationship between central and local government in the nineteenth century, is the practical, hard provincial experience of ministers and parliamentary staff at the Home Office. This aggregate of experience among personnel does go some way towards explaining an apparent respect for the autonomy of the locality on police matters. Between 1856 and 1886 there were only two short periods when neither the Home Secretary nor the Parliamentary Under Secretary had a _practical_ understanding of the nature of local government. Most parliamentary staff at the department in these years had been in their time a deputy lord lieutenant, a chairman of quarter sessions, or at least a magistrate, as shown in Table 1.1.

The aggregate of experience came down on the side of a clear understanding of the nature of _local_ administration. H. A. Bruce was even able to tell the National Association for the Promotion of Social Science about framing and administering law in Whitehall, and using it at home in recession, where he was Chairman of quarter sessions. (78) The important thing to note here is that it was county experience that was represented most firmly at the Home Office.

Table 1.1 Parliamentary Staff at the Home Office, 1856-80

Home Secretaries	Under Secretaries
1856 George Grey (JP, Deputy Lord Lieutenant Northumb.)	1856 W.H. Massey (Recorder Portsmouth)
1858 Spencer Walpole	1858 Gathorne Hardy (JP Workingham)
1859 Southeron Estcourt (JP Deputy Lord Lieutenant Wilts.)	1859 George Clive (JP Wokingham)
1859 Cornwell Lewis	
1861 George Grey (as above)	1861 H.A. Bruce (Deputy Lord Lieutenant Glamorgan)
1866 Spencer Walpole (as above)	1866 Lord Belmore
1867 Gathorne Hardy (as above)	1867 J. Fergusson (JP, Deputy Lord Lieutenant Ayr)
1868 H.A. Bruce (as above)	1868 E. Knatchbull Hugesson (JP Kent)
1873 Robert Lowe	
1874 R.A. Cross (JP Manchester, Chairman Quarter Sessions Cheshire)	1874 Selwyn Ibbetsson
	1878 M. White Ridley (Chairman Quarter Sessions, Northumb.)
1880 Vernon Harcourt R.A. Cross (as above)	1880 Arthur Wellesley Peel
1881 Vernon Harcourt	1881 Earl of Rosebury

Source: 'Hansard', Annual Series; Dod, 'Parliamentary Companion'; Burke, 'Landed Gentry', 'Peerage'; Walford, 'County Families of the UK'.

The Home Office's definition of its own role was the sum of some clearly understood administrative relationships, not all of which were bound by the strictures of statute. But definition of what a policeman was, was far more an outcome of contemporary thought and contemporary events. In the years immediately after 1856 the virtue not so much of individual police action, but of the single, unaccompanied policeman, was propounded by the Home Office. It was especially important to do this in the early 1860s, when a large and influential section of the game-preserving magistracy was proposing that policemen should patrol together in country districts so as to provide an effective force against poachers. 'The nature of the employment of the county police', said George Grey, the current Home Secretary, 'was that they patrolled singly.' (79) He believed that this was why they were generally popular with the smaller ratepayer. Game preservers who wanted to employ the police in the detection of poaching proposed giving them very wide legal powers for stopping and searching people on suspicion of their having been in pursuit of game. (80) Whilst Home Office officials believed along with influential sections of the national press that it would be 'monstrous' to leave legal matters to a policeman's judgment, and that policemen were 'taken from a class not very competent to judge what are reasonable grounds for a charge of felony,' (81) yet the 1850s and the 1860s witnessed a positive refusal on the part of the Home Office to eliminate the constable's individual accountability at law.

A well-publicised case of 1858, when an East Riding constable was charged with false imprisonment by the 'respectable' butcher he had accused of stealing some harness, and the charge was upheld, had led to pressure in legal circles for a quick passage through Parliament of a bill exempting policemen from liability for actions performed on duty. The Home Office resisted such pressure, and, partly because the Permanent Under Secretary of State at the department believed that the Home Office 'Instructions' of 1840 under which the constable acted, had misled him, recommended Treasury payment of the constable's costs. (82) In this way, on this and other occasions, the Home Office actually strengthened the definition of the single constable in his relationship with the law, and the governmental structure of the locality in which he worked. In fact, in the provinces police organisation was to become so structured, and so subject to a system of hierarchical decision-making, that it became extremely rare for a constable ever to have to make a self-determined move like the East Riding constable mentioned above.

In some boroughs this legal definition of the single, individually responsible constable resulted in a complete identification of policemen with their employing authority. Watch committees would hear complaints against the police, fine or dismiss a constable who had offended a ratepayer, and this procedure reinforced public perception of a watch committee as a kind of judiciary. (83) The individual legal liability of the individual policeman which was upheld by the Home Office was translated in provincial government into the single unit of masters and men, the servant absorbed into the watch committee's identity. When the head constable of Cambridge, for example, was accused in 1860 of 'outrageous exercise of power', the local press at least made little practical distinction between the position of the watch committee and the position of borough policeman: 'the defendent is Mr Turrell . . . or rather the defendents are the watch committee who have undertaken to idemnify their head constable.' (84)

It was then by both default and intention that the Home Office came to define a policeman in the years between 1856 and 1880. Yet in this time only one clear prescriptive statement about the position of constable was made by the department, and the statement itself was not for home consumption, but made in response to a French request for a comparison between the accountability of

French and English policemen. By the end of the 1860s it was possible to define a policeman as an individual personally responsible
for his official acts, and to say that in performing such acts he
was expected to live up to a commonly held idea of how a reasonable
man behaved. (85) The real man, not this cypher, but the social
reality of the policeman, was held in contempt — he was 'from a
class not very competent' — and we have yet to see how small was
a policeman's field of action made by police hierarchy and local
government. His field of action was made small, as the second part
of this book will show, because his capacity — his reasonableness —
had always to be measured against the fact that he was recruited from
the working class.

     Was this definition by the Home Office of the single, individual-
ly responsible policeman, an exact measure of the rejection of
militarism in the department? Administrative commentators have
seen it in this light, though it is true that they have not been
aware of the military debate, nor the background of war, that
ushered in the act of 1856. Henry Parris has noted that in 1860
Horatio Waddington, Permanent Under Secretary at the Home Office,
(86) checked the Home Secretary's willingness to sanction the use
of a county constabulary as the basis for a Volunteer force. (87)
But this refusal, when it was made, was really a rejection of the
proposal to arm and drill serving policemen rather than the rejection of a military ideal. There was no Home Office objection
to a county chief constable commanding a section of Volunteers (88)
and, indeed, it would have been impossible for a county constabulary
to avoid connection in the public mind with a soldiery. It was
in fact over the question of the police as a kind of soldiery that
the Home Office developed its clearest theory of police. It is
important to examine this theory, for it serves to put the official
account of the policeman's individual responsibility, the untested
cornerstone of most historical perception of the police, into
some perspective.

(vi)   Policemen as soldiers: the Murphy Riots

The County and Borough Police Act of 1856 (19 & 20 Vict. c.69) and
the rapid development of a uniform, countrywide system of police
made the use of military aid by local authorities a rare occurrence in the 1850s and 1860s, and it was not until the Fenian disturbances (of which the Murphy Riots of the late 1860s were a part)
that the role of the police as peace-keepers needed to be defined.
If Horatio Waddington made one point clear during his long years
at the Home Office as Permanent Under Secretary, it was that the
most important function of the department was to maintain the peace
of the localities. (89) Given the governmental reality of the
provinces, and a Home Office understanding of the structure of
police management, then, as a corollary to this conviction, disturbances of the peace came to be defined as a series of isolated,
incidents that could in their entirety be either be prevented or
suppressed.

     In the early 1860s the first reaction of a local authority facing
disturbance was communication with the Home Office. During the

Coventry Ribbon Strike of 1860 correspondence from the mayor, local notables and the Lord Lieutenant of Warwickshire were received at the Home Office. They contained a most detailed analysis of events, and in some cases, pleaded for guidance. The request for troops to be stationed in the town was granted, but the Home Secretary and the Permanent Under Secretary took a far more detailed interest in the preventative methods that might be embodied in the proper working of local law, advising magistrates to sit continuously, and to issue carefully worded, unprovocative statements dissuading local working people from action. (90)

The great majority of boroughs were in the same position as Coventry in 1860, that is, they did not have police forces large enough to deal with riots, and Home Office advice to them usually followed the same pattern: swear in as many respectable citizens as special constables as possible; call on the county constabulary, then the yeomanry (but if possible, swear the yeomen in as special constables); then finally, if necessary make application to the military. As the 1860s passed, local authorities were reminded more and more firmly by the Home Office that it was their duty to preserve their own peace and protect their own property. Official disapproval of stationing troops simply for show — 'Prevention' it was called — grew stronger in these years. There was constant reiteration from the Home Office of the virtues of 'a police force essentially civil, unarmed and acting without any assistance from a military force'. (91)

What came as a statement of principle from the Home Office was for panicking lord mayors simply another expression of administrative reality. In an election riot in Lincoln in 1862 the nearest station of troops was known by the borough authorities to be in Manchester. The reorganisation of the standing army in the 1850s meant that, like many borough authorities had before, and many were to do again, the Lincoln magistrates called on the county police. And entering Lincoln in military formation, all dressed exactly alike, batons displayed prominently in right hand, these policemen entered the city as an army. (92)

But whilst local political reality turned policemen into soldiers, the Home Office defined those policemen more rigidly as individuals. The Fenian disturbances and the Murphy Riots of the late 1860s enabled an important contemporary distinction to be made, between insurrection and rebellion, in the suppression of which the use of arms was justified, and 'mere riot', in which the use of arms were not justified and for which local police forces were primarily responsible. (93) Legally neat though the distinction was, it did not help the policeman very much:

A policeman who has the duty of suppressing a riot is in a very difficult position [ran a Home Office memorandum], for if by his acts he causes death, he is liable to be indicted for murder . . . and if he does not act he is liable to an indictment . . . for neglect. He is therefore bound to hit the precise line of his duty . . . . (94)

The series of riots known as the Murphy Riots ran from 1866 to 1871, reaching their peak in the summer and autumn of 1868. They were caused by the anti-Catholic orator and agitator called William Murphy who, when he set up his tent in a Lancashire or Black Country

town, was usually successful in provoking large-scale and violent
attacks on Catholic people, communities and property. (95) What
holds this series of riots together is their similarity of pattern in different places. All of them took place in urban situations where it was often assumed that geographically at least, disturbance would be easier to control, for in highly populated areas
the police could remain in close communication with each other and
were not spread out over a large terrain as they were in the
countryside. The riots drew on violently felt community antagonisms that were not created by, but were used by, Murphy and no
police hierarchy revealed itself to be unaware of such conflict.
Indeed, one of the few places where local police forces did enter a
national political arena during this period was here. 'Local knowledge', the principle of good policing vaunted by the Home Office,
had a peculiar meaning in these towns, during the Murphy Riots.

From June 1866 to April 1871 there were twenty-five riots, or
anticipated riots, caused by Murphy and his entourage. Places where
riot occurred intermittently over several days have been counted as
one occurrence. In ten of these twenty-five situations, troops were
called out. This is not necessarily to say that they were used.
But a town certainly knew that they were there: in Stalybridge for
example, in April 1868, they were billeted throughout the town,
though they fired not one shot, and never even appeared in military
formation. (96) The Volunteers were called out in two places (once
in conjunction with troops), and the militia was called out once
(again, in conjunction with the regular army). The same was true
of the Yeomanry on the one occasion when they were sent for. (97)
Police from outside the community in which the riot occurred were
used on eleven of these twenty-five occasions. Five boroughs with
their own police relied on county constabularies, five within county
police jurisdiction had extra men drafted to them, and one town
depended on detachments of police from Manchester to restore order.
Special constables were sworn in on eleven occasions: employing
'respectable persons', 'tradesmen', in defence of their own property
was a traditional response to urban riot, and their use in this way
during the Murphy Riots (and other disturbances of the 1860s) shows
that, although it may have been theoretically recognised that 'the
use of social and economic superiors as police exacerbated rather
than mollified class violence', urban manufacturers, tradespeople,
and ratepayers were often personally concerned in the armed protection of their own property in English cities in the late 1860s.
(98)

There were fourteen Murphy Riots in which no help from outside
was called on. Two of these occurred in towns where anti-Roman
Catholic feeling was not strong, though in Plymouth in June 1866
Murphy was able to rely on the allegiance of a body of Marines in
his audience to get him out of difficulties. (99) In Bradford in
June 1868, only twelve people turned up to Murphy's lecture, and
extensive police precautions proved unnecessary. (100) On other
occasions where outside aid was not applied for it was either because
disturbance was not anticipated, or because the lecture did not
take place in the later arena of conflict. In Stalybridge in
January 1868 disturbance was created by the invasion of a large
crowd inflamed by Murphy's oratory in a nearby town. On this

particular occasion a single policeman's action in isolating a possible 'cause' of trouble, an Irishman armed and ready to defend his
home, prevented further disturbance. (101)

On other occasions the careful guarding of buildings from
within and without by local policemen averted riots without resort
to outside help. In Oldham in February 1868, for example, the local
borough force co-operated with a body of 300 Irish people in
defending their church. (102) Other local police forces displayed
the preventative technique outlined above and isolated groups of
Catholics, arresting them for possession of dangerous weapons or
attempting to cause a riot. (103) In other places police success
depended on an ability to keep the streets clear. In a town where
the local police force came under the auspices of the surrounding
county constabulary it was easy to obtain extra help from within
the police hierarchy rather than by the application of a separate
watch committee to a county chief constable. The majority of these
urban communities that did not call on outside force were in fact
policed by the surrounding county constabulary.

What local authorities had learned from each other by the end of
1868 was that no police operation, however augmented, provided sufficient force to deal with the sort of riot that Murphy brought
about. However, by acting in a body, by providing a well-disciplined
human wall around a lecture theatre or a church under threat, a
police force could avert an attack. (104) Indeed, where policemen
acted individually, and with truncheon or baton tried to disperse a
crowd, they were singularly unsuccessful. Once a disturbance had
moved from the vicinity of a building, or a well-defined, enclosed
space (a square, an Irish ghetto, a cul-de-sac) the police were
generally powerless. In Birmingham in 1867 'there were great
crowds on the streets and it is not too much to say that from
3 p.m. to 8 p.m, mob law prevailed. The police, even with their
cutlasses had great difficulty in getting the best of the rioters.
In fact they failed to do so . . . ' (105) In Bacup in April
1868 'about 50 or 60 Irishmen . . . heavily armed . . . made an
attack on stragglers' who were following a Murphyite parade.
Street battle followed, but the police made only one capture. (106)
In Ashton in May of the same year a similar uselessness for police
purposes of 'open' battle was revealed. After 24 hours of disturbance news reached the town hall that an 'English mob' was
forming in the Irish quarter. 'Superintendent Ludlam of the
county constabulary with a company of about 30 men proceeded to
the scene.' The moment the police appeared, 'the mob divided',
one half racing over a nearby bridge. The other half formed a
procession and paraded through several streets, smashing the
windows of Irish homes as they went. Powerless in this situation,
the body of police moved to the vicinity of the Catholic church
and succeeded at least in protecting this from the crowd. 'Finding
the police then to be a match for them [the English mob] set out
for Stalybridge.' The police again attempted to form a closed and
limited encounter, and formed a barrier across the bridge leading
to Stalybridge 'which barred the progress of the rioters in that
direction; but they turned down the road leading to Dukinfield
. . . ' (107)

Policemen needed to have their backs up against a wall to act with any degree of success. However, given a situation of open confrontation on the streets, there were police tactics that showed a limited success. One has already been mentioned: that of arresting those seen, or believed, to be ringleaders. Indeed, what gave the policeman his ultimate power and advantage in a riot situation was his 'singleness' and individuality. What these qualities meant in reality was that he could arrest people and turn a crowd into a collection of isolate and powerless individuals. But to be able to make arrests, policemen needed to be backed up by great forces of physical power. In Manchester in August 1868, the scene of the most widely publicised Murphy Riot, the local police force provided its own army. Police tactics here were to charge the enormous crowd with truncheons, converging on obvious 'ringleaders'. This force of 100 city police then marched up and down the streets in closed formation, sealing off the area. Twenty of the county constabulary were held in reserve until this time, then 'rendered good service by arresting violence on the streets'. (108)

The impression that the army was not used at all during the Murphy Riots can only derive from a consideration of events in Manchester in August 1868. (109) The Manchester City Police were in fact the only urban force to deal with prolonged rioting without any resort to outside aid, except for a small force of Lancashire county policemen. Their success on the Saturday afternoon mentioned above depended on their appearance in a body, in military formation, armed with truncheons and a sophisticated method of charging a crowd and isolating elements within it. The Manchester disturbance took place in the middle of Murphy's meeting, in his presence. The meeting took place in the open air, and was the antithesis of the sort of situation with which the police dealt well; but the lecturer's presence did contain the crowd within a defined area. Most of the riots instigated by Murphy took place in the open street, after the conclusion of a lecture. The crowds he urged on were usually mobile, intent upon attacking Irish property. In cases like these the police might be successful, as we have seen, in creating a cordon round such property.

But it is misleading to speak of police 'success'. The only consistent end point to the riots was when William Murphy left town. The head constable of Manchester explained that policemen were dealing with a situation that had no defined end: 'there is no telling to what extent the excitement may go on . . . .' (110) Head constables reckoned success in terms of clearing the streets by midnight and making a substantial number of arrests. But Murphy chose his dates well, always lecturing on a Friday or Saturday evening, when riot would be free to extend over a day and a night and Catholics could be relied upon to be visible on the streets.

Overt public opinion turned to the preventative principle with the greatest alacrity: 'this riot must have been foreseen and ought to have been prevented;' 'no measures were taken to prevent the coming storm.' (111) In many cases of course, precautions were taken, by alerting the soldiery and swearing in special constables. But there is strong evidence that in the early stages of disturbance

in many towns, the police were prevented from acting as a riot force
by the pressure of local property owners, who insisted as ratepayers that they should patrol the streets in the normal way. (112)
Other precautions included the issuing of notices urging people
to stay at home, and some watch committees made speical efforts to
disarm the Irish — in both senses of the word. (113) All these
efforts showed a desire to contain the ingredients of riot within
doors, in a building, and this quest for 'precaution' belonged
especially to the urban ratepayer, for the burden on property was
heavy in a town where Murphy lectured. (114) Birmingham, having
the misfortune to house his headquarters, was the first city to
learn that in the kind of situation that Murphy engineered, '400
borough police, 180 county constabulary borrowed, 93 cavalry, 300
infantry, and 400 or 500 special constables' were not enough. (115)
Local authorities were increasingly to try preventing Murphy from
lecturing, or even from getting off the train that brought him to
his chosen battlefield. (116)

Though the soldiery was frequently called on during this series
of riots, they were only used in a traditional way on one occasion.
In Blackburn at the end of October, 1868, the Riot Act was read and
the Dragoons dispersed the crowd using cutlasses. (117) On the
other occasions when the Riot Act was read it was the local police,
the county constabulary, or a body of special constables, who provided the force behind the words. Looking at the whole series of
riots, it is clear that there was little difference in function
between the various peace-keeping force. Special constables and
Dragoons patrolled the streets like policemen, cavalry were spread
through a town in billets, the mere fact of their presence used
like a policeman's, as a warning. In general, it was the police
who acted as soldiers, and who appeared on the front line, troops
often being kept in the background. The local press was often
willing to compare these detachments of 'foreign' police to an
army. But the significant distinction revealed is that between
county and borough in the use of a police to protect property. The
contemporary understanding of a borough policeman as a servant of
the ratepayers is discussed more fully below, in section (viii).
However, it is important to recognise here that there was a legal
history in operation in mid-Victorian boroughs whereby relationships
between watch committees and constables were construed as those
pertaining between masters and servants. (118) County constabularies, on the other hand, were deployed by a magistracy which
understood the policing of areas to be, in part, the territorial
defence of property against an internal enemy. The Murphy Riots
brought these two histories of defence and policing face to face
with each other in the provincial England of the 1860s.

Most of the property damaged in the course of these riots was
that of the 'poorer classes', and the public buildings attacked
were usually Roman Catholic chapels. (119) Had damage been done
to property that belonged more to the mainstream of urban ownership and control and had large numbers of ratepayers been involved,
then the anomalous state of the compensation for riot damages
might have been revealed before 1882, when two Riot Damages Acts
were passed, the first in response to London's Sunday Trading
Riots, and the second (49 & 50 Vict. c.38), which extended its

provisions to the provinces. Damage done to the Catholic chapel
in Ashton in 1868 was remembered in 1882 when this second piece of
legislation was debated in Parliament. Under the law in operation
in the late 1860s it had been 'impossible to obtain compensation
. . . although buildings might be all but gutted . . . yet if those
who proceeded in the work of destruction had not the ultimate intention of entirely destroying the buildings, the owners could
obtain no compensation whatsoever . . . .' (120)

As the town clerk of Blackburn shrewdly pointed out in 1882, if
the provision of the act that had just been made to apply to London
was 'made of general application . . . the hand of every ratepayer
would be against the riots.' (121) In the northwestern towns of
1867-8 the hand of the most powerful borough ratepayers directed
the police towards their regular surveillance of property, and the
county police were called on to act in concert against those who
rioted.

(vii) THE GOVERNMENT INSPECTORS OF CONSTABULARY

The Home Office relationship with local government over police matters was defined both by provincial experience on the part of Home
Office staff, and by reaction to contemporary events. But there were
were more obvious and statutory links than these, as other commentators have noted. The County and Borough Police Act of 1856 (19
& 20 Vict. c.69) provided for the appointment of three government
inspectors for three geographical regions (north, Midlands, and
south), on whose favourable report the treasury grant to police
authorities was to depend. Five inspectors of police operated
between 1856 and 1880. Major General William Cartwright of Flore,
Northamptonshire, was by far the most influential of the five,
although he was the only one not to have had previous police
experience as a head or chief constable. In his teens Cartwright
had served in the Peninsula War under Sir John Moore, (122) and,
like another of the government inspectors, he belonged to that
generation of army humanitarians that never engaged in war during
the long stretch of peace between 1819 and 1855. (123) However,
in Cartwright's case, the county in which his family were major
landowners provided a domestic battle front, and he served as a
captain of the Northamptonshire Yeomanry in the 1830s. (124)

He was appointed as chairman of Northamptonshire quarter sessions
in 1851 after a long career as a poor law union chairman and magistrate. He remained on the commission of the peace during his life-
time and spent many years as chairman of the finance committee of
quarter sessions: 'he was ever exceedingly careful of the interests
of the ratepayers.' (125) His son, the conservative Member of
Parliament for Northants. South, was one of the more active parliamentary lobbyists for police superannuation.

Contemporary testimony to his understanding of local circumstances, and the ease with which he manoeuvred magistrates and
courts of quarters sessions, has been interpreted as tact. (126)
But it showed far more than that, and demonstrated rather a perfect
understanding, born of long personal experience, of the workings of
local government. The County and Borough Police Act became law on

1 January 1857, but Cartwright started his work in the last months
of 1856, visiting several Midlands courts of quarter session where
magistrates debated the precise formation of the new, compulsory
police. He carried with him an acceptable version of the Essex
model, (127) and the delicate hint that a system too much like the
old superintending constable system might not receive the government grant. (128)   In Buckinghamshire his influence routed a scheme
drawn up by Disraeli and supported by the Marquis of Chandos. (129)
What Cartwright negotiated in Buckinghamshire, he secured for
other counties in the Midlands region: one constable to 1,500
people. This was a smaller relationship of police to population
than the Home Office suggestion of 1/1,000, and Cartwright was to
work to improve the figures for the next fifteen years. The geographical ratios that Cartwright secured in 1856, of one constable
to 100,000 acres, is a rough average for all rural areas in the
years 1856 to 1880. What Buckinghamshire got in 1857, and what
the supporters of Disraeli's scheme had not wanted, was an increased
rate bill, a larger number of policemen, and a carefully graded system of classes of constable to provide promotion, which even at this
stage seemed to point to a severance of policemen from magisterial
control. (130)
     Other inspectors shared Cartwright's gentry background, though
they were not as well connected as he. Looking at the provincial
experience and status of these men, it becomes clear that the
impact of inspection after 1856 should not be interpreted as the
meeting of centralism and autonomous local government. It was
because the first inspectors were in a social position to understand that a local police was a part of local government that they
were so successful.
     The influence of the inspectors was two-fold. They outlined to
central government, and to an interested public, the needs of a
professional body, and second, in their annual reports they emphasised the virtues of a kind of local government policing, a wholesale system of ordering and disciplining communities that was
based on the administrative actions of local police forces. In
the years immediately after 1856 all three inspectors gave their
wholehearted approval to the employment of policemen in administrative functions. Cartwright's Midland district was one in which
the practice of appointing police officers as inspectors of common
lodging houses, of nuisances, above all as poor law relieving
officers, was far more widespread even by 1856 than it was in the
north and south. Cartwright, holding to Chief Constable MacHardy's
dictum, that the more a policeman was used, the better a policeman
he was, (131) advocated such appointments to quarter sessions with
a proselytising zeal. He was never to display the later reserve of
those ex-policemen Captain Willis (southern region inspector
1856-80) and Captain Woodford (northern region, 1856-68) who
both came to feel that many lineaments of Cartwright's complete
policeman were 'not appropriate'. To define this inappropriateness,
they employed a dividing line that Cartwright never needed to fix:
whether or not local administration 'interfered materially with
the proper performance of . . . ordinary duties'. (132)   It was in
a distinction like this that the voice of the ex-policeman was made
most plain.

Cartwright believed in 'vagrant crime', and one way of looking at his term as inspector of constabulary is as a mission to put into more general operation the lessons learned during his years as a poor law board chairman in Northamptonshire. The question of police supervision of the vagrant poor is dealt with in more detail below; but it is important to note here that Cartwright always received wide publicity for any scheme he suggested, and it was not only his local prestige but the local press that made him a powerful and influential man. All the inspectors' reports were published in the national press, and provincial papers too published the extracts that were applicable to their distribution area.

Compared with Cartwright, the other inspectors — ex-policemen all of them — understood part of their role as making a wider public aware of the police as something more than a workforce. All three supported the officer class campaign for a uniform superannuation policy. At first they understood the campaign as a question of reward for men of 'conspicuous merit', though after the mid-1860s their faithful recording of officiers opinion that a pension was a right, not a reward, became a means of making that opinion known in central government. (133) Yet before the 1870s all inspectors' suggestions concentrated on ameliorating a strictly local system of superannuation. Magisterial 'discretion', which resulted in so much local difference in the payment of pensions, was not condemned by a government inspector until 1880. (134) In this, as in so many other ways, the inspectors tended to sanction the differences inherent in local financial autonomy on police matters.

The government inspectors' ideas changed as those of professional policemen changed. Yet the only inspector without police experience came to his post with a far greater weight of theory than the others seem to have possessed. Cartwright was the first among them to outline the philosophy of rank, to urge the establishment of merit classes of constables, scheduled pay increases and a larger section of first class constables within police hierarchies 'so as not to keep good men down too long'. (135) The cornerstone of Cartwright's vision of police organisation was the sergeant: 'there is no rank more valuable to the well-working of a force than this, which not only gives deserving long service men promotion, but assists in outlying districts . . . remote from the superintendent . . . and keeps constables at such posts constantly superintended.' (136) Efficiency was not only organisational, but moral in intention, and Cartwright concerned himself with police welfare. He recommended the appointment of police surgeons, the establishment of station reading rooms and subscribed generously to the Police Mutual Assurance Association. He helped to finance and open a police orphanage at Brighton. (137) More than any other inspector, he displayed a sophisticated understanding of the pressures and conflicts that operated on a constable. (138) When he died in 1873 this conservative country gentleman was mourned as 'the policeman's friend'. (139) Country gentleman that he was, he saw the police as an improved soldiery. He saw obvious advantages in connecting county police forces with the Volunteers, and was sanguine about arming the police. He always approved of military drill for policemen, and on many occasions before the Fenian and Murphyite

disturbances of the late 1860s, urged rifle practice on rural
forces. (140)

The inspectorate was cynical about borough control of police
forces. They frequently asked the Home Office to provide statutory means for enforcing consolidation of boroughs with counties.
Their most precise criticism was of management by 'watch com-
mitiees and local interests and connections', especially where
there was a drink interest involved in police management. (141)
The inspectors did criticise county police management on many
specific points, but criticism of the boroughs rested on the very
nature of urban government, and it was questioned in a way that
police management by magistrates in the counties never was.

A concern for police welfare was often the platform for condemning the municipalities, for the County and Borough Police Act
of 1856 (19 & 20 Vict. c.69) had made it compulsory on county
authorities, but not on borough authorities, to establish superannuation funds (the argument in the counties was about whether
or not rural policemen ever got paid out of them). Borough funds
were in any case more likely to collapse because of their small
actuarial base. Disapproval for authorities that ignored the plight
of the 'broken down constable', were reserved for the boroughs.
Very close to the surface of a specific criticism like this lay
condemnation of the very nature of borough forces: they were too
small; only a force that could keep its own peace was truly 'efficient', and the only borough forces able to do this were those of
Manchester and Liverpool.

After Cartwright's resignation the other inspectors attempted
to remove administrative burdens from the complete policeman.
Colonel Cobbe, former chief constable of the West Riding, followed
Cartwright,and became government inspector for the Midland region
in 1869. In his first report to the Home Office he attributed the
high number of resignations from police forces to the large number
of extra duties that policemen were obliged to perform. (142) He
grew increasingly condemnative of magistrates who ignored Home
Office directions on the appointment of policemen to administrative tasks. (143)

By the late 1870s the inspectors' support for policemen as part
of a locally financed system of local government, had considerably
diminished. Yet it had been precisely that earlier support that
provided their success, and which enabled them to keep ratios of
police to population at a reasonable level. The first inspectors'
roots lay in the provinces, not only because they lived and worked
there, but by virtue of family background. As in Whitehall, the
provincial experience of the first inspectors was largely rural,
and Cartwright especially showed a clear commitment to the idea of
a locally controlled county government.

(viii)   BOROUGH VERSUS COUNTY

All questions of police management in the provinces were ultimately
financial questions. The history of local police forces from 1856
to 1880 is also an outline of the largely unwritten history of
ratepaying politics. The boroughs are particularly important for

this history, partly because the theory of ratepaying politics was
more clearly experessed there, but also because, on the question
of police and policing, the boroughs were not innovators, and
did not provide a pattern as they did in so many other aspects of
mid-Victorian legislation. The boroughs had to fight to maintain
privileges in police management, just as in 1854 and 1856 they
fought the compulsory consolidation clauses in two police bills.
They suffered in comparison with county forces and at the opinions
of county orientated Home Office officials, and the criticism
directed at them reveals what was approved of in rural governmental
relations.

It has been argued that the act of 1856 had only a very limited
effect on the boroughs, (144) but the first inspections under it did
have an impact on a number of municipal forces. In 1857 nearly a
third of boroughs made some changes in numbers or organisation.
Cartwright's Midland district provided the biggest proportion of
these, but all town councils were aware that a certificate of
'efficiency', and thus a government grant, depended on a minimum
number of policemen. (145) The inspectors took with them to the
boroughs the idea of district policing, a control and organisation
that would cross borough boundaries; but to town councils area
policing meant consolidation and the encroachment of a county into
municipal privileges. When a town council felt it had to defend
itself against this rural encroachment, then a public alaysis of
the shape and particularity of a community might develop. In the
pages of the local press at least the ratepaying citizens of Middlesbrough saw their town plain, with its particular needs for
discipline and control, discussed for the first time in late 1856,
when the implications of the County and Borough Police Act (19 & 20
Vict. c.69) were debated: 'the extent of their populations, its
growth, its character . . . a larger proportion of males than
could be found in any town of comparable size . . . .' (146) This
sudden perception of a community as a particular place on the map
of control was one of the incidental effects of the act of 1856.
The act itself also played a part in shaping ratepayers' understanding of their own status and powers. After the act was passed,
the Home Office demanded for the first time the collection and
return of statistics that had been required under the Municipal
Corporations Act of 1835 (5 & 6 Will. IV c.88). These returns,
detailing policing organisation, criminal statistics, the number
of licenced premises, and the number of vagrants passing through
in a year, were always printed in full in the local press after
1857. This kind of publicity clarified the relationship between
policeman and ratepayer, and the community in which they both
played out their roles was officially defined as belonging to
those who paid rates on their property and paid a police force to
protect it.

However, it would be misleading to suggest that there was any
fundamental change in borough police management in the years after
1856. Charges of 'bias' and 'interest' in watch committee control
of a police force did not alter, and though the government inspectors of constabulary developed a critique of some of the stranger
functions that urban policemen were called upon to perform, it was
difficult to find a formula for condemnation when in the very same

reports they were urging the appointment of county policemen in the administration of rural local government. (147)

The head constable of a borough was in a quite different statutory and bureaucratic position from that of a county chief constable: he was only the senior officer of a body of men that the watch committee of the town council had absolute power to select, direct and dismiss. The county chief constable, on the other hand, possessed these powers in law. A contemporary theory of municipal government drew great strength from this ability to control its own executive and thus to maintain complete control over the implementation of its own civil law: 'We have the power of making our own rulers, and expending our local taxes, and retain in our hands the entire management of our . . . local affairs . . . the greatest privilege is the power . . . of appointing our police.' (148)

A watch committee was the most prestigious of all a corporation's sub-committees. Usually very well attended, it met frequently, in most places, on a weekly basis. Meetings were less well attended in places where pressure of business was less, for example, where responsibility for public health, or scavenging, or hackney carriages was given to some other sub-committee. Members of a watch committee were chosen on the basis of long service and regular attendance at town council meetings. (149) In all towns the mayor, who under the Municipal Corporations Act of 1835 was also a sworn justice of the peace, was chairman of the watch committee. The loudest contemporary charge against watch committee management was changeability, and a fluctuating borough police management was compared with the long, uninterrupted years of magisterial direction in the counties. There was a requirement under the Municipal Corporations Act that a third of town councillors should relinquish their office every year; but in some towns, watch committee members did serve for very long continuous periods indeed — up to seventeen and twenty-seven years in Cambridge and Sheffield respectively, in the years between 1850 and 1880. Watch committees could, and did, pursue continuous policies. (150)

Local justification for borough police management drew strength from a well-defined relationship with the ratepaying public; but the legal position of a watch committee was anomalous. Being only a committee of a municipal corporation, it was not itself incorporated and could not therefore, be sued. Yet it had a statutory existence. (151) It was within this framework that some watch committees in some local communities came to establish themselves as a type of judicial body. In many places, even as late as the 1860s, it was watch committee members who were considered the peace-keepers, rather than the police. In Cambridge in the 1850s it was the custom of ratepayers to speak privately to a committee member, stopping him in the street, or calling on him at home, about the state of the pavements, the prevalence of street begging, or the improprieties of constables on the beat. By the 1860s a system of formal attendance at watch committee meetings to make complaints had developed. The watch committee constituted itself a committee of inquiry when complaints about police practice were made, and listened to police evidence. When damage was done to private property in the course of police duty, complainants might be recompensed out of the police fund. (152)

Supervision of the body of police was of course one of the statutorily prescribed functions of a watch committee. But there were
ways in which a system so liable to the vagaries of individual decision could lead to a very close identification of police and watch
committee, one which seemingly provided a closed circuit of detection and punishment, without any resort to a court of law. (153)
In Cambridge until the 1870s, the watch committee reviewed all
complaints against licenced premises that were made by the police:
'On Monday five or six were brought before the committee . . . they
promised not to offend again . . . all agreed it was their first
offence . . . they were discharged with a caution . . . .' (154)
The borough justices at licencing sessions deferred to watch committee investigation of beer houses — indeed the informal 'trial'
described above was seen as part of a regular procedure. (155)
In Cambridge, as in many other boroughs, there was a fairly high
and consistent number of magistrates on the watch committee, and
in this particular local context, where only the most casual distinction was made between the borough bench and the watch committee,
to talk of the latter as a 'kind of tribunal' (156) had a precise
meaning for the ratepaying public.

The Home Office grew eager to curb this sort of activity as the
1870s passed. The long-standing procedures in Cambridge came to an
end in 1871 after the new inspector of the Midland region complained of it to the Home Office. Ten years later when Rochdale
watch committee constituted itself a tribunal to deal with juvenile
crime, the practice was put a stop to, almost before it got under-
way. (157)

But a watch committee did not need the presence of magistrates in
order to act in this way. In Sheffield, where the only magistrate
on the watch committee between 1850 and 1880 was the mayor, it was
still used as a public, semi-legal tribunal in much the same way as
it was in Cambridge. It acted as a committee of inquiry into
union activity and trade 'outrage' in the 1850s, calling witnesses,
taking statements and listening to evidence from policemen and
public. Even as late as 1867 trade unionists knew that it was to
the watch committee, not the magistrates, nor the press, that they
must declare their innocence. (158)

Ratepayers demanded this activity on their behalf in the 1850s
and 1860s. They paid their money to a town council for the protection of their property, and the most significant feature of trade
outrage to the merchants and manufacturers whose works were theatres
of union conflict, was not damage to life, but to buildings and
equipment. Acting as a 'kind of tribunal' was anyway the most convenient way in which men involved in the iron and steel trade (fully
70 per cent of watch committee members in the years 1856-80) could
investigate attacks on their own workplaces and manufactures.

Sheffield watch committee revealed itself unwilling to maintain
this role as judicial body as the 1860s passed. In 1863 and 1864
the town council failed to receive a certificate of efficiency from
the Home Office and the government grant that went with it. This
failure, which centred on the watch committee's refusal to employ
enough policemen, revealed an antagonism between ratepayers and
rate-leviers, (159) and this antagonism revealed a context for
understanding why police and watch committee could not cope with

trade outrage in the city. Unlike the situation in Cambridge, which
has been briefly described, where once a licencing offence had been
committed and reviewed by the watch committee, it could be sent
before the borough bench, in Sheffield, if no murder was done during
a trade dispute then there could be no judicial investigation by a
coroner's court. If no insured property were damaged, then there
was no insurance office to institute an inquiry. (160) The watch
committee in Sheffield could not employ a judicial prerogative as
Cambridge watch committee could over licencing offences. The ability
of a watch committee to act in this way and to provide the sort of
judicial action that a ratepaying public demanded, depended ultimately upon the type of offence with which it dealt. (161) In
Sheffield, in the mid-1860s, public demand for action grew, and the
watch committee appealed to the Home Office for a commission of
inquiry into trade outrage.

In the late 1860s, the sphere of Sheffield watch committee's
influence broadened, as it abandoned its role as a 'kind of tribunal'. It and the police force were subject to radical reorganisation. The committee's concern with the surveillance and control of
vagrants passing through the town was promoted by the government
inspector. The head constable was appointed borough surveyor and
he flowered as a provincial social scientist, collecting statistics
on vagrancy, doing all the background work for the children's
employment commission of 1862, inquiring into street begging, writing
reports on common lodging houses and paying the scavengers' and
lamplighters' wages. His reports on the state of crime in his
borough contained the most minute calculations of the social and
moral state of those under his surveillance. The watch committee
came to see its central role as that of exacting 'cleanliness and
good reputation' from the town's inhabitants. (162) Indeed, so
numerous became its preoccupations that one town councillor complained that it obviated the need for a town council at all. (163)

However, in most boroughs the relationship between the watch
committee and the town council was not really problematic, though
it was frequently fuel for charges of aggrandisement. A wider,
town council control of a local police force was provided for by
the inter-relationship of committee membership. The watch committee enjoyed a good deal of financial autonomy, and it was an
accepted principle of local government that the work of the committee should not be too closely inquired into by the town council
as a whole. It was the only committee of the town council that met
secretly, and whose deliberations were not reported in the local
press. (164)

It is possible to distinguish the role of money in borough
police management in a very crude way. Clothing and equipping a
police force put money in the way of local tradesmen, for example.
(165) But the sinister figure of the Additional Constable tells us
more than this about the precise and clear link between money paid
out for protection within the context of a local community, and
services provided. Since the Police Act of 1840 (3 & 4 Vict. c.88)
it had been possible to appoint Additional Constables at the expense
of private individuals. These constables were not supported out
of the rates, nor by the government grant, (166) but they were

dressed in the uniform of the local force, and subject to the discipline of its officers. Sworn as constables by the justices, they were policemen to the public eye. They were permanently stationed to protect specific pieces of property, and use of them was the particular practice of dock and harbour boards and market commissioners. But they were also used by private factory owners and, in the counties, by owners of large estates: in 1855 the chief constable reported to Northamptonshire quarter sessions that:

> owing to the increase of crime in Pottersbury . . . and in compliance with a request from his Grace the Duke of Grafton he had availed himself of . . . 3 & 4 Vict. c.88 s.19 and had appointed a constable . . . and stationed him at Pottersbury to assist the policeman stationed there. The constable will be paid by the Duke . . . . (167)

In the 1860s and 1870s Additional Constables numbered up to 25 per cent of northern county and borough forces. They were usually appointed from the ranks of the local force (a plum for the long-serving, deserving man), and bureaucratically, they were meant to be dealt with separately; but the inspector for the northern region, himself an ex-policeman, always listed them as part of the total police establishment of a county or borough. They were used to detect pilfering from factories, and to control the picketing of works during trade disturbance. Such appointments were made at least up until the First World War, and the Additional Constable needs to be more closely examined as a means of industrial policing.

Town councils of course were not unaware of how the protection of their members' property through the agency of the Additional, might be viewed. Mr Vaughan, of Bolckow and Vaughan, Middlesborough, member of the watch committee, 'hoped that the public would not take up a false impression with regard to the policeman being employed at their works. They had one constantly employed . . . and if they could keep changing him . . . there would not be so much chance of his becoming known.' (168) It is clear that the public took up precisely the right impression, and saw policemen as being permanently stationed to protect wealthy men's property.

Reputation attached itself to a watch committee through the agency of its head constable in a way alien to county magistrates. Watch committee protection of a head constable was absolute, except in cases where such support could only be followed by loss of public esteem. A ratepaying public recognised that the chief officer of police was only a cypher. (169) In northern industrial towns there was a tendency among manufacturing watch committee members to interpret the status of policemen as workmen, making reference to 'workshop quarrels,' offering rewards in the shape of Christmas dinners, pooling public donations and handing them over to the men at holiday time, making easy reference to the pay of other working men when discussing police wages. (170) In this way, in larger towns, head constables came to be seen as faithful head servants to whom certain powers could be delegated, and who had specialised knowledge about the business of social control and discipline — choosing constables, for example. But there was not in the boroughs the social identification that was to be found between a county chief constable and the county magistrates. The county chief constable occupied a social position and an area of social assumption in

common with the members of the court of quarter sessions. The head
constable of the mid-Victorian borough identified himself with his
masters (or might find strength in opposing such identification).
Nothing attached to the office in itself. The borough head constable was part of a system of local government.

(ix)   THE PATTERN OF COUNTY POLICING

In the counties, arguments were no less about power and financial
interest, but the line of influence between ratepayer and policeman
is harder to trace. The magistrates who levied the county rate,
from which the police fund was extracted, were not elected to do so,
and mid-Victorian local politics were centred on this difference
between county and borough. Magistrates attempted to evade the
loss of power they saw implicit in the County and Borough Police
Act of 1856, and all such attempts were based on the idea of area
control and social control. In the majority of English counties
police distribution and organisation was based on existing petty
sessional divisions. In several counties, like Buckinghamshire, the
old superintending constable sub-committee of quarter sessions
formed the core of the new police committee after 1856. (171) The
way in which geographical and administrative power was retained
for the individual magistrate is examined in more detail below; but
the most pressing concern in the winter of 1856-7 was the selection
of a chief constable, for the act of 1856 confirmed his statutory
autonomy. It was on his selection that the weight of magisterial
preoccupation fell.

Between 1856 and 1880, forty-seven chief constables held office
in the English administrative counties. Twenty-three of them had
been appointed before 1856, under the Rural Police Act of 1839
(3 & 4 Vict. c.93). If the group of chief constables is divided
into two in this way, it is possible to see that magistrates'
perception of their role changed in the post-1856 period. The
small number of men active as chief constables in these years
demonstrates the extraordinary length of time for which most of
them served. (172) (See Table 1.2.)

Military experience was the binding experience between all
nineteenth-century chief constables, though the growth in magistrates' use of such experience after 1856 is striking. Fewer ,
men with experience of other British police systems were employed
in the mid-Victorian years, and there was an increase in the number
of men with rural gentry backgrounds serving as county chief constables. One effect of this type of employment was to bar the
promotion of police officers.

It is possible to be more precise about the chief constables
who came from a landowning background. As would be expected,
younger sons figured large, as shown in Table 1.3. Younger sons
were not always the impoverished scions of minor county families,
and it is clear that from the 1850s onwards county chief constables
served as an occupation for younger sons in much the same way as
the army had traditionally done. Becoming head of a county force
might enable a man to consolidate and extend an existing social
position and wed himself to the upper reaches of the county

TABLE 1.2 Background of chief constables, 1856-80

	CHIEF CONSTABLES ACTIVE BETWEEN 1856 and 1880:	47
(A)	APPOINTED BEFORE 1856	23
	Army/naval experience	7
	Landed gentry	5
	Metropolitan experience	3
	Royal Irish Constabulary experience	3
	Borough police experience	1
	Nothing known	11
(B)	APPOINTED AFTER 1856	24
	Army/naval experience	22
	Landed gentry	11
	Militia captains	5
	Royal Irish Constabulary experience	11
	Metropolican experience	0
	Borough police experience	0
	Nothing known	

Source: Bucke, 'Landed Gentry'; Boase, 'Biographical Dictionary';
Walford, 'County Families of the UK'.

TABLE 1.3 Chief constables with gentry backgrounds

CHIEF CONSTABLES APPOINTED AFTER 1856	24
Landed gentry	11
Younger sons	8
Eldest sons	3

Source: Ibid.

hierarchy: when a young army captain applied for the chief constableship of Staffordshire in 1867, one of his proposers wrote that he
was
   a gentleman of very good family and social position in Cheshire;
   he married the daughter of . . . the chariman of quarter sessions
   for Cheshire, and I think you will agree with me that a person
   who works . . . and a chairman of quarter sessions does work,
   really deserves some consideration when appointments of this
   description are being made. (173)
   But whoever they married, chief constables in the second half of
the nineteenth century occupied a social position that enabled them
precisely to understand their position in a governmental and political hierarchy. They did not need to learn what were the claims
of the lord lieutenant and the larger landowners who made up the
police committee of the court of quarter sessions: 'the police
committee is not composed of a few magistrates accidentally nomi-
nated by Quarter Sessions, but a number of noblemen and gentlemen

worthy of the greatest confidence,' asserted the member of one in
1866. (174)   It was knowledge of that governmental reality that
chief constables brought with them to the job. The Home Office,
drawing on and maintaining its experience of provincial government,
supported this set of social and political arrangements. When a
Welsh quarter sessions police committee wrote to the Home Secretary in 1873 asking if it were possible to appoint a chief constable from among their superintendents, the reply was plain:
experience showed that policing became inefficient where county
forces were under the charge of

> persons of inferior position . . . . In counties it is . . .
> most essential that the chief constable, who has immense powers
> in his hands, should be a person of equal standing to the jus-
> tices . . . and in a position equal to that of chief constables
> of neighbouring counties. (175)

The appointment of gentry chief constables increased as the
1870s passed: it was easier to manage a man who shared the same
social and governmental assumptions as the magistrates. In 1856 and
1857 Buckinghamshire had witnessed a ratepaying battle between the
retrenchment platform of the conservatives and the large liberal
landowners over the formation of its first police force. Quarter
sessions, led by its victorious chairman and large county landowner, Lord Carrington, appointed a chief constable who was presented as being 'free from party', because he was a 'stranger to
the county'. (176) Captain Carter, a former officer in the militia,
devoted much of his energy to breaking up the close administrative
relationship between the existing police force (parish constables
and superintendents) and the individual magistrates operating in
petty sessional divisions. (177) The smaller landowning magistrates gathered in quarter sessions were not to make the same
mistake again. When the 'man free from party' resigned in 1867,
they chose as his successor a man firmly moulded by county connection and prestige. The new chief constable's uncle was some
time deputy lord lieutenant and high sheriff, and the main branch
of his family owned nearly 6,000 acres of county land. (178) This
move in Buckinghamshire, away from the last vestiges of a 'professional' police, was a reaction to the delining powers of individual magistrates in police matters.

The County and Borough Police Act of 1856 (19 & 20 Vict. c.69)
had laid down clearly the separate spheres of magistrates and
chief constable. The functions of the former were financial,
and centred on the disposal of the police fund and the payment
of policemen. The police committee could not itself act (that is,
it did not have the powers of a borough watch committee) but its
composition in most counties, with the lord lieutenant, his deputy,
the chairman of quarter sessions and the high sheriff usually members, assured that its recommendations were accepted by quarter
sessions. It was with the chief constable that the power to appoint,
regulate and dismiss policemen rested. The very division of powers
between chief constable and police committee served to support the
autonomy of the chief constable. (179) The committee could only
make financial decisions on data received and needed the chief
constable's report before the police rate could be assessed and
the number of policemen for each division decided upon. The

detailed possession of information gave the chief constable considerable power. What is more the chief constable could use the
opinion of the government inspector to back up his opinion, and
finally, he could resort to quoting statute: 'There is no intermediary between me and my men. The Act of Parliament gives me the
power of dismissing any constable I think unfit.' (180)

A professional policeman might try to bring a professional notion
of policing to a county, but his task was never easy. In some
counties, the old lines of judicial organisation were broken up after
1856, and police divisions were made to supersede petty sessional
divisions. (181) But this picture should not be taken at face value.
In some forces the rank of inspector was created simply so that
one might be made resident in each petty sessional division, and in
the years between 1856 and the early 1880s the petty session still
remained the focal point of rural administration and policing.
The chief constable was expected to understand this. His travelling
allowance was paid so that he might attend the sittings of courts
of petty sessions on a regular basis. (182)

Throughout England as a whole officer staff of a county force
(inspectors and superintendents) were invariably drafted to petty
sessional towns. In Wiltshire, for example, in 1868 there was not
one town with a court of petty sessions that did not have a county
police officer permanently stationed there. Police work demanded
a readily available magistrate, not only to issue summonses, but
also to provide in court the climax to surveillance, detection,
pursuit and arrest. (183) Even in the late 1870s policemen saw
the magistrate as the final, essential part of the police hierarchy. Police organisation too demanded that its officers be
stationed near main roads, post offices and canals, and petty
sessional towns were usually this kind of communications centre.

In the post-1856 period, the magistrates of rural England
retained a strong control over the police. They were conscious that
the establishment of a county-wide police force might spell the
waning of the individual justice's power and that the focal point
of administration might move from petty sessions to quarter sessions. A continuing control of the police by the individually
acting magistrate was provided for by the choice of a chief constable, the distribution of policemen and, as the second half
of this book will show, by the choice of rural labourers as policemen and the discipline meted out to them.

(x)   THE STRUCTURE OF COUNTY CONTROL

Mid-Victorian police forces were small. The statistics returned
annually to the Home Office show that the median ratio was one
policeman to 1,446 people in 1858, one to 1,275 in 1868 and one
to 1,221 in 1878. In 1858 the county policeman had 4,360 acres
under his surveillance, 4,030 in 1868 and 4,037 in 1878. (184)
But these figures are the stuff of statistical abstraction: the
whole of a force was counted as operational — an office of clerks,
the chief constable, a detective force, grooms and lock-up keepers
were all counted as perambulating policemen. (185)

Another set of figures, published annually in the 'Police and

Constabulary Almanac and Guide' show clearly that it was the police division, rather than the county as a whole, that formed the basis for operation and dispersal. This division, with the superintendent or inspector at its head formed a hierarchic unit of operation. Theoretically, police work recognised no division boundary, but the very nature of daily activity — perambulation, meeting at conference points, communication of reports to the superintendent — were based on it. The police division also marked the boundaries of public relations, for whilst there was not a great difference of police to people in the separate divisions, there was a very big difference in the ratio of policemen to area, as can be seen from this brief account of Cheshire and Leicestershire in 1868, as shown in Table 1.4.

TABLE 1.4   Ratio of police to population and area in Cheshire and Leicestershire, 1868

(A) CHESHIRE: WHOLE COUNTY		(B) LEICESTERSHIRE: WHOLE COUNTY	
Effective police/pop.: 1/1,835		Effective police/pop.: 1/1,783	
Effective police/area: 1/3,028		Effective police/area: 1/5,371	
Divisions: 9		Divisions: 8	
pol/pop.	pol./acre	pol./pop.	pol./acre
(1) 1/1,322	1/1,629	1/1,872	1/5,422
(2) 1/1,344	1/2,203	1/2,281	1/4,278
(3) 1/1,788	1/6,072	1/1,877	1/3,224
(4) 1/1,549	1/3,816	1/1,569	1/7,671
(5) 1/1,794	1/3,522	1/1,067	1/7,451
(6) 1/1,005	1/2,745	1/1,671	1/5,395
(7) 1/1,613	1/ 843	1/1,556	1/5,938
(8) 1/1,716	1/4,617	1/1,881	1/5,305
(9) 1/1,391	1/2,156		

Source: 'Police and Constabulary Almanac', 1858-.

Division 7 of Cheshire represented a densely populated urban are area, and there are represented here as well vast tracts of uninhabited land that were never traversed by a policeman. But it is still worth contemplating the medians of 3,000 and 5,000 acres that these figures offer. Should a constable have walked without stopping, and never have returned to his cottage or headquarters, he could not cover this area, even in a working day of twelve hours in which he walked some 12 to 16 miles. He was not meant to. His beat was a well-defined route that took in the major farms and manufactures of his division. He kept to the road, not just because that meant faster walking, but because the Night Poaching Prevention Act of 1862 (25 & 26 Vict. c.114) rendered his position off it untenable after that date. The suppression of vagrancy and watching for suspicious persons were all a matter of the highway. County policemen were not often seen: 'There is

no policeman . . . a policeman in the agricultural parishes has
generally four to look after . . . you must first of all find the
policeman . . . .' (186)

There was a coherent principle of government at work here. The
type of place a policeman lived in was important, for it was there
that contact with a local population was most consistent, and there
that the policeman was most consistently seen to be <u>doing</u>. If the
distribution of one county constabulary is looked at over a period
of eight years (1861/9) certain factors clearly emerge. The
Leicestershire police were, during this time drafted to 75 villages, towns and hamlets in the county. Excluding the eight large
divisional centres, which were also market towns with their own
court of petty sessions (and quarter sessions in the case of
Leicester), it emerges that out of 69 communities where the police
were stationed, 23 had populations of over 1,000, 31 had populations of 500-1,000, and only 13 had populations of under 500. The
figures for communities without resident policemen reveal a striking
difference. There were 244 of these, and only 6 of them had a population of over 1,000, and 206 of them were communities of under 500
souls. (186)

These places were not unpoliced; except for some isolated villages on the county border, all of them were surveyed from a
central hamlet. But policemen did live in centres of population
that were rather larger than was usual for the county as a whole,
and for police purposes what this meant was that a developing system of communications could be drawn upon and used. (188) For more
general governmental purposes it is clear that the police fitted
into a pre-existing pattern of social discipline. There were
proportionately more resident magistrates and clergymen in the
villages where the police were stationed than in villages where the
they were not as shown in Table 1.5.

TABLE 1.5 Provision for social discipline in villages with
and without police, Leicestershire, 1861-9

COMMUNITIES WITH POLICE:	67	COMMUNITIES WITHOUT POLICE:	244
Resident magistrates in	22% (15)		13% (31)
Resident clergy in	92% (62)		54% (133)
Resident gentry in	40% (27)		38% (94)

Source: 'Police and Constabulary Almanac', 1868; White, 'Directory
and Gazetteer of Leicestershire', 1863, 1877.

Magisterial control of the police depended on this sort of physical proximity. Yet the influence of the individual magistrate
over the singly stationed constable declined in the 1870s, and it
was the nature of police work done within the context of county
government that provided that decline.

(xi)   THE RISE AND FALL OF AN ADMINISTRATIVE POLICE

The police act of 1856 broke new administrative ground by empower-
ing magistrates to oblige the police to perform work other than
that involved in keeping the peace. (189)   The administrative work
that was devolved onto the police in this way can be divided into
three types.   The police were expected to perform traditional functions of county government, functions that involved the mediation
of local statutory bodies of fairly recent creation, and administrative functions thrown directly on the police by central legislation in the 1870s.   Between 1856 and 1880, 40 of the 43 English
administrative counties used the county police force to inspect
weights and measures, collect the county rate, survey roads, inspect
bridges and to survey market trading.   Every English county used its
policemen as impounders of stray cattle.   These traditional administrative functions were dictated by district need and remained under
the direction of the resident magistrate rather than the court of
quarter sessions.   Inspection of weights and measures was the only
function of this kind that embraced whole counties, and the other
appointments were always partial.
   When the police were used in this traditional work of county
administration the government inspectors usually disapproved,
because there was little in its intrinsic nature that could wed
it to police organisation.   Organising and disciplining the vagrant
poor under a joint appointment by poor law guardians and magistrates was seen as a different matter, because the vagrant was
understood to be, on many occasions, a criminal, and a policeman
supervising him was seen to be efficiently and cheaply performing
a police and an administrative function, both at once.   But policemen themselves disliked working as inspectors of weights and
measures: 'The acts relating to weights and measures being them
into contact with men who are not really criminals and make them
unpopular,' explained one Northamptonshire superintendent in 1875.
'It brings them into contact with the more respectable classes . . .
makes life very irksome if they happen to offend them.' (190)
Thirty-eight counties used policemen as inspectors of weights and
measures until the beginning of this century.   Often a superintendent and several constables were permanently detailed off
for the work, and travelled about the county division with the test
weights in a cart, and set up test stations in pre-arranged
places. (191)
   The second group of administrative functions introduced an intermediary agency into the relationship between policeman and magistrate.   Between 1857 and 1880, 35 counties in England employed
their police as assistant poor law relieving officers for periods
lasting over ten years, and 33 counties used them as inspectors of
common lodging houses, again, for ten years or more.   They were
employed as inspectors of nuisances in nine counties.   The use of
the police as poor law relieving officers had spread to some
extent before 1856, especially in the boroughs, and it had been
sanctioned by the Poor Law Board in 1848. (192)   Under the County
and Borough Police Act of 1856 (19 & 20 Vict. c.69) sanction rested
with the court of quarter sessions in the counties, and payment was
made by the local board of guardians.   A board of guardians may

have become a board of health in 1858, (193) and the officers of
boards of health were ratepayer elected. The joint control of a
local police, by unelected magistrates on the one hand, and elected
officials on the other, sharpened the demand for elective county
government in many areas. (194) The other effect of such appointments was to remove power from the individual magistrate in petty
sessions to the court of quarter sessions.

That the surveillance of vagrants and common lodging houses could
be turned into the surveillance of the potentially criminal was
recognised by police officers, police committees and watch commi-
tees. Indeed the 1860s and early 1870s witnessed something like
an inspection fervour, with professional witnesses before select
committees suggesting that policemen be appointed as inspectors of
factories, of employed children not covered by the factory acts, of
midwives (should they be forced to register) and of truants under
the educational legislation of the 1870s. Carried away by the
vision of a thoroughly policed and inspected society, some, including county chief constables, suggested that the homes of the poor
should be inspected by the police, for cleanliness and against over-
crowding. (195)

Yet as the 1870s passed, many county chief constables came to
assert the needs of police work and police organisation over those
of local government. The process of self-definition by which the
permanent officer class began, in the 1860s and 1870s, to understand
themselves as members of a specialised, nation-wide body, possessors
of a unique role, is examined in the second part of this book. But
the county magistrates who watched this process of self-definition
perceived that it involved, on the part of many of their officer
staff, a rejection of the role of executive agent of local government, and a positive preference for finding the misdeed, the
offence, the improper act. Many officers choose to detect crime
whilst acting as inspectors of weights and measures, or inspecting
market traders' stalls. (196)

The three government inspectors of constabulary were assiduous
in reporting to the Home Office these feeling on the part of chief
constables and officers of police who had come to see the performance of local government administrative functions as detracting
from their 'proper' duty. In the early 1870s the Home Office
issued several circulars to local authorities suggesting that they
stop using their police in this way. (197) The use of policemen
as inspectors of nuisances was the first extraneous function to be
removed from the list of those that did not affect the payment of
the government grant. Magistrates knew that in losing an executive
officer who was also a constable, they lost real local power. (198)

The tendency of central government to devolve administration
directly on to the police without any intermediary agency accelerated in the mid-1870s as local appointment, through the magistrates, declined. The Explosives Act and the Adulterated Foods
Act of 1875 (38 & 39 Vict. c.17; 38 & 39 c.63) are not unimportant
examples. These two statutes named local police forces as executors, and the administrative division was defined as the police
division. (199) The police collected information, issued licences,
initiated action and took proceedings, and they did not need a
magistrate to do any of this. (200)

In both counties and boroughs these legislative developments had the effect of loosening the relationship between policemen and masters, and in the boroughs the changing statutory significance of the police cut them off, to some extent, from overt influence by a local ratepaying community. Throughout the country in borough police archives are testimonials to the impact of the innocuous seeming legislation fo the mid-1870s. The Petroleum Act of 1875 shook the head constable of Stratford-upon-Avon in a way that nothing else had in the past ten years. In the longest report he ever made to the watch committee he detailed his own statutorily required actions under this act, and with growing confidence offered his first opinion as an officer of police that had ever appeared in his report books:

Mr Farmer, Butcher, who occupies the adjacent premises to Mr Newton is making an alteration to his Sausage Engine and He has had constructed a new chimney . . . which I consider dangerous as I have been informed that sparks have been seen to fall . . . close to where Benzoline is kept on Mr Newton's premises. (201)

Two other changes supported this loosening of bonds between policemen and police authority. First of all the grant from the consolidated fund to local police authorities was increased from a quarter to a half of the cost of pay and clothing; (202) second, various changes in local government organisation removed a good deal of autonomous police power from police authorities. The Public Health Act of 1875 (38 & 39 Vict. c.55) named all municipal corporations urban sanitary authorities, which were obliged by law to put into effect a formulated code of public health. Police activity in the sphere of inspection and policing was in any case declining, and continued to do so. But where the police continued to perform policing functions they now operated under written, codified statutory law, and not under local law. In the counties, the Local Government (County Councils) Act of 1888 (51 & 52 Vict. c.41) is noted for having severed judicial control of the police; but in fact the earlier legislation described above had already made the local policeman a less powerful weapon in the individual justice's armoury of control. (203)

In contrast with continental systems of policing, centrally designed to promote general good order, social discipline and 'cleanliness and good reputation,' England's administrative police grew out of a system of local government, and at its foundation lay locally conceived theories of the management and control of populations. (204) This local theory of social order, and the provincial government that allowed it to be put into effect, did translate often into a more general, national rhetoric. But it was a set of beliefs and policies that originated in the provinces that central government reacted to, and sometimes used. This process is made plainer if the role of the police in one administrative function, their supervision of the vagrant poor, is considered briefly, in more detail.

(xi)   THE POLICE AND THE VAGRANT POOR

Under common law, constables had always had responsibility for controlling vagrants: at large, on the highway, with no visible means
of support, the vagrant was not only potentially criminal, but he
also represented a mobile anomaly in the structure of social control, which was based on the dispersal of buildings with inhabitants
of them either in control, or to be controlled, depending on whether
or not they paid a property tax for their protection.

Throughout the nineteenth century (and right through to present
times) (205) the police acted under the Vagrancy Act of 1824 (5 Geo.
IV c.83). This was a consolidating act, which confirmed the tendency of eighteenth-century legislation in its three-part distinction between 'idle and disorderly', 'rogue and vagabond', and
'incorrigible rogue'. A first conviction made vagrants 'idle and
disorderly', and they could work up to the label of 'incorrigible
rogue' being bestowed on them with a third conviction. The Vagrancy
Act provided a daily context for police work in the nineteenth century, and that so many officers were in the 1860s and 1870s eager
to submit a wide range of offences to this three-part distinction,
and proposed the labels 'habitual drunkard' and 'habitual criminal'
for those who had been given a fair chance and failed to take it,
is possibly explained by their long use of the vagrancy acts. (206)

Mid-Victorian legislators found the structure of the vagrancy
acts useful for erecting barriers against a wide range of social
offences, for were any category of people to be named vagrant in
a statute, then police powers against them became automatic. In
the 1850s, for example, a series of statutes ostensibly dealing
with the education of pauper children incidentally defined desti-
tute children as vagrants, and in 1868 and 1872 the description
vagrant was extended to any person found gaming in a public place.
(207)

The vagrancy laws therefore conferred a statutory and universal
power on all policemen in the surveillance of poor people mobile on
the roads; but within specific local government areas the use of
the police in this way was particularised, and the constable's
individual powers in law were employed as part of a local system of
social control.

The process by which theories and beliefs, articulated and
refined in the localities, came close to becoming central government policy is well illustrated in police action against vagrants.
A brief consideration of the theory and practice of vagrant control
in Northamptonshire, and the dissemination of its experience by
Major Cartwright, the Northamptonshire magistrate who became one of
the three government inspectors of constabulary in 1856, is important for two reasons. It makes clear the specific practice of a
specific provincial place, and it also reveals a wider vision of
order and control used by local authorities in the direction of
its police.

The metaphors used by local administrators in the revelation of
this vision were geographical. The county was a terrain defined
by rates levied for its own internal good ordering. Each administrative unit within this terrain, each petty sessional division,
each poor law union, was similarly defined as an official financial

community that was in some way beleaguered, either by the dangers of its borders, or the anomalous nature of those unofficial people who passed through its ordered landscape. Midland counties, like Northamptonshire, were particularly vulnerable in the years before 1856 when the establishment of county police forces was only piece-meal. The county was traversed by vagrant routes: 'We touch upon eight counties,' William Cartwright reminded the court of quarter sessions in April 1856 'in only two of which was there any police . . . the number of parishes was 286 . . . 68 were on the border.' (208) It was the long unsupervised road, the miles from one work-house to another that alarmed a tremulous public. The 'footloose army' returning home from the Crimea in 1856 had immediately been clad by this public imagination in the uniform of the professional criminal vagrant. The suppression of vagrancy was the preamble to and the justification of, the County and Borough Police Act of 1856. (209)

William Cartwright believed in 'vagrant crime,' and from his very first appointment as the chairman of Brackley Poor Law Union in 1835, sought to separate the 'criminal tramper' from the respec-table working man, tramping in search of work. The first letter written by the Brackley Board of Guardians was to the commissioners of the Metropolitan police asking them to recommend two police officers to be appointed as poor law relieving officers. Two men were appointed in this capacity and moved permanently to Northamp-tonshire. (210) Under Cartwright's direction the Brackley Union experimented with various work tasks for able-bodied trampers, formed a parochial watch to police the parishes of the union and report on vagrants at large. (211) Cartwright was instrumental in diverting parochial funds for the renting of a previously privately funded Mendicity House for the reception of people on the tramp. (212) Such experiments were watched by the central Poor Law Board, which in fact had encouraged the use of police as poor law relieving officers in large boroughs before 1856.

After 1856, the limited local experimentation of Northampton-shire became nation-wide, and out of the 43 English administrative counties 37 employed their police in this way for a decade or more between 1856 and 1880. The practice was most general in the Mid-lands area under Cartwright's direction, and he worked hard to persuade local authorities to appoint their police as assistant poor law relieving officers on the grounds that this was the only effective way of supervising the professional criminal tramper. (213) The police were also extensively used in this way in the boroughs, but Cartwright never urged this kind of appointment on watch committees in the way he did on courts of quarter sessions. Boroughs it is true, had other methods of surveillance, such as inspection of common lodging houses, and the appointment of police-men as relieving officers actually declined in boroughs after 1856. But what really lay behind Cartwright's lack of interest in the supervision that a borough police could offer, was his vision of area and geographical control. He placed a great deal of emphasis on the general supervision of vagrants en route and made many changes in the existing ticket-of-way system. In many areas people on the tramp were issued with a ticket that directed them to the next workhouse on their journey. The ticket-of-way was to be shown to a policeman on demand and was meant to prevent people straying from the road or taking too long over their journey. (214) When distances between workhouses were too great to be covered in a day's walking Cartwright suggested that tickets might be issued by the workhouse master for a lodging house on the road that was 'under the supervision of a police constable who would see the applicant on arrival and departure'. (215)

By the early 1860s the practice in counties using their police as relieving officers was fairly uniform. As vagrants entered a town or village, they were directed by the policeman on the beat to the police station where the desk sergeant's practiced eye looked them over. The respectable were sent on to the overseers, and the 'criminal' were retained. The practice of building a tramp ward next to the police station developed in the 1860s, and by the mid-1860s many policemen who acted as assistant poor law relieving officers were empowered to grant food as well as shelter. It was efforts like this, to make the practice uniform and efficient that it practically impossible to isolate the 'criminal' from the 'respectable'. (216)

The response on policemen's part to the system they worked under was to blur the very distinction that the system had been designed to clarify: 'estimated roughly,' said the head constable of Chester to a poor law inspector, 'I am decidedly of the opinion that 75% of them never work, but spend their time tramping from union to union.' (217) In the 1860s there developed a very strong move for handing the entire supervision of the vagrant poor over to the police. County chief constables and officers of police appointed as relieving officers who thought in this way had their opinions given wide circulation by Cartwright in his reports, and every piece of local administrative practice that he wrote about and publicised revealed its police purpose. When he enthused about a system in use at Oswestry House of Industry, and described in detail purpose built vagrant wards, the separation of the sexes, the work task imposed, the careful watching by a constable through the night, he echoed those police officers who also knew that a bath and fumigation served quite another purpose than a hygeinic one: 'by removing every vestige of clothing, the facilities afforded for searching them are most effectual.' (218)

Cartwright retired as government inspector in 1868 and returned to his original scene of experiment in the county of Northampton-shire. Still a magistrate and member of the court of quarter sessions he drafted extensive and detailed proposals for handing the supervision of the county's vagrants over to the county police: as he had reported to the Home Secretary three years earlier, 'with very little difficulty a system might be organised which would supervise the whole of the vagrant population.' (219) Such arguments were to be played out in central government a few years later; but by the early 1870s there already existed an idea of what constituted the 'proper' duty of the police, and to make local police forces into the executive arm of local boards of guardians was no longer seen as an appropriate use of policemen. The other government inspectors had never displayed Cartwright's enthusiasm for the system and had in many instances detailed the difficulties experienced by local forces when they worked for two authorities. (220) National supervision of a vagrant population by police forces was rejected partly because of the administrative problems involved. But it was a system that served local government well in some areas for a quarter of a century, and was available still as a vision of an ordered and supervised system óf control in the early years of this century. (221) Whether local magistrates and boards of guardians appointed their local police officers assistant poor law relieving officers or not, the legacy for police forces and for ratepaying populations was considerable. Poverty was united with crime, and all people who were mobile were viewed as potentially delinquent.

(xiii)   RATEPAYING AS THEORY

At the basis of all nineteenth-century provincial government and its deployment of police lay the payment of the rates, and it was this handing over of cash to a local authority, on the basis of the value of property owned or occupied, that defined a multiplicity of official communities. Different rates were levied over different geographical areas, and the smallest official community defined in this way was the parish, the largest the county, and the borough itself defined a separate financial community.

What delineated these communities was money paid out for services to be rendered and for benefits (among them, the benefit of police protection) to be received. (222) All the uses of the term community in this book have so far been in this financial, official, sense, and it has been indicated how beliefs and ideas about social discipline, government and policing might enter into administrative practice at the county or borough level because those ideas and beliefs were accompanied by sums of money handed over. Yet at each point the official, financial community was in conflict with the unofficial community. Areas of social relations and of rights and obligations were based on the geographical areas defined by the property tax that paid for services, and where working-class people came into contact with the official community, where, for instance, they met the operation of the poor law, they came face to face with a practice and an ideology informed by a particular set of financial theories. They were outside this official community not only for all the reasons we know about, such as not possessing the right to vote, but because, not paying rates, they dwelt outside the 'real' structure of ownership, responsibility, obligation and government. It was understanding of this reality that lay at the basis of police dispersal and management.

County administrators in particular possessed well-developed, articulate and very old ideas about wedding the unofficial community to the official in an ordered and hierarchic harmony for the defence of an area's peace. We have seen these arguments at work in magistrate's rejection of the 'alien' peace that seemed to be embodied in the paid police force of the Rural Police Act of 1839, in the revival of the militia under threat of war, in the desire to use police forces as the basis of a Volunteer force, and in the image of a county policeman as a man joined to the official structure of county control for the defence of a territorial peace. Indeed, the interesting and important point about the development of police forces in mid-nineteenth century England is that policemen, people from the unofficial community of the rural poor, were asked to join the official community as servants-as policemen. They brought with them the experience and attitudes of the unofficial community, and these were used as a tool of governmental policy by their employers. This development is dealt with in the second part of this book. In order to make the background to this development plain, it is important to look at the financial basis of provincial theories of police and policing. The financial model that the counties, as opposed to the boroughs were seen to provide, also heightens the evidence there is that it was the virtues of the unofficial <u>rural</u> community that were sought in recruiting policemen, in both rural and urban areas.

Each speech in Parliament that introduced a police bill was a body of suggestions for the improvement or property protection. Each court of quarter sessions knew this, and either approved or rejected the police acts of 1839 and 1842 in this light. None of this is surprising, for both the theory and practice of rating for police purposes rested on a double distinction between real property and personal property, and between property and people, that rendered the last impermanent and fragile in the face of the needs of the first. Such a theory, and the practice that followed it in nineteenth-century communities, distinguished between the stationary, limited way in which property needed protection, and the mobility of the people it needed protecting against.

A local police was almost entirely a local charge, and was completely so before 1856. After that date, a police force was supported almost entirely out of the rates, for the government grant only covered a quarter of the cost of paying and clothing policemen. The Rural Police Act of 1839 (2 & 3 Vict. c.93 s.20) had provided for forces to be paid out of an increased general count rate, but the amending act of 1840 (3 & 4 Vict. c.88 s.28) replaced this arrangement with a separate police rate. County ratepayers knew exactly what their police cost them for the rest of the century. The change between 1839 and 1840, and the substitution of one rate for another, had been due to the pressure of strictly local feeling, and it had been argued that if a petty sessional division produced more crime than the neighbouring ones, then the police rate should be higher in the first. (223) Under the Municipal Corporations Act (5 & 6 Will. IV c.88), borough policemen were paid out of the borough fund, as were all officers of the corporation.

In accounts of nineteenth-century local government that have been written since 1900, the practice of levying rates on local communities has been seen as distinguishing between beneficial services, where 'assessment was made according to the proportion of the <u>benefit</u> from the expenditure which it was estimated the individual ratepayer received,' and onerous services, where 'assessment was made according to the <u>ability</u> of the ratepayer to pay.' (224) The Webbs saw the onerous and beneficial bound together in the parish, the geographical area in which rates were levied. The parish was seen by them as a unit of 'obligation', where arrangements were made for 'the due performance of . . . collective

regulations and common services'. (225)   Mid-nineteenth-century
ratepaying citizens certainly appear to have operated with this
distinction between onerous and beneficial services in mind when
they petitioned quarter sessions and town councils for more, or for
fewer police, or when they complained about the police rate, or the
distribution of constables.

But an understanding of what sort of arrangement they were par-
ticipating in by paying out lump sums to a local rating authority
was dictated far more by the actual practice of assessment in local
communities, where the visible value of a man's property was taken
as a measure of his ability to pay for services.   The Parochial
Assessment Act of 1836 (6 & 7 Will. IV c.96) defined the poor rate
as being levied on the basis of the net annual value of occupied
property, that is, the amount for which such property might be
rented out from year to year.   This in fact had been a rating
practice of very long standing, and the act merely gave it legal
status. (226)

Farmers and landowners had rates levied on them according to
the value of their acres and their buildings, not according to the
profits they might make from them, and as farmers were to complain
throughout the century, they saw themselves paying out money to a
police authority for something which a police force could not protect: 'there is nobody in the place that objects to the police
. . . but it is the land . . . you assess us upon the rental of
the land, which we receive no benefit from.' (227)   The invidious
comparison between a poor rate and a police rate was always present for critics like these to draw on.   A poor rate was viewed
with greater favour by ratepayers because 'it is the practice to
exampt . . . (property) which is not beneficially occupied at the
time of making the rate, on the grounds that such property cannot
furnish any complainants on the parish funds.' The official theory
of rating for police purposes on the other hand was that it was
essentially a rate levied for 'purposes always consistent and
similar: the protection of property in its widest sense, and the
prevention of crime'. (228)   In fact in this way, the practice of
rating for police purposes in local communities did outline a
national community of concern with crime and property protection.
But local concerns, and the needs of local property were asserted
against this latent principle: 'those that are getting rich in the
manufacturing districts', said one rural landowner in 1852 'should
pay tax according to the crime they create.' (229)

Tension in rural areas between ratepayers and rate-leviers often
rested on a confict between rates levied on property, but spent
on people, that is, spent according to density of population. All
counties, but particularly those that contained industrialised areas
could furnish examples of places where the rateable value of each
acre was not matched by a distribution of policemen, and where in
districts valued at a lower rate, more police were stationed. In
rural areas there was an enormous range in the number of valued
county acres given to individual policemen to protect: in Hertfordshire in 1868 a policeman protected on average £1,175 worth of
assessed property, whilst in the same year in the East Riding a
constable protected £12,114 worth. County ratepayers knew as well
that in terms of property protection, borough ratepayers received

a better deal, with borough policemen protecting on average only
half of that which county policemen protected.

Police legislation in the nineteenth century recognised two
principles at the same time. In the years before 1856 it was
generally recognised in this legislation that a locality should
pay for its own crime and its own protection, by defraying payment for a police force from rates on specific police divisions.
At the same time, policemen themselves were recognised as performing a general service, for county and borough policemen had powers
outside the areas that paid for their services. The treasury grant
authorised under the act of 1856 was seen by its promotors as
breaking new ground, and further defining local police forces as
part of a national, general service. (230) But grant-in-aid did
not have this effect, partly because the contribution was so small.
It covered only a quarter of the local cost of paying and clothing
the police; buildings, transport, stabling, police equipment,
stationery and so on fell entirely to local charge. But even had
the grant been larger, a local theory of police would have prevented any central aid from defining local police forces as part
of a general provision. The local theory was clear, based on sound
book-keeping principles, and it had a long history: the most mean-
ingful way that ratepayers had of understanding police presence was
as a type of <u>insurance</u>, not as an onerous or a beneficial service.

When George Grey made his most persuasive point in defending his
police bill of 1856, his words met a body of experience that was
competent to understand that where the Rural Police Act of 1839 had
been applied, the result had been an 'enhanced value of property'.
(231) A legacy of the pre-1856 period was a view of a policeman as
an agent of the protection of property against people: 'Whatever
would give protection to property must give increased value to
property' . . . ' Police presence was form of insurance, under the
terms of which the man who paid the premiums had a right to a say
in its management.

The people against whom property needed protecting were mobile.
Crime, as has been seen, was popularly equated with vagrancy, and
protection against the projected and alarming mobility of post-war
vagrants was one of the precise reasons for drawing up the police
bill of 1856. Much police effort was devoted to the suppression
of vagrancy in the years after 1856, and in the 1860s the county
police forces of England came close to providing a systematic and
general surveillance of people on the road, moving from one place
to another. It was the counties that provided this wholesale system: they bordered each other, and were not geographically isolated
as the boroughs were. They provided an operative reality that could
be called a national system of police. Thus the national needs of
property, to be protected against a national community of crime,
came to be recognised, not through the intentions of statute and
the operation of central government, but through the agency of
locally governed, locally financed police forces in the years
after 1856.

Whilst bricks and mortar were static, the depredator could move.
Forgotten legislation of the mid-Victorian years can demonstrate
how this fear of mobility was translated into legal precedent.
A recent historian has noted how a revered liberal legal reformer

in 1858 was pushed by a public panic at the idea of burglary to propose that those convicted of such crimes should have the onus of proof put upon them, after their release from prison, that they earned their living by honest means. (232) This was not just an isolated and fearful suggestion. The principle of placing the onus of proof of honest possession of property on to the accused was enshrined in two pieces of Victorian legislation. Convicts released on licence under the Penal Servitude Acts of 1864 and 1871 (27 & 28 Vict. c.47; 34 & 35 Vict. c.112) — ticket-of-leave men — were assumed guilty of the possession of stolen property until they could prove themselves innocent. Supervision of these men was de-volved on the police by central statute, and mobility, actually being at large, was defined as criminal in these acts.

More thorough-going in its effect than the Ticket-of-Leave Acts was the Night Poaching Prevention Act of the 1862 (25 & 26 Vict. c.110) which placed upon any man or woman walking along the highway whom a policeman cared to stop, the legal onus of proving lawful possession of game and of demonstrating that on the land they had just left they had not been attempting to poach. All working people in rural England were in this way subject to a systematic surveillance and discipline, and it was being mobile, moving from one place to another, that placed them at risk. (233)

People who were not ratepayers, working people, vagrant or settled poor, were seen by their betters as belonging to a dif-ferent order of community from themselves. They belonged not to that local community of district need, of payment precisely reckoned for services rendered, of insurance taken out, but were increasing-ly seen, through the operation of local police forces and the atti-tudes created by legislation, to belong to a national community — of disorder, impropriety and legal aberration. The evolution, throughout the period under discussion here, of a police force con-ceived of as acting in a general or national interest was partly a response to this outlining of a national community of impro-priety.

Part two

MEN AND POLICEMEN

The fourth and last sort of people in England are daie-labourers,
poor husbandmen, and some retailers (which have no free land),
copie-holders, and all artificers, as tailors, shoe-makers, car-
penters, brick-makers, masons and etc . . . They have neither
voice nor authoritie in the commonwealth, but are to be ruled, and
not to rule others: yet they are not altogether neglected; for
in cities and corporate towns they are fain to make up their in-
quests of such manner of people. And in the villages they are
commonly made churchwardens, sidemen, ale-conners, now and then
constables . . .

Harrison, 'A Description of England', 1587, quoted to the Con-
stabulary Commissioners in 1839; pp. 1839, xix, p. 211. William
Harrison, 'The Description of England' (Cornell University Press,
New York, 1968), p. 118.

The voluntary and involuntary actions of working people brought
face to face with provincial government and policing in the second
half of the nineteenth century can help to reveal its contemporary
purpose and meaning. The first part of this book has suggested that
provisions were made for the coercion and control of local populations through the agency of local police forces, and that examples
of this process can be seen in the Additional Constable clad in
the uniform of the local force permanently stationed at the iron
works; in a detachment of county policemen entering a borough to
put down riot, and properly being called an army; in the man on
the road looking for work being handed a ticket to the tramp ward
by the policeman appointed as relieving officer. But when William
Broadhead, trade union activist of Sheffield offered in 1860 to
attend a closed meeting of the watch committee in order to explain
his innocence of trade outrage, he not only casually revealed his
own perception of power and government, the way things were, in
Sheffield. He also demonstrated quite clearly what a pursuit of
watch committee members through thirty years of trade directories
and local newspapers can also reveal: that in the 1850s and 1860s
the great merchant manufacturers composing the committee that paid
and directed the police <u>were</u> the law in Sheffield. (1)

Such relationships between government and the pattern of life
within local communities were, at many points, overt and visible,
but none the less complicated for that. Silence greeted the first
compulsory and universal police act in 1856. A pre-existing
middle-class experience of what a policeman was, the slow-witted,
dilatory ex-farm labourer — the 'fool in blue' — goes some way
towards explaining an ensuing twenty years of silence, in Parliament, in novels, in pictures and paintings, on the subject of the
police. The respectable knew of course, that policemen were still
the servants of the ratepayers, in spite of new treasury grants-
in-aid and government inspection after 1856. They understood how
things worked: policemen were not important; they were agents,
not actors. Yet where another public's perception of policemen
seems to give them substance and make them visible, as for example
in the weekly reports in all provincial newspapers of street
assaults upon constables, it is unwise to translate this action

immediately into a simple attitude of dislike and resentment. Working-class people seem to have known on many occasions that policemen were unimportant, that power was located elsewhere, with a magistrate for example, using the police as executors and servants in the ancient centres of rural administration, or with the rate-paying oligarchy of a city directing its policemen to patrol particular streets, watch particular pieces of property. The evasion of the licencing laws, for instance, quite clearly indicates how much general understanding there was of a policeman's inability to act outside the hierarchy of local administration and local government.

If working people understood on occasions that policemen were unimportant in this way, then policemen were assaulted and beaten up, and very occasionally killed out of that understanding, not in spite of it. When a Sheffield fork-grinder returned to his trough after 11 months in the borough police in 1859 — 'trade was very bad and prices very low . . . I entered the police force to better my condition' — he was greeted with gunpowder. He was attacked thus not because he had joined the police, or not simply for that reason, but because his employer, a member of the watch committee, had got him a job policing when times were hard and had asked him to return to fork-grinding (to find out what he could?) after a series of 'outrages' at firms where watch committee members were partners. (2)

The second part of this book is designed to show how, partly through a process of self-definition, policemen changed themselves from a collection of unimportant working-class men wearing the uniform of local power and authority, into the beginnings of a recognisably modern police force, cut off from overt influence by local government.

Chapter 2

MAKING A COUNTY FORCE

This chapter is designed to show the pattern of recruitment to one Midlands police force in the year of its creation, that of Bucking-hamshire in 1857. Comparisons are made with another constabulary, that of Staffordshire, which was 17 years old in 1857, in order to show how national and local changes in political and economic cir-cumstances influenced both recruitment and a man's decision to be-come a policeman. Other more general contemporary evidence on these questions shows that the pattern discernible in these two counties holds substantially true for other areas, both rural and urban, in the 1860s and 1870s.

Both Staffordshire and Buckinghamshire are Midlands counties, and belonged to the same inspection area; but the pattern of recruitment to these two forces in the mid-1850s demonstrates larger differences in their local circumstances than is apparent from a simple description of one county as partly industrialised, and the other as rural and agricultural. (1) Constabulary records, and what they can reveal of movement and motivation in the lives of working people, are a minor, but useful source for social and economic history. Buckinghamshire and Staffordshire are repre-sented here because their records are extant, and in the county archives; (2) but it needs making clear that the Buckinghamshire records are unusually good ones, listing the birthplace, trade, last employer, last residence, previous public service, age, marital status and number of children of each recruit. They thus contain a much fuller account of some working lives than most material in county record offices, and because they are so full they can allow a reasonable interpretation of the much scantier material from Staffordshire. (3)

Much of the material in this chapter is presented in tabular form, for reference purposes. The argument draws on these tables, and comments on particular aspects of the material contained in them, but it is not necessary to study the tables in detail whilst reading.

After 1856 more policemen were employed than ever before. The County and Borough Police Act (19 & 20 Vict. c.69) outlined a career structure, and though as a workforce policemen were most

intimately tied to local government, the conditions of their life
across the country were, after 1856, remarkably uniform. This
meant that a more rigid police hierarchy than had existed before
exploited through a recruitment policy a pre-existing set of social
relationships. The background and experience of the majority of
recruits meant that these relationships were, to a large extent,
rural in nature: the image of rural class relations dominated law-
keeping and policing in Victorian England, in both city and country.

Yet some contemporary commentators indicated that the social
source for policemen, though it consistently remained the countryside, changed in its class composition during the late 1840s and
1850s. In his research on the Staffordshire constabulary from
1843 to 1860, David Philips found a large proportion of 'farmers'
joining the force; (4) this was not the case in the 1860s or 1870s
except where the 'farmers'' background was Irish. The chief constable of Cumberland and Westmorland complained in the 1870s that
over a quarter of a century, the pattern of recruitment had changed:
before the act of 1856 'I used to get many sons of the small yeomanry
of which there are many still in Cumberland . . . men of that stamp
have left me.' (5) In the 1840s, small scattered police forces,
many of them utilising parish constables in superintending constable systems (6) provided a familiar social opportunity for sons
of small farmers. The rapid expansion of forces after 1856, drawing on working-class recruits, marked a decline in police forces'
use of this section of the rural community.

It was a mid-Victorian truism mutually held among the profes-
sonally concerned and the unprofessionally observant, that the provincial policeman had formerly worked the land. But observers past
and present have often got it wrong. It was a generation of
fathers' memories of the 'hungry forties' according to one modern
commentator, that drove their sons, that 'great army of the unskilled who would otherwise look to the field or the factory or
colliery', into the arms of the police forces of provincial
England. (7) Yet only a tiny proportion of colliery and factory
workers are to be found among those who gave their names to police
recruiting sergeants. Yet another proportion was composed of men
who became policemen because factories could find no use for them.
These were skilled men, craftsmen, many of whom still defined themselves by their trade years after becoming policemen. Men such as
these turned to a local police force in a kind of temporary des-
peration. Some stayed and became policemen. By discovering more
precisely who they were, and where they came from, it is possible
to suggest more realistic motives for becoming a policeman than
their hypothetical fathers' memories of times past.

'Some farm bailiffs, some shoemakers, some labourers, some of
all sorts; we have soldier pensioners . . . all sorts,' said
Superintendent Cockeridge of the Hertfordshire constabulary in
1875. (8) There were in fact more than 'some' labourers in this
force, as in all English police forces, and very few farm baillifs.
There were not many ex-solidiers either (the great difference
between recruits at all levels in the pre- and post-1856 periods).
All chief constables objected to soldier recruits because they saw
drinking as part of institutional life, and, out of all the successful policemen (men who stayed to receive pensions) examined for

this study, only one had army experience. In parading before the
select committee to which he was giving evidence the great panoply
of social ranks that made up his county police force, the superintendent alighted on the farm bailiff because he was an interesting, though statistically not very likely, type of social casualty,
respectable and fairly certain to make a good policeman. Police
forces dealt in failure and casualties, and the craft shoemaker
was a more common entry on the constabulary register page.
   Superintendent Cockeridge's chief constable knew, as well as
must have the superintendent, that 'the best recruits for police
. . . are agricultural labourers.' (9) In the 1890s chief constables were still saying the same: 'the night patrols are so long,
and so very lonely that . . . I find the only man who can stand it
is a . . . labourer fresh from the plough.' (10) Rural labourers
did form the largest work group in a county constabulary's intake,
making up between a third and two-thirds of it in Staffordshire and
Buckinghamshire in selected years between 1856 and 1880:

TABLE 2.1   Number of labourers as recruits to Buckinghamshire and
            Staffordshire constabularies for selected years

	1856/7	1863	1866	1876	1880
BUCKINGHAMSHIRE					
Number of recruits	154	22	32	18	17
Number of labourers	41	11	14	10	12
% of intake	27%	50%	41%	49%	59%
STAFFORDSHIRE					
Number of recruits	112	135	79	90	72
Number of labourers	35	59	36	57	31
% of intake	31%	52%	47%	62%	47%

Source: Buckinghamshire Record Office, Constabulary Records, Constabulary Records, Register of Members of the Force, 1856- .
Staffordshire Record Office, Constabulary Records, Register of the
Members of the Force, 1842-94; Descriptive Register 1842-63; Return
of Members of the Force, 1842-1863.

However, labourers did not show themselves to be significantly more
successful than other work groups in enduring until pension time.
In Staffordshire, as in Buckinghamshire, the majority of long-
service men between 1856 and 1880 was always composed of ex-rural
labourers, but in the more industrialised county other work groups
contributed long-service men out of proportion to their numbers
at recruitment.
   The description 'labourer', which was the most common entry in
both counties' police recruitment books, in fact raises more
questions than it anwers. For Buckinghamshire, where the name
and address of a man's last employer was recorded, it is possible
to decide whether the recruit was a farm labourer or a general

labourer. It is necessary to make the distinction because the label
was given equally to the former employee of a farmer at Little
Milton, Oxfordshire, and a former worker in a biscuit factory at
Reading. There is no such way of checking the Staffordshire recruits, for neither a man's last employer nor his last residence
was recorded. Yet among the scores of entries reading 'labourer'
there is the occasional 'agricultural labourer', or 'rural labourer'.
Usually these descriptions applied to men born outside the county,
and who had presumably worked in other areas before becoming Staffordshire policemen. But some Staffordshire recruits were labelled
in this too, and the majority of those had been born in the rural
parts of the county. This of course, is no indication of what
they had been doing just before becoming policemen, but their
birthplace and background does add some weight to the more substantive data from Buckinghamshire, which shows that the majority
of 'labourers' had some agricultural background and experience.
(11)

What detailed constabulary records can help to show is a kind
of social dislocation, the fragmentation of a social pattern, changes
in local circumstances (more rarely national circumstances) made
manifest in the lives of working men and their families. The
Police Act of 1856 was in itself partly a response to the wider
social dislocation of war and the domestic fears that it engen -
dered, of the 'footloose army' returning home from the Crimea.
A constabulary in the process of formation in 1857, like Buckinghamshire recruiting in one year more men than it was to in the
next five put together, can show the reverberations of a national
dislocation very clearly. In the following account of the trade
background of Buckinghamshire's police recruits in its year of
formation, only 2 men gave their trade as soldier; but 21 of them
had spent some time in the army, and 19 of those had just been discharged from the Crimean regiments. The results are shown in Table
2.2.

Out of the 41 recruits listed who gave their trade as 'labourer',
15 joined the force directly from the land, and it is clearly possible to call them agricultural workers. Two other labourers had
worked for some time on the railway, one had worked for an agricultural implement-maker in Aylesbury, 1 had worked on the canals,
1 in a London shipyard, 1 at a tailoring firm, 1 at a public house,
and 1 at various unskilled labouring jobs in London. These 8 men
were clearly 'general labourers', and thought of themselves as
such. The other 18 'labourers' are harder to interpret. All of
them had had previously immediate experience either in the army or
in a police force. Six of the 18 were Buckinghamshire born and
had worked in the Metropolitan or City of London police for
several years. The formation of a constabulary in Buckinghamshire and over 150 jobs to be filled perhaps gave them something
to come home for. The 5 'labourers' who had joined the police
force directly from the army had all, except for one man, been
born outside the county, as had the 6 men who had worked for other
police forces before joining that of Buckinghamshire.

The level of previous public service was high in this year
of intake, when a police hierarchy had to be created, and men
appointed as officers. Two of the labourers in Table 2.2 with

Table 2.2 Previous trade of Buckinghamshire constabulary
recruits, 1857

'Labourer'	41	Soldier	1
(farm labourer	15	Bailiff	1
(general labourer	26	Coach painter	1
Farmer	15	Coachmaker	1
Shoemaker	9	Dairyman	1
Servant	7	Dealer	1
Gardner	6	Editor	1
Grocer	6	Greengrocer	1
Groom	6	Ironmonger	1
Lawyer	5	Marble mason	1
Tailor	6	Merchant traveller	1
Baker	4	Needlemaker	1
Clerk	4	Plumber	1
Carpenter	3	Ropemaker	1
Porter	3	Saddler	1
Wheelwright	3	Salesman	1
Bricklayer	2	Sawyer	1
Draper	2	Stoker (at a gas company	1
Gamekeeper	2	Thongmaker	1
Police officer	2	Watchmaker	1
Potter	2	Wire ropemaker	1
Railway worker	2	'No trade'	1
		TOTAL	153

Source: Buckinghamshire Record Office, Constabulary Records,
Register of Members of the Force 1856- .

previous police experience were appointed to the rank of sergeant
and inspector, and men who had worked under the county's old
superintending constable system were appointed to officer posts
in the new police force. A high proportion of farmers were Irish
— 8 out of the 15 listed above — and all but one of these Irishmen had previous experience in the Royal Irish Constabulary. Five
of the English-born farmers had already worked as policemen in other
forces. Recruits with a background like this were actively sought
out in this year of formation as a deliberate tool of policy. The
proportion of men with previous public service was never to be so
high again. This is shown in Table 2.3.

For some men army and police force had already distanced them
from their trade. Nine shoemakers joined the Buckinghamshire
constabulary in 1857 (Table 2.2); 6 of them had already had a
spell in a police force or in the army. Experience and geography
marked this distance. One of the wheelwrights recruited in 1857
(Table 2.2), a native of Lincolnshire, spent two years in the
army and on his return to England in 1853 didn't go home, but got
a job as a labourer with a soda water manufacturer in Luton Bedfordshire, and joined the Buckinghamshire constabulary in October
1857.

Service in the army is the most obvious indication of a fracture

TABLE 2.3   Previous public service experience of Buckinghamshire
            constabulary recruits, 1857

No such previous experience	44	Listed as 'police'	12
Metropolitan police	22	Borough police	9
Army	21	Royal Irish Constabulary	9
Old Buckinghamshire super-		Militia	6
intending constable system	18	Marines	1
County police forces	12		
		TOTAL	154
			(12)

Source: Buckinghamshire Record Office, Constabulary Records,
Register of Members of the Force 1856-

between a man's past and his present. But the constabulary records
reveal other men who had spent time doing work other than at their
trade:

TABLE 2.4   Immediate previous work (other than public service) not
            as trade given, Buckinghamshire constabulary 1857.

TRADE	LAST EMPLOYMENT
Shoemaker	Railway worker
Grocer	Railway worker
Potter	Railway worker
Saddler	Railway worker
Gardener	Prison service
Merchant traveller	Labourer for Commissioner Woods and Forests, London.
Wheelwright	Labourer at soda water manufacturer

Source: Buckinghamshire Record Office, Constabulary Records.
Register of Members of the Force, 1956-.

It is possible that the incidence of dislocation indicated by military experience, and in Table 2.4, was much higher than these numbers represent.
    But the sort of change suggested here could take place within a
relatively small geographical area. In Buckinghamshire in 1857,
the majority of recruits were natives of the county. Taken with
those who were born in counties that border Buckinghamshire, they
accounted for well over half the total intake. as shown in Table
2.5. A comparison between the birthplace of these 153 recruits,
and their last place of residence, as shown in Table 2.6 shows a
kind of contraction, with men moving closer to the south Midlands,
nearer to London. Garrison towns in Kent and Hampshire discharged
soldiers to the labour market in these counties, and discharge from
the army also accounts for the large proportion of men living in
London prior to joining the Buckinghamshire constabulary. However,

TABLE 2.5   Birthplace of Buckinghamshire constabulary recruits, 1857

Buckinghamshire	54	Lincolnshire	1
Bedfordshire	6	Suffolk	4
Hertfordshire	6	Kent	2
Berkshire	5	Sussex	1
Oxfordshire	10	Somerset	4
Warwickshire	1	Devon	1
Northamptonshire	2	Herefordshire	1
Rutland	1	Cheshire	3
Cambridgeshire	2	Lancashire	2
Essex	3		
London	7	Wales	1
Middlesex	1		
Surrey	3	Scotland	2
Hampshire	5		
Wiltshire	2	Ireland	12
Gloucestershire	3		
Worcestershire	2	Malta	1
Shropshire	1		
Staffordshire	3	Gibraltar	1
		TOTAL	153

Source: Buckinghamshire Record Office, Constabulary Records,
Register of Members of the Force, 1856–.

TABLE 2.6   Last residence of Buckinghamshire constabulary recruits,
1857

Buckinghamshire	63	Gloucestershire	1
Bedforeshire	6	Staffordshire	1
Hertfordshire	3	Norfolk	1
Berkshire	7	Kent	2
Oxfordshire	3	Lancashire	3
Warwickshire	2		
Northamptonshire	1	Wales	1
London	41		
Middlesex	2	Scotland	1
Surrey	1		
Hampshire	3	Ireland	10
		TOTAL	153

Source: Buckinghamshire Record Office, Constabulary Records,
Register of Members of the Force, 1856–.

several Buckinghamshire-born men travelled straight home on being
discharged. Charles Rose, by trade a watchmaker of Chesham, Buckinghamshire, had, at the age of 27 just spent 11 months in the Crimea

with the Turkish contingent and was working for a Chesham watch-
mender when he joined the county police a couple of months after
his discharge.

Though Buckinghamshire, in lying closer to London and the great
garrison towns of the south-east, shows more clearly in its pattern of recruitment the impact of national crisis on individual
lives than does that of Staffordshire, nevertheless the background
of their policemen can be directly compared. (Table 2.7) In both

TABLE 2.7   Previous trade of Staffordshire constabulary recruits,
1856

'Labourer'	35	Soldier	2
Shoemaker	10	Chimney sweep	1
Butcher	5	Coachman	1
Potter	4	Cooper	1
Baker	3	Dyer	1
Engineer	3	Engine cleaner	1
Groom	3	Gamekeeper	1
Miner, collier	3	Grocer	1
Painter	3	Horsebreaker	1
Policeman	3	Iron refiner	1
Weaver	3	Lath cleaver	1
Blacksmith	2	Last maker	1
Brickmaker	2	Locksmith	1
Carpenter, joiner	2	Nail maker	1
Clerk	2	Plasterer	1
Farmer	2	Plate layer	1
Gardener	2	Tailor	1
Maltster	2	Wheelwright	1
Servant	2		
Silk twister	2		
		TOTAL	112

Source: Staffordshire Record Office, Constabulary Records, Regiseter
of Members of the Force, 1842-1894; Descriptive Register 1842-1863.

counties labourers accounted for about 33 per cent of recruits and
craftsmen for about 14 per cent. As far as deductions can be made
from Staffordshire's much sparser records, a local geographical
source for native-born policemen can be discerned. Twenty of the
35 'labourers' were Staffordshire born, and 12 of those were from
the rural parts of the county. None of the native labourers were
born in the Black Country, and the remainder were natives of the
rural areas bordering the Potteries or the district around Leek.
(13)

As in Buckinghamshire, the previous trade of police recruits
reflected the employment pattern of the locality.   In Staffordshire
country crafts were not represented to the degree that they were in
the Buckinghamshire registers, and a small but significant proportion of Staffordshire policemen had previously worked in some
branch of the Staffordshire iron trade. The constabulary also

provided employment for a small number of Staffordshire miners in
1856. The Buckinghamshire force on the other hand gave employment
to more ex-servants than Staffordshire did, and also to more men
who had previously worked in the retail trades and at office jobs.
Contemporary policemen knew what figures for other selected years
of intake for these two counties will show: that a local police
force formed part of the local context of employment. It was part
of the local map of change, opportunity, and despair.

The half-dozen Staffordshire recruits who had previously worked
in the iron trade were all natives of the county or of one of its
immediate neighbours; but not one of them was a native of the iron-
working Black Country. They, or their families had already made
one change through local migration, and their later joining of
the police force fitted into this pre-existing pattern. The pattern can be seen elsewhere. The names of referees in the Staffordshire records allow a life to be followed for a brief period, for
instance that of a coachman from Shropshire working on the railways,
who, like the butcher from Gloucestershire and a young Irishman,
gave his trade as policeman, all of them thus indicating a self-
conscious break with their past.

A map drawn from Table 2.8 would show a roughly similar distribution of recruits' birthplaces as would one made from the Buckinghamshire figures (Table 2.5). Yet it is striking that the number

TABLE 2.8 Birthplace of Staffordshire constabulary recruits, 1856

Staffordshire	70	London	2
Leicestershire	5	Kent	1
Warwickshire	3	Suffolk	1
Shropshire	4		
Cheshire	5	Wales	1
Derby	4		
Nottinghamshire	3	Scotland	2
Buckinghamshire	2		
Oxfordshire	1	Ireland	4 (14)
Wiltshire	1		
Gloucestershire	1	Germany	1
Herefordshire	1		
		Unknown	1
		TOTAL	112

Source: Staffordshire Record Office, Constabulary Records, Descriptive Register 1842-1863; Register of Members of the Force
1842-1894.

of recruits who were natives of the county where they became policemen was much lower in Buckinghamshire than it was in Staffordshire
(36 per cent in the former, 62 per cent in the latter). This difference cannot be attributed to the aftermath of war in the way in
which much of Buckinghamshire's recruiting in 1857 can. In fact,
until the mid-1870s Staffordshire was to employ more county-born

men than Buckinghamshire did. (Table 2.9) Some of the difference
is of course explained by the proximity of Buckinghamshire to
London, the vagrant routes that traversed it, and the efficient
railway system that served it. But the kind of migratory patterns

TABLE 2.9   Recruits who were natives of Buckinghamshire and Staffordshire, for selected years, 1856-80.

	1863	1866	1876	1880
BUCKINGHAMSHIRE				
Number of recruits	22	32	18	17
Number native born	5	10	9	9
% of intake	22%	31%	50%	53%
STAFFORDSHIRE				
Number of recruits	135	79	90	72
Number native born	77	43	38	43
% of intake	66%	56%	43%	60%

operating in police recruitment that have already been indicated
may explain more. Police officers often spoke of the movement of
labourers from the 'poorer agricultural parts' not only to towns
but to industrialised counties, in order to become policemen. It
is possible that the industrial towns and counties of mid-nineteenth-
century England employed a proportionately greater number of rural
labourers than the rural counties did. The head constable of Sheffield told his watch committee in 1875 that

> Ten only of the 60 men appointed in the year belong to York-
> shire. 12 came from Lincolnshire, 5 from Notts., 3 from Derby-
> shire, one from Beds. 2 from Bucks., one from Cambridge, 2
> from Essex, one from Gloucestershire, one from Hants., one
> from Herefordshire, one from Hunts., 2 from Lancs., 1 from
> Leicestershire, 2 from Norfolk, 5 from Northamptonshire, 4 from
> Rutland, 2 from Suffolk, one from Surrey, one from Bombay and
> 4 from Ireland. (15)

To recruit from the constant source for policemen, which was rural
poverty, a net had to be spread from Sheffield over a very wide
area. But Staffordshire, so clearly divided into its three areas —
the Black Country, the Potteries, the rural parts — contained within
its own borders the eternal geographical and economic source for
policemen.

It is clear as well from this brief glance at two Midlands police
forces — one well-established, one its year of formation — that the
local economic background that made a local police force an employment opportunity was understood and used by police hierarchies.
This was particularly to be seen, and will be seen again, in police
forces' use of Irishmen. Most police forces, for instance, employed
Irishmen, certainly Buckinghamshire and Staffordshire employed many,
though the latter's use of them declined after 1856.(16) In
Buckinghamshire's year of formation only 1 of that county's 12
Irish-born recruits came from the six counties that now form Ulster,

whilst half of Staffordshire's much smaller number of Irish recruits were Protestant (at least by name and birthplace). (17)   In Staffordshire there were violently held community antagonisms that made the employment of Catholic policemen a foolish administrative act, whilst in rural Buckinghamshire such a police presence did not much matter.   In this way the facts of social and economic life of a locality — in this case the existence of migration routes from Ireland through Staffordshire — were used and deployed by police authorities.

Chapter 3

ORIGINS

This chapter elaborates the questions raised in 'Making a County Force', by looking at recruitment in Buckinghamshire, Staffordshire, and other places, over the quarter-century after 1856. The details discussed here will provide a framework for a later consideration of both the attitudes and assumptions bought by police authorities when they paid a policeman's wages, and the changes that men themselves had to make in order to become policemen.

The men who joined England's police forces after 1856 were not particularly young men. The most common experience over the country as a whole was to join between the ages of 20 and 25, though men joining borough forces were generally slightly older than this. (1) As the 1880s approached, recruits started to get younger, and between 1856 and 1880 the median age of men joining the Buckinghamshire constabulary dropped from 24 to 21 years, and from 25 to 23 years in Staffordshire. There were no Home Office rules about minimum age, though most county rule books put the lower limit at 18 or 19. It was rare for a man under 20 years to join a county police force.

Most police recruits then had at least ten years of working experience behind them, and many had a good deal more than that. Their age at joining enabled them to make detailed comparisons between a past and present life. 'I must be very thankful I have never been out of employment or without a Shilling since I first took to Keep myself at the Age of 13 years and 9 months,' wrote John Pearman in the memoirs he compiled after his retirement from the Buckinghamshire constabulary in 1882.

I have been very lucky . . . . Working at my trade (Sawyer) until I was 21 I thought it time to give up such hard work which brought little more than a liveing for myself but much for my employers. The Railway started and Joined the Great Western . . . not Likeing London I was far from being settled although we made good wages and not worked hard . . . one day I had a tiff with the Superintendent . . . so I made up my mind to be a Soldier . . . soon went to the east Indies. Now of all my life this was the most worth liveing . . . Mr Officer was not the same Tyrant as in england . . . with all the faults of a Military life there is more to live for then the poor man who

in england is a free born Slave.   I cannot say much for the
Policeman's life he must be a special man & Look after other
men's faults and shut his eyes to all virtues I must say I done
well in the Police Force . . . (2)
In 1863 70 per cent of Buckinghamshire recruits and 96 per cent
of Staffordshire's were single men.   Some county recruitment posters
carried the warning that 'No Married Men Need Apply,' and in urban
centres even fewer recruits than this were married.   Yet policemen
did get married.   In all the English counties in 1863 the number
of married men ranged from 63 to 85 per cent of the force. (3)
Security of housing, being past first youth, and a police moral
welfare system that whilst it found a married man a burden on the
police fund, nevertheless had to encourage marriage — all these
factors outline a motivation for becoming a policeman more certain
than any hypothetical father's memories of the hungry forties. (4)
The decision taken by a man in his mid-20s to become a policeman is
immediately traceable to his own circumstances, and his own perception of them.

There are some qualifications to make to the mid-Victorian truism
that the police constable had formerly worked the land.   The over-
whelming tendency of contemporary evidence, from city and countryside, does suggest that this was true, and the figures from Staffordshire and Buckinghamshire indicate that a large proportion of men
came directly from the farm to police work.   However, they also show
that other categories of rural labourer accounted for a significant
portion of recruits.   What coloured mid-Victorian evidence on the
origins of the police was partly the desire, which has already been
indicated, to believe that the policeman was an ex-agricultural
labourer, and partly in ignorance, especially in urban areas, of
what labouring in the countryside might actually involve.   It is also
probably true that many more farm labourers applied for the job of
policeman than were accepted.   The experience of seeing young men
go off to try to be policemen was evidently a common one in some
country places.   But this does not mean that they became policemen;
that depended on how strict was a police authority's interpretation
of the Home Office rules on literacy. (5)

The farm labourer was also seen as the most common policeman
because of his motivation was easy to interpret: 'Our recruits all
come from districts where work is bad and wages light,' said the
chairman of Bristol watch committee in 1875. (6)   'We generally
recruit them from the villages round our locality,' remarked the
head constable of Northampton.   'We do not get them from the town,'
affirmed the head constable of Nottingham.   'As a rule they come
from Lincolnshire and North Derbyshire.' (7)   As the last chapter
indicated, each police headquarters was the centre of a neighbourhood mapping of rural poverty. The distances traversed on this map
between 1856 and 1880 changed very little in Staffordshire and
Buckinghamshire, though it is only in the latter that we can be sure
of the exact timing of the journey.   The more substantive date for
Buckinghamshire in 1863 (Tables 3.2 and 3.3) repeats the pattern
of movement and migration that was discernible in 1856 from the place
of birth to the geographical area in which policing was taken up.
This pattern remained consistent in sample years up to 1880.

Table 3.1   Birthplace of Staffordshire constabulary recruits, 1863

Staffordshire	77	West Riding of Yorkshire	1
		East Riding of Yorkshire	1
Leicestershire	8	Suffolk	1
Warwickshire	2	Sussex	2
Worcestershire	3	Dorset	1
Shropshire	4		
Cheshire	3	Wales	1
Derbyshire	7		
Buckinghamshire	1	Ireland	3
Wiltshire	1		
Herefordshire	1	Nothing known	18
		TOTAL	135

Table 3.2   Birthplace of Buckinghamshire constabulary recruits, 1863

Buckinghamshire	5	Northamptonshire	3
		Hampshire	2
Bedfordshire	1	Wiltshire	1
Hertfordshire	1	Norfolk	2
Berkshire	2	Somerset	1
Oxfordshire	2		
Warwickshire	1	Ireland	1
		TOTAL	22

Table 3.3   Last residence of Buckinghamshire constabulary recruits, 1863

Buckinghamshire	9	Hampshire	1
		London	3
Berkshire	2	Norfolk	2
Oxfordshire	2		
Northamptonshire	2	Ireland	1
		TOTAL	22

Table 3.4   Birthplace of Staffordshire constabulary recruits, 1866

Staffordshire	43	Nottinghamshire	1
		Wiltshire	1
Leicestershire	5	Devon	1
Warwickshire	2		
Worcestershire	3	Wales	1
Shropshire	3		
Cheshire	9	Scotland	2
Derbyshire	3		
Lancashire	1	Ireland	4
		TOTAL	79

Table 3.5   Birthplace of Buckinghamshire constabulary recruits, 1866

Buckinghamshire	10	Norfolk	1
		Dorset	1
Berkshire	1	Devonshire	1
Oxfordshire	4	Cheshire	1
Warwickshire	1	Lancashire	2
Northamptonshire	1		
Hampshire	4	Ireland	3
Wiltshire	1		
Gloucestershire	1		
		TOTAL	32

Table 3.6   Last residence of Buckinghamshire constabulary recruits, 1866

Buckinghamshire	14	Norfolk	1
		Kent	1
Bedfordshire	1	West Riding of Yorkshire	1
Berkshire	2		
Oxfordshire	2	Wales	1
London	6		
Surrey	2		
Wiltshire	1		
		TOTAL	32

Table 3.7   Birthplace of Staffordshire constabulary recruits, 1876

Staffordshire	38	Dorset	3
Warwickshire	1	Wales	1
Worcestershire	3		
Shropshire	5	Ireland	26
Cheshire	3		
Derbyshire	2	Norway	1
Nottinghamshire	1		
Buckinghamshire	1		
Berkshire	1		
Wiltshire	1		
Herefordshire	1		
London	2	TOTAL	90

Table 3.8   Birthplace of Buckinghamshire constabulary recruits, 1876

Buckinghamshire	9	London	1
		Lincolnshire	1
Bedfordshire	3	Devonshire	1
Berkshire	2		
Oxfordshire	1	TOTAL	18

Table 3.9   Last residence of Buckinghamshire constabulary recruits, 1876

Buckinghamshire	7	Lincolnshire	1
Bedfordshire	3	Ireland	2
London	3	Canada	1
Devon	1		
		TOTAL	18

Table 3.10   Birthplace of Staffordshire constabulary recruits, 1880

Staffordshire	43	Scotland	1
Warwickshire	4	Ireland	5
Leicestershire	1		
Worcestershire	2	Unknown	1
Shropshire	2		
Cheshire	5		
Derbyshire	1		
Hertfordshire	1		
Buckinghamshire	1		
Herefordshire	2		
Northumberland	1		
Devon	2	TOTAL	72

Table 3.11   Birthplace of Buckinghamshire constabulary recruits, 1880

Buckinghamshire	9	Wiltshire	2
		Middlesex	1
Oxfordshire	1		
Hertfordshire	2	Canada	1
Staffordshire	1		
		TOTAL	17

Table 3.12   Last residence of Buckinghamshire constabulary recruits, 1880

Buckinghamshire	10	Wiltshire	2
		Essex	1
Northamptonshire	1	Middlesex	1
Hertfordshire	1	London	1
		TOTAL	17

Source: Tables 3.1–3.12: Buckinghamshire Record Office, Constabulary Records, Register of Members of the Force 1856- . Staffordshire Record Office, Constabulary Records, Register of Members of the Force 1842-1894; Descriptive Register 1842-1863.

It is clear that recruitment to a local police force was often used as a way of returning home in a minor variation of the way in

which discharted soldiers used Buckinghamshire's new establishment
in 1857. For instance, in Buckinghamshire in 1876 the two men
immediately resident in Ireland were both Buckinghamshire born,
both of them grooms, both of them with long periods of army
service behind them from which they were discharged in Ireland.
In the same year, the recruit from Canada, an Aylesbury-born blacksmith who had worked in Ontario for four years, returned home. Like
many men who used the police force in this way, his term of service
was short — under six months.

There remains a division between those men who used a local
police force as a deliberate and calculated means of survival, and
those who, usually over greater distances, were in some sense forced
into its arms. Contemporary police wisdom did not really distinguish between the two: 'We have men leave our force who have been
farm labourers . . . put (themselves) under a shoemaster . . . and
bounce and tell us he can earn 5/- a week more than I can,' said one
disgruntled Northampton sergeant in 1875. (8)   Urban officers saw
this as opportunism, and a two-way traffic:

I do not mean [said the head constable of Sheffield] that they
come direct from the countryside. They come from the service
perhaps of a railway company, or a firm of railway carriers . . .
and after residing in the town for some time, they leave and come
to us . . . We [lose] them this way . . . when they have been
drilled and smartened up there is a great demand for them. (9)

But it was not opportunism that brought annual quotas of Canon
Girdlestone's wretched Devonshire labourers to the police forces
of Lancashire and the West Riding in the years between 1868 and
1872, though the gentlemen sitting on the police committees of those
counties may be accused of it, in their nice calculations that the
degree of poverty that led one Devonshire conscript to the Lancashire police to ask if his journey would involve a sea crossing,
would prolong the time until he was tempted by an industrial
wage. (10)

The number of recruits to Staffordshire from another depressed
peninsular county in 1876 (Table 3.7), and the unusually high
number of Irish recruits in this year indicate a surer motive for
such long journeys than northern officers' dismissive formula that
attributed to countrymen a desire for the transient glory of wearing
a uniform and walking about the city streets like 'a fine gentleman'. (11)   The figures for Buckinghamshire and Staffordshire,
taking sample years as they do, show similarities in the social
sources for, and the migratory patterns of, men becoming policemen,
and cannot show any trend or change in that source. Yet constabulary records could be used as a fine local indicator of trade
cycle, of depression and unemployment. Certainly in the 1870s
these two Midland police forces were used by men who were not only
finding an individual solution to their problem of poverty, but
who were responding to a wide, national depression of circumstances.
These reverberations were small, and are difficult to interpret.
A chairmaker and a french-polisher joined the Buckinghamshire constabulary in 1872. The Wycombe furniture industry was in decline,
and several local workshops had recently closed.   Only two, out of
the dozens thrown out of work, joined the local police force, but
their action shows one effect of local crisis. One joined in

February, the other in March. How much did they want to stay? One
was dismissed within the month, the other after nine. The trade
background of recruits in Staffordshire and Buckinghamshire for
sample years up to 1800 (Tables 3.13-3.20) can serve to indicate
these varying circumstances of becoming policemen.

Table 3.13 Previous trade of Staffordshire constabulary recruits,
            1863

'Labourer'	59	Bricklayer	1
Miner, collier	6	Carrier	1
Groom	5	Clerk	1
Shoemaker	5	Engine driver	1
Farmer	4	Engine tenter	1
Butcher	3	Footman	1
Carpenter, joiner	3	Girder riveter	1
Wheelwright	3	Maltster	1
Brickmaker	2	Policeman	1
Gamekeeper	2	Potter	1
Gardener	2	Platelayer	1
Miller	2	Saddler's tool maker	1
Moulder	2	Seaman	1
Puddler	2	Tailor	1
Smith's striker	2	Nothing known	18
Blacksmith	1		
		TOTAL	135

Table 3.14 Previous trade of Buckinghamshire contabulary recruits,
            1863

'Labourer'	11	Market gardener	1
Baker	2	Thatcher	1
Carpenter	2	Wheelwright	1
Blacksmith	1	Woodranger	1
Gamekeeper	1		
Groom	1	TOTAL	22

    In Staffordshire, in 1863 (Table 3.13) 35 of the 59 'labourers'
were Staffordshire born and 27 of that 35 had been born in the rural
part of that county. Yet the land delivered up its workers over
greater distances than the journey from Offlow Hundred to Stafford
police headquarters. Two young farm labourers from Brighton to
Sussex travelled together to Stafford in January 1863. When one
was dismissed in July, the other resigned. It is unlikely that
they set off to become policemen. It is far more likely that,
one cold January morning they asked the policeman in the tramp
ward, properly appointed poor law relieving officer and tramp
master, what the job was like, and he, an eye open for 'the genuine
working man' as he had been instructed, directed them to the
station sergeant at county headquarters.
    It is unlikely that these two brothers made a career of polic-
ing elsewhere. Like the majority of recruits, they left very soon.
Yet that journey from the south to the midlands had been more

successful for some.   Ten years before, in 1851, Robert Dunham, 23 year old shoemaker of East Coker, near Yeovil in Somerset, had travelled to Reading and joined the borough police.   Thomas Dunham, labourer, 20 years old, joined him in 1852 and William Dunham, servant, had joined the other two in Reading in 1855 at the age of 25.   All three of them joined the newly formed Buckinghamshire Constabulary in March 1857.   Robert was dismissed in 1859, but his two brothers (or cousins) stayed on in Buckinghamshire until they were pensioned off.

In 1863 in Buckinghamshire, the majority of the 'labourers' (whose individual histories strongly suggest they had previously worked the land) had already journeyed some distance from their background.   Two of the 11 had been labouring on the railway, 2 had spent the last few years in the Metropolitan police, 1 had just left the army, 1 had been labouring at Millbank Prison in London and 1 had been a groundsman at a Northampton park.   Only 3 had immediately been working the land.

As in the more turbulent 1850s, for many men coming out of the army precipitated an application to join a local police force. In Staffordshire in 1866 (Table 3.15) a Chester-born labourer with ten years in the 15th Hussars joined the county constabulary.   By 1866 Stafford's boot and shoe trade was in severe decline, and 5 of the 6 shoemakers who joined the county police force in this year were born in or around Stafford itself.

Table 3.15   Previous trade of Staffordshire constabulary recruits, 1866

'Labourer'	36	Engine driver	1
Shoemaker	6	Engine maker	1
Miner	4	Farmer	1
Servant	4	Gamekeeper	1
Blacksmith	3	Grinder	1
Butcher	2	Groom	1
Carpenter	2	Hawker	1
Gardener	2	Locksmith	1
Miller	2	Painter and glazier	1
Potter	2	Printer	1
Baker	1	Silk weaver	1
Boiler maker	1		
Drainer	1	Unknown	1
Edge tool striker	1		
		TOTAL	79

Table 3.16   Previous trade of Buckinghamshire constabulary recruits, 1866

'Labourer	14	Carpenter	1
Groom	4	Clerk	1
Grocer	3	Coppersmith	1
Farmer	2	Gardener	1
Footman	1	Poulterer	1
Baker	1	Veterinary surgeon	1
Blacksmith	1		
		TOTAL	32

Local police forces also absorbed the small-time failure in business. In 1866 a single 24-year-old Gloucestershire veterinary surgeon last 'in business at Malmesbury, Wilts.,' joined the Buckinghamshire police force. He made a success of it, and retired with a pension in 1910. The 23-year-old poulterer last 'in business at Stoke Mandeville, Bucks.,' on the other hand, stayed only 18 months and resigned in 1867. Police hierarchies usually looked kindly on this small number of recruits whose status was higher than that of a labourer. The 29-year-old farmer of Little Milton, Oxfordshire, who joined the Buckinghamshire force in 1866 had four children, and had been running a small-holding in his native village. He rose fast and well through the ranks and was a second-class constable within nine minths. He failed again, was demoted to third class in 1870, and was dismissed in 1871. (12)

But police forces were usually the resort of those who had lost the means to use a skill rather than of the failed businessman. In the Staffordshire intake for 1876 (Table 3.17) was a man who had formerly worked in the London ship-building industry. In 1870 the cutter and driller in Table 3.17 had left the declining London iron ship-building trade and joined the Metropolitan police. Six years later he made the journey north to Stafford and promotion.

Table 3.17   Previous trade of Staffordshire constabulary recruits, 1876

'Labourer'	57	Gardener	1
Miner	12	Painter	1
Groom	3	Potter	1
Puddler	2	Servant	1
Seaman	2	Shoemaker	1
Baker	1	Smith's striker	1
Blacksmith	1	Stone mason	1
Cutter and driller	1	Textile worker — beetler in	
Engineman	1	linen factory	1
Engine cleaner	1		
Footman	1	TOTAL	90

Some men travelled where annual migration routes were well established. The recently discovered route from East Anglia to Burton-on-Trent along which young farm workers went to the maltings perhaps provided the scattering of Suffolk labourers that can be identified in the Staffordshire constabulary record books during the 1870s. They all joined the police in June or July: 'the malting season had to finish in June because the brewers were unable to malt in the summer seasons'; 'roll on the 31st of May . . . ' (13)

It is important to note that it was not universally the case that poverty was the main motive leading men over long distances to become policemen, though it was the most common cause. In Table 3.18, which shows recruitment to the Buckinghamshire force in 1876, the one miner represented came from the prosperous silver and lead-mining village of Teighsham in Devon. He was 21 and single when he left, and in a position to ask the mine overseer for a reference. If adventure led him to Aylesbury, it took him no further, for he stayed to receive a pension from the force in 1906.

Table 3.18 Previous trade of Buckinghamshire constabulary recruits, 1876

'Labourer	10	Servant	1
Groom	2	Shoemaker	1
Blacksmith	1	Silversmith	1
Miner	1		
Porter	1	TOTAL	18

By 1880, the end of the period under discussion here, the social source for policemen was generally consistent with what it had been a quarter of a century before. However, the trade background of Staffordshire's recruits in this year (Table 3.19) raises some interesting points. There were 15 Staffordshire-born 'labourers' recruited in 1880, but only a third of those had been born in the rural areas, as had been usual in the past. There was a discernible increase, then, in the number of men who originated on the fringes of Staffordshire's quarrying or iron-working districts calling themselves labourers. Without details of their immediate history it is impossible to talk of a shift in the background of recruits. But the two metal workers joining in this year do point to a real shift, not so much by their background (Staffordshire had always absorbed as policemen men with this trade experience) but by their urban roots: one was from Walsall and the other from Stafford. They are also conspicuous by their success. Both of them stayed to receive pensions, and very few policemen who had worked in Staffordshire's iron trade over the past twenty-five years had been as successful as policemen as that. It is possible that after the 1870s some police authorities began to draw more on the experience of men who came from an urban, industrial background rather than a rural one. However, in rural Buckinghamshire the pattern of movement away from birthplace and occupation was consistent with what it had been at the beginning of the force. Half the Buckinghamshire 'labourers' came directly from the land; the railways had claimed three of the others before the constabulary did.

When police authorities, like the chairman of Middlesbrough watch committee in 1875, said that police recruitment was 'simply, a matter of wages,' (14) they ignored an administrative motive with which they operated. Chief constables and watch committees wanted to employ rural labourers 'fresh from the country'. The constantly reiterated preference for the former agricultural worker was not merely negative, rejecting old soldiers (who drank too much) and tailors and potters (who had not the stamina to walk 12 miles on a wet night), and nor was it simply a reflection of recruitment statistics, for agricultural workers were not consistently the majority of labourers who joined police forces, and other types and trades of men joined and were successful. But to police officers and police authorities the farm labourer was desirable because he represented docility, because he implicitly understood a way of life and a system of social relationships, and because he could be 'drilled and smartened up'.

Table 3.19   Previous trade of Staffordshire constabulary recruits, 1880

'Labourer'	27	Ironstone miner	1
		Joiner	1
'Farm labourer'	4	Mill furnaceman	1
		Painter	1
Miner	6	Platelayer	1
Groom	3	Puddler	1
Bricklayer	2	Saddler's tool maker	1
Clerk	2	Shoemaker	1
Draper	2	Stocktaker in iron works	1
Gardener	2	Stone mason	1
Metal worker	2	Tinplate worker	1
Railway worker	2		
Silk weaver	2	None/No information	2
Smith's striker	2		
Carter	1		
Farmer's son	1		
Grocer	1	TOTAL	72

Table 3.20   Previous trade of Buckinghamshire constabulary recruits, 1880

'Labourer'	12	Musician	1
		Seaman	1
Groom	2		
Carpenter	1	TOTAL	17

Source for Tables 3.13-3.20   Buckinghamshire Record Office, Constabulary Records, Register of Members of the Force, 1856- , Staffordshire Record Office, Constabulary Records, Register of Members of the Force, 1842-1894; Descriptive Register 1842-1863.

This mattered particularly in a county force. Being a village policeman demanded of a man much the same set of social assumptions that living in a tied cottage did. Being single and living in a station house demanded the same hierarchical bowing to discipline that being a farm worker did. And a county policeman had to bow to the same men as he bowed to in his former life: the farm bailiff-become-superintendent, the chief constable married to the shire's land and money. Some chief constables indeed saw in their policemen (clothed in their mind's eye no doubt in the virtues of the farm labourer whether ex-butcher or ex-baker) the vision of a golden age rural community, classes united by defence against a larger enemy, the community no longer scarred by the wars of ratepaying politics, made whole once more. Captain Ruxton, magistrate of Broad Oak, Kent, before he became that county's chief constable in 1856, drilled his army of farm labourers against a possible French invasion and worked hard to get them issued with arms. He hoped to raise by 'sections . . . additional constables to be paid and clothed at the expense of the government . . . giving preference in joining to the married agricultural labourer of 25-45 years.' (15)

So the decision made by some rural workers to become policemen was applauded and actively sought out by police authorities. But decision taken, recruiting book signed, uniform on, most recruits showed themselves unwilling to become policemen.

Chapter 4

BECOMING POLICEMAN

This chapter examines the influences that went into the making of a
small minority: the long-term policeman who endured until pension
time. By looking at the factors that brought success to the few,
it is possible to consider what intention and motivation lay behind
the consistently high dismissal and resignation rate from police
forces in the mid-Victorian years. As in the last two chapters,
data from Staffordshire and Buckinghamshire for selected years is
considered in detail, and much of it is presented in tabular form,
for reference purposes.

Turnover and variations in police establishments were consistently high in the period 1856-80. Whilst national figures show
that the median percentage of a force leaving for all reasons in
the southern counties was halved between 1866 and 1880, from 15 to
8 per cent, it still stood at 15 per cent in the northern counties
at the end of the period under discussion here. It had been nearly
double that twenty years before. Men left borough forces in greater
numbers than these, though the position was more stable in non-
industrial areas. Resigniations, the voluntary leaving of a force,
counted throughout the country for the greatest proportion of men
leaving. In the south of England the number of men resigning from
county forces increased from 50 to 70 per cent of a year's turnover between the mid-1860s, and 1880.

Dismissal accounted for the next highest proportion of men
leaving all police forces. (1) The median figure for dismissal
as a proportion of a year's turnover in the southern counties was
43 per cent in 1866 and 27 per cent in 1880. Throughout English
police forces as a whole the dismissal rate declined in this way
as discipline became less harsh, much less harsh in the northern
counties, where difficulties in recruiting policemen tempered
punishment, and the median figure there in 1880 was only 18 per
cent of a year's turnover.

The pension rate was by 1880 still very small (16 per cent of
that year's turnover in the southern counties, 10 per cent in the
north) but it is still important to discover what distinguished
these men — successes in a police hierarchy's terms — from that
vast army of men who left, or were told to go. 'If the men stay
two years, there is some hope of them staying longer' said a chief

Table 4.1   Totals leaving southern and northern counties, for all
reasons, 1880 (turnover expressed as % of total force)

Southern Counties 1880

West Sussex	20	Cornwall	9	Devon	7
Hampshire	15	Berkshire	8	Somerset	6
Gloucestershire	13	Dorset	8	Surrey	6
Kent	10	Wiltshire	8	Herefordshire	5
East Sussex	10				

Northern Counties 1880

Cheshire	20	County Durham	14	Nottinghamshire	8
North Riding, Yorkshire	20	West Riding, Yorkshire	14	Northumberland	7
Cumberland and Westmorland	15	Lanchashire	13		
Derby	15	East Riding, Yorkshire	11		

Source: Report of Her Majesty's Inspectors of Constabulary for 1880,
PP 1881, li.

constable in 1874, 'but the vast proportion of men change within
the year, or the first few months.' (2) Looking at the career
pattern of one force over a stretch of time can help to bring the
long-term, successful policeman into perspective.

Table 4.2   Length of service in Buckinghamshire for selected years,
1857-80

No. of recruits	(154)	(26)	(26)	(33)	(17)	(17)
Years	1857	1862	1867	1872	1877	1880
Periods of service	%	%	%	%	%	%
Under 1 year	47	35	38	42	47	41
1-2 years	15	15	23	18	10	18
2-5 years	13	23	19	18	7	18
Over 5 years	26	27	19	21	35	23
Pensions (as % of total intake)	12	11	11	18	35	12

Source: Buckinghamshire Record Office, Constabulary Records,
Register of Members of the Force, 1856-

Men who left with under one year's service were always to provide the largest proportion of an intake's turnover. The surprisingly high number of men who left with over five years' service,
leaving as they did not only the possibility but the likelihood of
becoming pensionable policemen, is not only a reflection of a continued rigour of discipline (see below Table 4.3) but also of what
contemporaries knew: that police work provided not only part of the
employment background of working men's lives, but also provided
a limited freedom of manoeuvre on the labour market. (3)

Fewer men stayed so long in the more industrial Staffordshire, and a comparison between that county and Buckinghamshire shows the former to be a force always composed of much shorter-service men. Fewer men in Staffordshire left after becoming reasonably well established in the force.

Table 4.3   Length of service in Staffordshire and Buckinghamshire for selected years, 1856-80

Staffordshire

No. of recruits	(112)	(135)	(79)	(90)	(72)
Years	1856	1863	1866	1876	1880
Periods of service	%	%	%	%	%
Under 1 year	46	41	43	43	15
1-2 years	26	29	23	23	20
2-5 years	15	10	18	9	20
Over 5 years	13	20	16	24	44
Pensions (as % of total intake)	2	13	15	10	26

Buckinghamshire

No. of recruits	(154)	(23)	(32)	(18)	(17)
Years	1857	1863	1866	1876	1880
Periods of service	%	%	%	%	%
Under 1 year	47	34	34	33	41
1-2 years	15	18	19	12	18
2-5 years	13	18	15	22	18
Over 5 years	26	30	31	33	23
Pensions (as % of total intake)	12	13	19	28	12

Source: Staffordshire Record Office, Constabulary Records, Register of Members of the Force, 1842-1894; Descriptive Register 1842-1863. Buckinghamshire Record Office, Constabulary Records, 'Register of Members of the Force 1856-   .

The influences on a man's police career were many, and the choice of movement that can be seen in the numbers above was severely curtailed by a police hierarchy's expectations of men become policemen. Dismissal rates were expressions of an institution's dissatisfaction with its servants, as shown in Table 4.4.

In Staffordshire, dismissal accounted for over half the turnover of a year's intake, and a significant percentage of a year's total number of recruits were dismissed even with five year's service behind them. For men who stayed this long, and who were, in contemporary police officers' estimation, likely to make permanent policemen, the likelihood of dying was roughly equal to the likelihood of being dismissed. Yet in both of these Midland

Table 4.4   Reasons for leaving Staffordshire and Buckinghamshire
             constabularies at each stage of employment, 1856-80

Staffordshire

No. of recruits	(112)	(135)	(79)	(90)	(72)
Years	1856	1863	1866	1876	1880

No. of men leaving with
under 1 year's service

Reasons under 1 year	%	%	%	%	%
Resignation	47	49	46	46	55
Dismissal	53	51	50	54	45
Death	-	-	3	-	-

No. of men leaving with
1-2 years' service

Reasons 1-2 years	%	%	%	%	%
Resignation	68	50	50	48	80
Dismissal	31	48	44	52	20
Death	-	2	6	-	-

No. of men leaving with
2-5 years' service

Reasons 2-5 years	%	%	%	%	%
Resignation	70	76	64	38	57
Dismissal	29	8	29	62	43
Death	-	15	7	-	-

Reasons over 5 years	%	%	%	%	%
Resignation	46	26	38	32	15
Dismissal	13	7	15	13	9
Death	20	7	15	13	15
Pension	20	59	31	41	59

Buckinghamshire

No. of recruits	(154)	(23)	(32)	(18)	(17)
Years	1857	1863	1866	1876	1880

No. of men leaving with
under 1 year's service

Reasons under 1 year	%	%	%	%	%
Resignation	46	75	63	33	43
Dismissal	53	25	36	67	57
Death	-	-	-	-	-

No. of men leaving with
1-2 years' service

Reasons 1-2 years	%	%	%	%	%
Resignation	43	75	83	50	66
Dismissal	56	25	17	50	33
Death	-	-	-	-	-

continued........

No. of men leaving with
2-5 years service

Reasons 2-5 years	%	%	%	%	%
Resignation	76	–	80	100	100
Dismissal	24	100	20	–	–
Death	–	–	–	–	–

No. of men leaving with
5+ years' service

Reasons 5+ years	%	%	%	%	%
Resignation	24	57	30	17	25
Dismissal	6	–	–	–	–
Death	8	–	10	–	25
Pension	51	43	60	83	50

Source: Staffordshire Record Office, Constabulary Records, Register of Members of the Force, 1842-1894; Descriptive Register 1842-1863. Buckinghamshire Record Office, Constabulary Records, Register of Members of the Force, 1856- .

counties, the longer a man stayed the more likely he was to resign rather than be dismissed the service. A few of these resignations after five years' service were motivated by promotion to a higher rank in another police force (these were the only occasions when reason for a resignation was recorded). The opportunism that the head constable of Sheffield ascribed to his very short-service men coming up from the countryside and staying to be drilled and smartened up just long enough to be made desirable as door-men and time-keepers, operated with still greater benefit to long-service men. Habits of 'regularity and punctuality' were noticed by local businessmen. For a few policemen the job was a useful way of making contacts: 'people will take them without being recommended . . . they know everything about the police and from the methodical habits, the effect of discipline, they perform their duties better.' (4)   'Of those who have resigned,' said this same head constable to his watch committee in 1875, 'the majority alleged that they had obtained more remunerative employment, many of the others saying they disliked working on Sundays or that night duty injuriously affected their health.' (5)

In Buckinghamshire, a small stable rural force, 60 per cent of the intake of 1880 had left within two years; in Staffordshire throughout this period over 40 per cent of a year's intake left within a few months (see Table 4.3). The details of resignation rates in these two counties show that the majority of recruits did not want to become policemen, and had no stake in the job. Urban and rural chiefs of police knew this, and believed that forces were used by working men as a temporary relief from unemployment or as a means of migration. Given these factors, it becomes clear that it is not possible to speak of policemen pursuing such wholesale policies as the 'constant surveillance of all the key institutions of working-class neighbourhood and recreational life'. (6) Certainly the police were an important factor

in the implementation of legislation that sought to discipline work
and leisure, and we have yet to see how deeply and emotionally
involved were some police <u>officers</u> in the condemnation and suppression of working-class pleasure. But this is not to talk of
most policemen: out of the 1000 policemen whose lives were followed in order to compile the tables for Buckinghamshire and
Staffordshire, only 4 rose through the ranks to become inspectors
or superintendents. The mid-Victorian policeman, sent onto the
streets of Burslem with instructions to watch the beer houses,
was most likely to be a rural labourer who at the age of 23 had
walked from somewhere in the rural district of Staffordshire, or
over the county border from Leicestershire or Shropshire to the
police headquarters in Stafford, and who was soon — within a few
months — likely to be a policeman no longer. The tensions between
that policeman's life and the social life he was — often ineffec-
tually — sent out to control will be examined later. But it was
not a simple relationship: it was provided for by both a recruit's
background, his own reasons for using a police force, and by the
expectations of the local government which, in employing men whose
experience of life and work was overwhelmingly rural, thought that
they bought poverty and passivity.

The longer a man stayed in a police force, the more likely was
he to endure. In Staffordshire, considering the intake of 1876,
though only 23 of the 90 recruits stayed for over five years, 12
of those 23 eventually received a pension. In the intake of the
same year in Buckinghamshire only one of the men who stayed
longer than five years failed to make it to pension time. It was
in the shape of the long-term, long-suffering ex-rural labourer-
become-policeman that his betters made most clear their assumptions
aout the community government of mid-Victorian England. It is
possible to be quite precise about the factors that made the permanent, pensioned policeman. Table 4.5 shows the careers of policemen in the Buckinghamshire force for the intakes of 1862, 1867,
1872 and 1877. What they reveal in fact is that it was not <u>con-
sistently</u> ex-farm labourers that made up the ranks of the pensioned.

In the intake of 1862 the 4 pensioners were: a general labourer
from a neighbouring county; a farmer from southern Ireland with
four years' experience in the Royal Irish Constabulary behind him;
a groom who was a native of Norfolk and who had been working in
Buckinghamshire immediately before becoming a policeman; and a
blacksmith, a native of a neighbouring county. The 3 pensioners
who survived the intake of 1867 had all had previous police experience before joining the Buckinghamshire force. One labourer
who was successful in this way was a native of a neighbouring
county, the other was from Essex. The baker who stayed to receive
a pension was a county man who returned home in 1867 after working
for eight years in the Lanchashire constabulary and two years
working in London. In the intakes of 1862 and 1867 former police
experience does seem to have been a factor in creating the long-
term career policeman.

The success of men who had a knowledge of a terrain that came
from birth or residence in the county is seen more clearly in the
1970s. Out of the intake of 1872, 3 of the 6 pensioners were

Table 4.5   The success of Buckinghamshire police recruits in the intakes of 1862, 1867, 1872 and 1877

Intake of 1862 (26 men)

YEARS OF SERVICE

1 2 3 4 5 6 7 8 9 10 11 12 13 14 15 16 17 18 19 20 21 22 23 24 25 26 27 28 29 30 31 32 33 34 35

..... Dismissed
----- Resigned
——— Pensioned

'Labourer' (farm)
'Labourer' (farm)
'Labourer' (farm)
'Labourer' (farm)
'Labourer' (general)
'Labourer' (general)
'Labourer' (general)
'Labourer' (general)
Farmer
Farmer
Farmer
Farmer
Groom
Groom
Groom
Groom
Shoemaker
Shoemaker
Blacksmith
Carpenter
Cattle dealer
Coach painter
Coachman
Glazier
Miller
Stone mason

Table 4.5 (cont.)

Intake of 1867 (25 men)

YEARS OF SERVICE

....Dismissed
----Resigned
——Pensioned

1 2 3 4 5 6 7 8 9 10 11 12 13 14 15 16 17 18 19 20 21 22 23 24 25 26 27 28 29 30 31 32 33 34 35

Labourer (farm)
Labourer (general)
Labourer (general)
Labourer (general)
Labourer (general)
Labourer (general)
Labourer (general)
Labourer (general)
Labourer (general)
Labourer (general)
Labourer (general)
Labourer (general)
Labourer (general)
Labourer (general)
Shoemaker
Shoemaker
Baker
Blacksmith
Chairmaker
Gardener
Gamekeeper
Groom
Porter (railway)
'No trade'
'No trade'

Table 4.5 (cont.)

Intake of 1872 (34 men)

YEARS OF SERVICE

Legend:
- ..... Dismissed
- ----- Resigned
- ——— Pensioned

Years: 1 2 3 4 5 6 7 8 9 10 11 12 13 14 15 16 17 18 19 20 21 22 23 24 25 26 27 28 29 30 31 32 33 34 35

Occupations:
- Labourer (farm)
- Labourer (farm)
- Labourer (farm)
- Labourer (farm)
- Labourer (farm)
- Labourer (farm)
- Labourer (general)
- Labourer (general)
- Labourer (general)
- Labourer (general)
- Labourer (general)
- Labourer (general)
- Baker
- Bricklayer
- Brickmaker
- Butcher
- Butcher
- Butcher
- Carpenter and Wheelwright
- French polisher
- Gardener
- Gardener
- Gardener
- Gardener
- Grocer
- Grocer
- Groom

cont.

Table 4.5 (cont.)

Intake of 1872 (cont.)

YEARS OF SERVICE

1 2 3 4 5 6 7 8 9 10 11 12 13 14 15 16 17 18 19 20 21 22 23 24 25 26 27 28 29 30 31 32 33 34 35

..... Dismissed
----- Resigned
——— Pensioned

Cellarman
Letter carrier
Printer
Chairmaker
Servant
Ropemaker
Ropemaker

Intake of 1877 (17 men)

Labourer (farm)
Labourer (farm)
Labourer (general)
Labourer (general)
Baker
Blacksmith
Butcher
Gardener
Groom
Groom
Groom
Groom
Groom
Groom
Porter
Servant
Servant

Buckinghamshire born and had been working the land just before
joining the police. The general labourer and the cellarman were
natives of neighbouring counties and had both previously served in
another police force. The servant was a native of Devon who left
his birthplace in 1869 to work in the City of London police force.

The intake of 1877 produced 6 pensioners, 4 of whom were natives
of Buckinghamshire or a neighbouring county. The groom and the
servant were from the south-west peninsular counties and had already
put some distance between themselves and their past when they
joined: one was already working in Buckinghamshire and the other
had been in a Midlands' borough police force for several years.

These are brief and isolated success stories, and in many ways
they conflict with accounts from Staffordshire, where, for instance,
previous police experience was not a factor in becoming a long-term,
pensioned policeman. In that county's intake of 1863, only 1 out
of the 16 pensioners it produced had previous police experience, and
this was consistently true for all Staffordshire pensioners considered from sample years between 1856 and 1880. Buckinghamshire,
geographically positioned on migration routes from the depressed
south-west, close to London and the garrison towns of the south,
absorbed into its constabulary men who had already abandoned a
past life, and who had already sought in Metropolitan and Midland
borough police forces a way out. Distance and poverty made permanent policing attractive to the two men from Devon and Dorset
who joined the Buckinghamshire force in 1877, and who stayed to
obtain pensions.

In both counties birth within the locality (the county or one
of its neighbours) was the most consistent factor in success. What
a chief constable approved of when he looked at the rural labourer
become policeman was the quality of physical strength. Though
Staffordshire-born shoemakers joined the county force in some
numbers in the 1860s, not one from these sample years ever received
a pension. Miners, on the other hand, who joined in roughly the same
proportions as shoemakers, did occasionally make pensioners, as did
occasionally smiths' strikers and other metal workers. No potter
in Staffordshire ever lasted beyond a year, no tailor or baker in
either Buckinghamshire or Staffordshire, for their trade had
weakened them. Butchers, however, born and working in rural
districts in both counties were remarkably successful as policemen. Ex-servants, particularly grooms, made pensionable policemen
out of proportion to their numbers at joining. The ability to care
for and manage horses was a vital skill in a county police force.

The factors that made permanent, pensionable policemen were
then an extension and elaboration of the factors that sent hundreds of men to the recruiting office in the first place. Pensioners were in general local men, natives of the county or one
of its neighbours. Knowledge of the terrain was an important
factor in success. Physical strength was also reckoned by police
authorities, as was the collection of attitudes implied by a long
period in domestic service. The ex-farm labourer was used as an
example of the good and successful policeman because he embodied
all of these attributes, and he did in fact make up the numbers
of the most represented work group to receive pensions.

Stranded high on this island of approbation and success, the

policeman working towards his pension was a lonely figure. Most
of the men who had joined with him would have left within their
first couple of years. Yet some who left actually returned. 'The
men joining the police come out of the country,' said Constable
Nicholls of Sheffield in 1875,'and they get into conversation with
those at the works, and leave, thinking they can better themselves
. . . sometimes they do not like the work; they are put out and
come back and settle in the force.' (7) Certainly, a consideration
of the men in Staffordshire's intake of 1863 who used the force
over a period of fifteen years, confirms what Constable Nicholls
said (see Table 4.6). In both counties, use of the police force
was never to be so high again as·it was in the 1860s, not even in
the depression years of the 1870s. All except 2 of the 'users'
presented in Table 4.6 were natives of Staffordshire, which suggests that a force was used in this way only when it was geographically easy to return to a past life. But only rarely did these
men 'settle in the force'. Looking at the Staffordshire intakes
of 1856, 1863, 1866, 1876 and 1880, it is possible to count 26
men who acted in this way. At the end of their final period of
unemployment 13 of them resigned, 5 died and only 5 of them
received pensions. (8) Police work was, then, a job that fitted
into the pattern of some working-class men's lives, and did not,
in the vast majority of cases, indicate a change of life.

Physical strength was recruited, and in as far so it is possible to measure it by a man's former trade and his subsequent
endurance as a constable, it was important for the making of a
permanent policeman. Yet Home Office rules demanded literacy.
All police work at what ever level demanded a reasonable pro-
ficiency in reading and writing, but particularly in writing.
County forces especially were spread thin, and the writing of
reports and entries in occurrence books was an effective means
of supervising constables at outlying stations. 'This book',
ran the notice pasted into the front of the journals that were
issued to all members of the Northampton constabulary, 'is to be
kept in the form of a daily Journal by the Inspector, Sergeant
or Constable (as the case may be) in charge of divisions or
stations. He will record in a neat and legible manner his proceedings during each day of 24 hours . . .' (9) Some magistrates
obviously heard complaints about diary writing: 'I have heard
the men complain that their whole time is taken up with writing
and reports and that after walking God knows how many miles, they
had to sit down and write out endless statements of what they
had seen and heard.' (10) Many recruits were turned down for
being functionally illiterate, (11) but it certainly seems to
have been the case that some skills were taught as much as they
were recruited. The West and East Riding constabularies and
those of Dorset and Kent employed schoolmasters to teach penmanship to new recruits. Probably only a minimal literacy was
demanded of many recruits, and in any case, journal-keeping is
an effective and economical method of improving writing and
spelling, and the Stratford borough constables who jointly
filled in the police report books over the year 1865 and 1866
certainly improved dramatically in penmanship and spelling. Their
head constable evidently believed that he had an educational role

Table 4.6 Users of Staffordshire constabulary in the intake of 1863

1863 64 65 66 67 68 69 70 71 72 73 74 75 76 77 78 79 80 81 82 83 84 85 86 87 88 89 90

1 labourer
2 shoemaker
3 blacksmith
4 seaman
5 groom
6 miner
7 no trade
8 farmer
9 labourer
10 labourer
11 labourer
12 labourer
13 no trade
14 labourer
15 labourer

---   Resigned
...   Dismissed
———   Pensioned

to play in their supervision, and he usually underlined the words
that they mis-spelled and helped them to learn the correct form.
(12)

However, far more important than the ability to write well was
the qualification implied by a man's former trade, and there is
considerable evidence that many men refused to abandon their definition as worker for one as policeman. Though the level of former
police experience was high on recruitment, only a tiny proportion
gave their trade as policeman. Those few who did, like the future
head constable of Colchester and Cambridge, Gilbert Turrall, had
joined very young and had 'consequently never had an opportunity
of learning any trade'. (13) When Mr Justice Mellor questioned a
Chesterfield policeman suspected of perjuring himself to protect
three members of a nailmakers' union accused of trade outrage
in 1862, he could not estimate the worth or respectability of the
man before him by the mere knowledge that he was a county police
sergeant: 'What were you before you entered the police?' he asked
— 'An engine tenter at Chesterfield Station,' replied the sergeant,
defining himself in a way comprehensible to both protagonists. (14)
Men clearly sought to hold on to their distinction of a trade.
James Robinson, a small-time brick manufacturer from Sheffield,
remembered five years later how one of his cows had been maimed
during a trade dispute of 1862: 'this policeman who was at hand
said he was a butcher and understood the matter. He advised me
whatever I did to sell it . . .' (15)

But the life that policemen were made to lead, and the work
that they did, developed a new trade, that of policeman, in the
years between 1856 and 1880. As a job of work and a set of skills,
it developed out of the abilities demanded by a specific task,
and out of an older ideal of servitude.

Chapter 5

A POLICEMAN'S LIFE

When a new police force was created a hierarchy had to be appointed, but after the formative period, no man joined at any level higher than that of third class constable. By the 1880s a rigid pattern of promotion through the grades of constable to the hierarchy's final accolade to the respectable working man, the position of sergeant, had been established. Some forces had as many as seven grades of constable in order to provide the most finely regulated system of reward and check. (1) Very few recruits reached as high as the position of inspector; this was the rank reserved for the bankrupt businessman, the failed farmer, the dismissed agent. In fact, most pensioners were still first-class constables on retirement. By the mid-1860s the government inspectors were urging the opening of ranks; but little changed over the next twenty years. In the English police forces, officers — most inspectors, all superintendents — were appointed, not made.

The officer class was composed of long-term men, a permanent contrast to the fluctuating lower ranks. Officers were <u>policemen</u> in precisely the way that constables were not: inspectors and superintendents in the Staffordshire force did not have their trade recorded in the way that constables did. Out of a total of 25 officers appointed in Staffordshire between the year of formation in 1852 and 1863, 20 died in the force or were pensioned off. Most of these men had had previous police experience, and had travelled to Stafford in the cause of furthering their careers. These distinctions between officers and men were partially a result of the theoretical distinction that police authorities made between officers and rank and file: classes had to be kept closed and men in their places.

The pattern of promotion and checks through discipline acted on the third-class constable in the following way: in Buckinghamshire in 1857 a third-class constable had only to wait about four months to be promoted to the second class. The next stage was slower, and it took eleven months to reach the first class. Very few men went further than this. Out of the 21 men who made their unimpeded way from third to first class, 4 became sergeants (it took 2 of them twenty years to get there), 2 became inspectors, and 1 (a true exception to the general rule) became deputy chief constable in

1887. (2) Men appointed to the second class in 1857 were promoted
faster than this, and like first-class recruits, provided proportionately more sergeants. The good promotional opportunities of
this year of formation meant that 40 years later the structure of
the officer class was still based on this particular intake.

In 1867 promotion for third-class recruits (and all recruits
were third class now) was slower. Reaching first class took the
average recruit three years. In 1877 promotion was more reliable,
but even slower. In Staffordshire in 1866 it took a third-class
constable eight years to become a sergeant, and much longer in
1876, by which time twenty years was normal. 'Classes in forces
are limited to a particular number,' remarked one of the government inspectors, 'so that unless a vacancy occurs, no promotion
can be granted . . . a clog is placed upon the exertion of the
lower grades.' (3)

In the mid-1860s police authorities began to deal with the problem (for it was believed that slow promotion drove good men away)
by creating a 'merit' class intermediary between first-class constable and sergeant. As a reward, not for exertion, as the government inspectorate would have liked, nor yet, as many policemen
wished, for acts of personal bravery, it offered a penny a day
more than basic pay for a blank discipline sheet, and sheer staying
power. In the Buckinghamshire intake of 1876, for example, all but
one of the constables who stayed to receive a pension were 'merit'
men. This response to pressure by the government inspectors to
'open up classes', confirmed, rather than by-passed, a hierarchical
system of promotion that rewarded endurance and passivity with
money and status.

Discipline and de-ranking worked against the inexorable, if slow,
upward climb. Dismissal was a form of discipline concerned with
the inability to be a policeman (the police surgeon's diagnosis
of a lung complaint, literacy too close to illiteracy) as well as
with punishment for offence. The majority of dismissals in these
years were for drunkenness, and whether this was on or off duty
doesn't seem to have mattered much, though in Buckinghamshire at
least officers were allowed to get privately drunk. (4) Frequently, in the Buckinghamshire records, other offences were noted
which men, had they been sober, might have been able to avoid, such
as insulting language to officers, disobedience and the missing
of conference points. 'Gaming in a public place,' that is, play-
ing dominoes in a beer house, indeed any relations with a local
population other than official ones, were discouraged, and during
the very early years of Buckinghamshire's establishment, were a
sure way of being dismissed.

The longer a man stayed in this county, the less likely he was
to be told to go; yet even should he stay five years, his chances
of being dismissed were still high. Drunkenness counted for just
as high a proportion of dismissals among these long-service men
as it did for men who left with under twelve months' service.
Dismissal for 'contracting large debts' was also just as likely
for long-service men as it was for short-stayers. It was a very
common cause of dismissal in all forces, county and borough. It
probably meant living on tick at a local shop and being found out
for not setting up. Several county rule books forbade such

common domestic economy. This was hard on the county policeman, who was paid not weekly, but fortnightly or monthly. (5)

Through thirty years, discipline became less harsh, but the categories of administrative disapproval outlined above endured. Though drunkenness still accounted for the majority of dismissals in boroughs in the 1880s, some watch committees had long held to the governmental thesis that one needed to set a drunkard to catch one:

they could not get the most pious and moral men to be policemen. Such persons would be unfitted for the vocation. It was some- times necessary for policemen to appear to be fit company for the bad characters they might have to associate with. Some had to get liquor in order to get others into a similar state. (6)

In cities, a drunken policeman was more likely to be fined, and not dismissed, as he most invariably would be in a county force. In 1875 the entire Birmingham police force defended their 'right to a glass of ale,' against the teetotal faction of the watch committee. ·'The work they had to do could not properly be per- formed unless they did have some refreshment', and this was a defence of beer on duty, which no county authority would have entertained for a moment. (7)

In the counties, after dismissal and fining, de-ranking was the most common punishment. In Buckinghamshire in the late 1860s and 1870s it took two years for a demoted constable or sergeant to regain his former rank. A reduction in wages of 1s. a week (the difference between first and second-class constables' pay in 1868) for two years was a high price to pay for being absent from duty and visiting a pub. When Constable Raynor of the Cambridge borough police was reported absent from his beat and seen sitting in an ale house for half an hour in 1869, he was fined two days' pay. (8) But in both counties, and in the seemingly more lenient borough forces, offences that cast doubt on the governmental decorum of local authorities, such as policemen accepting bribes, were nearly always punished by dismissal.

All disciplines imposed were pecuniary in effect. Yet when policemen complained about their wages they rarely mentioned this, nor the drastic reduction in wages that sickness entailed. Ex- rural labourers and shoemakers used to the vagaries of payment for piece work knew that a working life brought a multitude of times when there was not enough coming in 'for his family to live on'. (9) Policemen in the counties did in fact receive half pay for a limited period of sickness, and this was a security not enjoyed by other members of the uniformed working class. (10)

But a policeman's complaint about wages rested not on these points of security and consistency, but rather on a comparison between his wage and that of other work groups. Wages in the counties were far more standardised than those of boroughs, and were laid down in a government circular. In boroughs wages were not only subject to a finer degree of scrutiny by the ratepayers than they were in the counties but also to 'the facilities of obtaining more remunerative employment, expense of living, cost of house rent . . . ' (11) These median figures disguise a wide range of wages. Borough police wages were dependent on local revenues: small boroughs with small ratepaying populations paid

Table 5.1 Wage rates for borough and county policemen for selected years, 1856-80

(A) NATIONAL MEDIAN FIGURES FOR BOROUGHS

	CONSTABLES				SERGEANTS		
Class	3rd	2nd	1st		3rd	2nd	1st
Year							
1857	18	19	20		23	23	23
1858	18	19	20		22	23	23
1862	19	19.6	20		23.4	24	24
1863	19	19.6	20		23.4	24	24.6
1865	19	20	21	Pay shown	24	25	25
1866	20	21	21.6	in	25	25	25
1867	20.3	21	22	shillings	25	26	26
1872	22.6	23.4	24.2		29	29	29
1873	23.8	24.6	25		30	30	30
1876	25.6	26.3	26.7		32	32	32
1877	25.6	26.1	26.7		32	32	32
1880	26	27	27		32.6	32.6	32.6

(B) NATIONAL MEDIAN FIGURES FOR COUNTIES

	CONSTABLES			SERGEANTS			INSPECTORS		SUPTS.		
Class	3rd	2nd	1st	3rd	2nd	1st	2nd	1st	3rd	2nd	1st
Year							£/annum		£/annum		
1858	18	19	20	22.6	24	25	75	80	100	109	115
1859	18	19	20	24	24	25	75	80	100	109	115
1860	19	19	21	23.4	24	25	75	80	100	110	115
1861	19	19	21	23	24	25	75	80	100	109	115
1862	19	19	21	23	24	25	75	80	100	110	130
1863	19	19	21	23	24	25	75	80	100	110	130
1864	19	20	21	24	25	26	75	80	100	112	130
1865	19	20	21	23	24	27	80	80	105	112	130
1866	20	21	23	25.6	26.3	28	80	90	108	112	139
1867	20	21	23	26	26.3	28	85	90	120	130	139
1868	21	22	23	25	26.3	28	85	90	120	130	139
1869	21	22	23	26	26.3	28	85	90	120	130	139
1870	21	22	23	26.6	28	28	85	90	135	135	140
1871	21	22	23	26.10	27	28	90	95	135	135	140
1872	21	23	24	26.10	27.3	29.2	99	104	140	137	140
1873	23	24	24	28	27.8	29.9	100	104	146	155	150
1874	23	24	25.6	29.2	27.8	32	100	107	146	155	150
1875	23	24	26	30.4	29.2	31.6	100	107	146	142	164
1876	23	24	26	30.4	29.2	31.6	100	107	146	142	164
1877	24	24	26	32.1	29.2	31	100	107	146	142	164

continued.......

Class	3rd	2nd	1st	3rd	2nd	1st	2nd	1st	3rd	2nd	1st
							£/annum		£/annum		
Year											
1878	24	24	26	30.4	30.4	31.6	100	110	146	150	164
1879	24	24	26	31	29.2	31.6	100	110	146	150	170
1880	24	24	26	32	29.2	31.6	100	100	146	150	170

Source: Annual Reports of Her Majesty's Inspectors of Constabulary, PP series, 1857-80.

very low recruiting wages — 14s. a week was the wage offered by boroughs with under 5,000 population as late as 1862. This had risen to a recruiting wage of 20s. by 1877. In that year boroughs with populations of 10,000-30,000 were offering nearly 24s. to their recruits. The larger the borough, the higher rose the recruiting wage in these years, though in 1867, when boroughs of a comparable size were offering 19s. to their recruits, Hereford City offered 10s. In very large boroughs a recruiting wage was lower: authorities could rely on a migration from rural areas to make it attractive. Boroughs with populations of 30,000-50,000 offered recruits 17s. in 1857, 19s. in 1867 and 24s. in 1877. These were the wages that the majority of policemen working in these places received during their life as policemen, before early resignation or dismissal took them back to the labour market. In very large towns there were often many classes below that of third class, for instance in 1866 Salford, Liverpool, Birkenhead, Preston and Manchester had more than eight classes of constable. The wage for a seventh-class constable, calculated nationally, shows only a little deviation from the national third-class median. Such fine divisions of rank were used for training purposes and men were usually removed from them, one way or the other. But the largest number of borough constables resigned or were dismissed from these classes, so throughout the majority of — brief — police careers many men received 6d. or 1s. less than these figures shown above.

County forces offered less than the boroughs as a recruiting wage: 17s. in 1857, 19s. in 1867 and 20s. in 1877. They too had classes below the third, and they served to provide a probationary period for new recruits. Such classes were also seen as a means of paying lower wages than those laid down in the Home Office pay scales to men not yet part of the police hierarchy proper. It was the large, old, professional county forces (like those of Lancashire and County Durham) that first established this ladder of grades in the 1850s, and the practice extended to the Midlands and the south over the next fifteen years. Men in these low ranks were often employed — in the knowledge that they would soon be likely to leave — in order to make up the numbers of personnel on which the government grant ultimately depended. The qualification of literacy was not always demanded of these men.

Nineteenth-century policemen's own evidence was that joining a police force was a response to an immediate situation rather than a calculation of future benefits. Police authorities knew this: no man 'of 20 or 21 thinks about superannuation,' said the chairman of Bristol watch committee; 'when he gets a family and when he

reaches forty years [he does] . . .' (12)   To the shoemaker and the
tailor joining was an escape from poorly paid and uncertain work
to a poor, but regular, wage.   It was regularity of payment that
police authorities believed attracted men who in better times were
used to higher wages than police wages.   In the case of the former
farm worker, fairly substantive comparisons can be made between
his income from the land, and his wage as policeman.

Table 5.2   Weekly earnings, after payment of rent, of farm labourers
and county police recruits in four counties, 1861 and
1868 (shillings)

DEVONSHIRE 1861

Farm labourer

Wage (summer employment)	8.0-11.0
Possible wage with extra earnings	8.0-15.0
+ cider	
- house rent (average)	-1.6
= a possible wage range of	6.6-13.6
Some work for women in season	

Police recruit

Wage	16.0
+ free uniform, no rent, no coal allowances	
+ boot allowance	+4d.
- 2½% superannuation	-5d.
- house rent (estimate)	-2.0
= an average wage of	13.11
Wife expressly forbidden to work	

COUNTY DURHAM 1861

Farm labourer

Wage (summer employment)	13.6-18.0
Possible wage with extra earnings	15.0-20.0
+ potatoes (in some areas)	
house rent free (in some areas)	
= a possible wage range of	13.6-20.0

Police recruit

Wage	17.0
+ free uniform, no rent, no coal allowances	
no boot allowance	
- 2½% superannuation	-5d.
- house rent (estimate)	-2.0
= an average wage of	14.7
Wife expressly forbidden to work	

BUCKINGHAMSHIRE 1868

Farm labourer

Wage	11.0-13.0
Possible wage with extra earnings (this includes harvest beer)	12.6-15.6
- house rent (range)	-1.0- 3.6

STAFFORDSHIRE 1868

Farm labourer

Wage	12.0-13.0
Possible wage with extra earnings (little chance of this)	13.0-15.0
- house rent (range)	-1.0- 2.6

continued........

Table 4.2 continued......
—

= a possible wage range of	9.0-14.6	= a possible wage range of	9.6-14.0
A little field work for women in season		Some field work for women in season	

Police recruit		**Police recruit**	
Wage	17.6	Wage	19.6
+ free uniform, no coal allowance; some rent subsidy worth 1.0 a week to recipients		+ free uniform, no coal allowance	
+ boot allowance	+5d.	+ boot allowance	+7d.
$-2\frac{1}{2}$% superannuation	-5d.	$-2\frac{1}{2}$% superannuation	-6d.
House rent (average)	-2.3	- House rent	-1.0-2.6
= an average wage of	14.1	Wage range of	17.1-18.7
but if in subsidised housing (unlikely for recruit)	15.1-16.0		
Wife expressly forbidden to work		Wife expressly forbidden to work	

Source: PP 1861, 1, Return of Agricultural Labourers' Earnings; PP 1868-9, xiii, Report on the Employment of Women and Children in Agricultura; PP 1868-9, 1, Report on the Weekly Earnings of Agricultural Labourers. Reports of Her Majesty's Inspectors of Constabulary, 1858-80, passim.

In some counties there were real gains in wages to be made by becoming policemen. But houses still had to be paid for. In the southern counties in the mid-1860s a married sergeant expected to pay 2s. 3d. a week house rent out of a wage of 26s., and a married constable paid on average about 2s. out of a wage of 21s. There is no indication of how many men occupied this kind of subsidised housing — probably well under half a county force. Herefordshire, for example, threw all its policemen on to the open housing market, and it is likely that it was the officer class that benefited the most. 'A nice home and a good garden,' noted John Pearman of the station house at Great Marlow which he was drafted to in 1863 when he became a second-class inspector. (13)   A good garden was a valuable item for any man with a family to feed.

Much less information on accommodation exists for the northern counties, though a rent scale for County Durham policemen in 1866 shows that a superintendent was charged 3s. 10d. for house and stable accommodation, and that married inspectors, sergeants and constables were charged 1s. 6d. Single men paid 1s., and all these rents were deducted at source. (14)   Rents charged to borough policemen were a far less regulated affair.   In the southern region in 1867 only 9 out of 58 boroughs provided some sort of accommoda-

tion, and none of it was for single men. In northern industrial
cities there was more accommodation than this, much of it,
like Manchester's and Liverpool's, in the form of barracks. (15) But
it was far easier to find suitable accommodation in boroughs,
for no one place in a town could be very far from a policeman's
beat and the central police station. The same dictates restricted
choice for rural constables, and one West Riding constable of 1866
thought local high rents were the very basis of his troubles: 'Men
with families paying £7-£10 a year in rent are poor, badly kept and
a few years' service in the police unfits them for other labour.
Then they . . . become a sort of "come day, go day, God send pay
day" men . . . .' (16)

   Some county forces provided coal, a ton for the winter, 5 cwt
for the summer months. Later in this period, some paid gas and
water bills, some footed the rate bill. Where subsidised housing
was provided, it was then a valuable addition to income. There
were others too. There was a regular boot allowance paid to many
county constables — 7d. a week was the norm in the 1860s. This
allowance was adjusted to pay — the higher the wage, the lower the
allowance. Most boroughs though were not at all consistent about
paying this allowance. There was also, in many counties, a random
scale of allowances for the performance of local government administrative functions. But it was the officer class who stood most to
gain here. Whilst a policeman appointed assistant poor law relieving officer could add an average of £13 a year to his income, no
rank lower than sergeant ever performed this function. It was particularly the inspectors' plum. There was undoubtedly the opportunity there to earn something extra for a very small number of
merit-class constables: acting as javelin man at assizes could earn
them 2s. a day; escorting a prisoner some distance or attending
sessions or assizes could earn a constable 1s. 6d. a day. But these
rare jobs were in the fee of the officer class. Other allowances,
for serving summonses and executing warrants, went by law to the
police superannuation fund. Very few constables indeed earned anything above their wages.

   Money, then, defined a policeman's status, and measured the
limits of his ambition: 'a man must have some object in view, and
in the case of the constable, that at present only consists of the
chance of promotion to a higher rank, bringing with it greater res-
ponsibilities, but also increased comforts.' (17) This ambition
was not just defined by the structure of a local police force, but
also by a set of external circumstances of which policemen still
felt themselves to be a part. Head and chief constables certainly
knew that police authorities functioned as part of a wider employment market, and a wider social structure. 'We are on a par with
the working man except that the policeman works seven days and
the working man only about five and a half days,' said the head
constable of Birmingham in 1874. (18) 'Relatively, the wage is a
fair average, about 4s. per day,' said the chief constable of Cumberland and Westmorland in the same year. He was calculating a
six-day week for a first-class constable. 'You cannot get labouring
men in Cumberland for less than 3s 6d or 4s a day . . . it is very
much below the pay of the agricultural labourers.' (19) Men in
his position knew that the working man's hold on the position of

constable was tenuous indeed: the average rate of wage 'in the city
is £1 a week' reported the head constable of Norwich in 1874, 'and
in the agricultural districts 15s . . . I think a policeman would
rather obtain agricultural employment if he got a 1s a week more,
than remain a constable.' (20)

Yet a decade before these head and chief constables made these
casual comparisons between working men and policemen, constables
had been making a more subtle analysis of their own position. In
the mid-1860s policemen saw themselves still as working men, but
of a particular sort:'viz, the mechanic, and the most intelligent'.
(21) A deputy chief constable might reply in statistically de-
flating tones to this constable that twenty-seven years' police
experience had shown him that 'out of a hundred candidates taken
consecutively . . . 52 were labourers . . . only 8 belonged to the
mechanic class . . . the others were servants, discharged soliders
. . . railway porters . . . ', (22) yet it was the social and
economic position of the skilled mechanic that policemen felt themselves most comfortable at the thought of occupying.

Identification with the artisan was partly made for the purpose
of pay claims, and on the streets the divorce from a man's origins
that this identification implies might not be so clearly emphasised. Constable Green of Birmingham asked his fellow workers
in 1875 'whether 4s a day was adequate wages when a common
labourer would refuse 5½d an hour?' He told of a meeting between
himself and an old friend in a Birmingham street one Saturday
afternoon. They compared their financial positions, and Constable
Green concluded that he had the worse bargain: 'the man, who was
only a common labourer, was earning 6d an hour with half time for
overtime and double time for Sundays.' (23) John Pearman, one
of the rare constables who rose through the ranks to the position
of officer, saw his police career within the context of a working
life, and at the end of it, on his retirement from Buckinghamshire constabulary in 1882, understood his position still to be that
of a working man: 'as poor men we cannot find much to live for ours
is a life of heavy toil to get a bare living and to amas (sic.)
money and Whealth (sic.) for the great men of the day.' (24)

There was also a confusion of identification among police
authorities. In many boroughs in the 1850s it was easy enough
to associate the officer class of a local force with other emer-
gent groups of uniformed workers — in the post office for instance
— as this exchange between the Huddersfield improvement commissioners makes clear: 'What is the salary of the Superintendent
[that is, the head constable]?' — '£78 a year.' — 'It is sadly
too little.' — 'It is less than the clerks in the post office get.'
— 'It is more than superintendents get in other towns.' — 'If we
get a corporation we can have £100 a year.' (25) Watch committees
in industrial towns often saw constables as another version of
their hands, as employees — 'as for the quarrel among the police,
it is simply a workshop quarrel' — and considered that the borough
bound them to the job only in the same way that a factory bound
its workers. (26)

The County and Borough Police Act of 1856 (19 & 20 Vict. c.69)
provided for the professionalisation of local police forces. It
was the statutory basis for a growing awareness among policemen

that theirs was a life apart. But this awareness also found its
roots in the enforced isolation of policemen from local social and
political life. In this changing situation, the function of watch
committees remained the same: to estimate how much a community
needed to spend on its internal good order, collect the monies
obtained in rates by the town council, and pay them out for the protection of property and life. In a governmental situation where
the accounts were clear, where ratepayers had a vote in the spending of their money, then watch committees found it easy to see themselves as employers. Members of watch committees were always to
hover uneasily between the idea of a policeman as a worker, and the
idea of him as a servant. It was a change of identification on the
part of policemen, part of their own reaction to their isolation,
that made the label of servant become more precise and more mean-
ingful to urban ratepayers in the years between 1856 and 1880.

By the 1870s policemen had begun to look further afield than the
structure of their local force for their identity. For the main
part, this search was contained within the national agitation for
pension rights. But firing that search, and making it overt, was
an already existing structure of promotion. Though it remained
the most abstract and theoretical of structures for the majority
of men who joined forces, it was nevertheless the idea of the steady
upward climb that marked police work off from work done in a former
life. This structure was developed by policemen into a way of life.
By the late 1870s, English police forces began to look increasingly
inwards, ceased for the main part making comparisons with other
working lives, and began to look only to themselves for identity.
An enforced way of life became the lineaments of an ideal. The
next chapter considers the process by which this happened.

Chapter 6

AN ENTIRELY NEW SITUATION

'It is incessant walking, and work every day of the week, including Sundays.'

'It is most essential that they keep under control their private feelings. They become police officers and are in an entirely new situation.' (1)

Police discipline was a way of impressing the social virtues on a body of employees. But the goal was broader than the creation of the respectable, temperate working man. Discipline extended to policemen's families, and the majority of policemen had families. In some county forces, constables had to present their future wife to the chief constable so that her respectability might be gauged. County forces generally forbade police wives and children working. This was not a legal restriction, but was seen by police committees as a necessary corollary to that section of the act of 1856 that forbade a policeman's taking other work. Some rural constables felt that life would be easier if a wife could 'keep a cow if he lives in the country, and a small shop if he lives in the town'. (2) Possibly, joining a workforce that offered limited advancement as part of its very structure enabled men to dream such dreams. That particular dream was firmly and paternally dismissed by a chief constable: 'a police constable's wife with 5 ot 6 children would not have much time to spare . . . neither should the risk of bad debt be overlooked.' (3) This restriction on family employment was not at all rigorously applied in the boroughs. Police wives who worked in northern industrial cities seem largely to have been confined to the genteel trades of dressmaking, bead working and feather curling. One deputy chief constable wrote to the policeman's newspaper detailing instances of police wives in boroughs 'earning money by bonnet-making . . . keeping schools . . . grocers' shops . . . cows, pigs, poultry'. (4)
    The married recruit who joined the Staffordshire and Buckinghamshire constabularies in the 1860s had on average two children. Staffordshire indeed, refused to employ men with more than three. But more children followed, and talk of half a dozen was common in the columns of the 'Police Service Advertiser': 'I am expected

to keep a wife and six children in a respectable condition, and provisions at the rate they are . . . .' (5) All of John Pearman's
children were born after he became a policeman: 'My own married
life as been a life of much care haveing to raise eight Children
out of Eleven borned. Well I have always been a very careful man
never making any wast of money . . .' (6) For all policemen there
was pressure to maintain a respectable family facade and to educate
their children: the world looked at a policeman's family. (7) The
wife of a policeman lived with a particular tension: 'the irregular
hours, the constant anxiety . . . the seclusion in which we are
bound to live to avoid the inquisitive gossip of prying neighbours
. . . .' (8) A report in the policeman's newspaper in April 1871
of a City of London constable's wife who tried to drown herself as
the only way of escape from the cellar dwelling she and her husband shared with another family, brought in many letters form men
an women living under great strain. (9)

The isolation that these men and women complained of was many
stranded. Most county forces seem to have been consistent about
stationing recruits and their families at some distance from their
most recent home and birthplace. (10) The countryman who travelled
to the city to become a policeman in one sense made that most
familiar and lonely of nineteenth-century odysseys. But his
journey was different, and his loss perhaps sharper, for he knew
precisely where he was going. Had the recruiting sergeant visited
his village, and had he signed his name, then he would have done as
his grandfathers had done, and taken the King's shilling. He,
though, would walk freely into the citadel, and put on the uniform
of the enemy.

Nevertheless, the borough policeman did not lead the physically
isolated life of a county constable. In town directories policemen's names are to be found listed next door to greengrocers'
shops, and dairies, in Sheffield at least, in rows of small resi-
dential houses. Only the very largest of boroughs provided the
sort of communal living accommodation that some of the northern
counties did. The number of northern county policemen living in
communal housing increased substantially in this period, though
the number of men living in barracks in Lancashire and Yorkshire
actually declined. The general pattern for earlier years, and
still later in the southern counties, was a married sergeant, his
wife and a single constable as a lodger living together. A married

Table 6.1   Station accommodation for men in northern county forces
            (expressed as % of force)

	1857	1867		1857	1867
Lancashire	50	30	Cheshire	28	16
County Durham	28	31	Cumberland and		
East Riding,			Westmorland	7	18
Yorkshire	18	22	Northumberland	–	34
North Riding,			West Riding,		
Yorkshire	15	23	Yorkshire	–	17

Source: Reports of Her Majesty's Inspectors of Constabulary; 'Police
and Constabulary Almanac', 1858, 1868.

policeman was an expensive item for a county police committee, but at the same time, a valuable feature of a disciplinary system. The police units shown in Table 6.1, were not large; but the pattern of living in five Lancashire station houses in 1878 shows an extension of this basic police accommodation unit:

Table 6.2 The pattern of living in five Lancashire station houses, 1878

	Inspector	Sergeant	Constables (married)	Constables (single)	TOTAL
Waterloo		1	1	5	7
Nelson		1	1	2	4
Standish		1	1	2	4
Moss Side	1	-	1	5	7
Radcliffe		1	1	6	8

Source: Reports of Her Majesty's Inspectors of Constabulary; 'Police and Constabulary Almanac', 1858, 1868.

In the late 1870s the experience of the young unmarried recruit in the northern counties was still that of the barracks, where he would undergo a period of training. (11) Such a life was not private — 'fifteen or twenty young men and two or three older ones living together' (12) — and it wasn't particularly private in smaller police communities either, with constables 'constantly coming and going at all times of the day and night'. (13) This pattern of living deliberately made police wives auxiliary policemen. Prison bedding was frequently sent out for washing to police wives. In Cambridge Mrs Turrall, wife of the head constable, earned £10 a year as 'female searcher', (14) and in the Radnorshire village where Francis Kilvert was curate, he saw Mrs Lewis, wife of the village constable, as a cut above the other women, and able to do what her husband could not do: for example, examine a little girl for evidence of her father's ill-treatment of her. (15)

Substantial myth attaches itself to the 'singleness' and isolation of the rural policeman's life. Witness, for example, Flora Thompson's memories of the Candleford Green constable devoting his working hours to the cultivation of his garden, (16) and the order issued in the 1890s to the West Riding police forbidding their entries at local horticultural exhibitions because they won too many prizes. (17) Yet in contrast to an extraordinarily stable officer class, a large majority of whom occupied the same house in the same village for anything up to twenty years, life in the lower ranks was a shifting, impermanent affair: 'I was only in the county force for two years and two months and I was in six different stations during that time.' (18) Removal from station to station was a frequent and arbitrary punishment for the lower ranks, but even John Pearman, whose rise from third-class constable to first-class inspector was accompanied by an excellently blank discipline sheet, was moved three times between joining the Buckinghamshire force in March 1857 and his arrival at Eton (where he stayed eighteen years) in 1864. (19)

There were 621 county officer staff in the villages, towns and hamlets of England in 1868 (this total excludes chief constables and sergeants). Of these men 376 had been officers in the same county since the creation of their forces; 230 of them had been stationed in the same house in the same village for ten years or more. A decade later, 55 of them were in exactly the same place as they had been in 1858, and 29 of them were in the same force but in a different district. A similar pattern emerges if the officers appointed between 1860 and 1868 are considered.

Table 6.3 County officers appointed after 1860 and before 1868

Employed in the same county in 1879	79
Living in the same village, etc.	63
Retired, moved to other forces, etc.	103
TOTAL	245

Source: 'Police and Constabulary Almanac' 1860-8.

It was officers that provided the stability that has been ascribed to mid-Victorian police forces. Their backgrounds, their pattern of life and their daily work cut them off from the great fluctuating, impermanent army of the rank and file. Stationed in social and institutional security in petty sessional towns, housed at the meeting of roads and the confluence of rivers, a post office at hand, in daily communication with the local magistracy, theirs, as we shall see, was the formation of English police forces.

For the officer class in boroughs, permanence of housing was also the pattern. But this was largely the case for all borough policemen, officers and rank and file. According to an urban theory of policing, a policeman was best living on his town beat, (20) and most watch committees did not employ enough men to operate a system of shifting personnel, even had they wanted to.

But all constables, borough and county, were to a very large extent cut off from the community. Large numbers of men recruited at the formation of a force might show themselves unwilling to mark themselves off. The chief constable of Buckinghamshire had to issue a general order in December 1857 insisting that the plates inscribed 'County Constabulary' be fixed up over police cottage doors. (21) But there was no effective way of disguising the enormity of the change from man to policeman. A policeman must always be a policeman. He must, until the mid-1860s, wear his uniform on and off duty. The concept of being off duty is a twentieth-century one anyway, and was not recognised until the 1890s, when the larger forces instituted regular days of rest, as of right. (22) Policemen were not allowed to drink, gamble, smoke in public, nor to attend fairs and race meetings. If the craft shoemaker, in the county force for nine months until something better came along, was presented with the task of disciplining working-class society by the 'monitoring and control of the streets, public houses, race courses, wakes and popular fetes', (23) then some different perspective on governmental intention must be obtained by seeing that the man inside the policeman's uniform was only permitted to be on the streets, and that the pubs and race courses were closed to him, as man and as policeman. (24)

The extremes of such internal discipline applied far more to the rural than to the urban constable. The clearest indication of the respectability that county police extracted from their men is seen in the operation of an enforced religiosity. In many ways this was simply an institutional identification with the observed principles of county life: the great turnout one March Sunday in 1857 when the entire Buckinghamshire police force marched to Aylesbury parish church, hymn books held purposefully in left hand, (25) was not uncommon in these years:

The duties on Sundays and other days appointed for public worship will be arranged as to permit the attendance of the Constabulary at divine service at least once a day (they) are
expected to show an example of due respect for an observance of
the Sabbath day and a strict attention to their religious
duties . . .

said the chief constable of the North Riding. (26) In some areas dissenters were expected to make this overt acknowledgment of the established church:

the chief constable . . . considers it far better that constables should be church men rather than chapel-goers, and that
those who have no decided inclination for chapel should be
encouraged by the Superintendent to attend church. . . .
Superintendents who are dissenters would exercise a wise discretion if they went occasionally to the parish church. (27)

In the journal of George Williamson, an inspector in the Northamp-
tonshire constabulary, he noted attending chapel once between January 1866 and November 1867. On every other Sunday divine service was noted as taking place at 'church'. (28)

How much this enforced religiosity conflicted with policemen's personal beliefs, it is difficult to say. Certainly Catholics and dissenters did become policemen (though the police orphanage opened at Brighton in 1866 did not cater for the former). (29) The head constable of Wolverhampton was a Roman Catholic (much to his disadvantage when he applied to be chief constable of Staffordshire in 1867). (30) About half the Irishmen in Tables 2.2-3.20 were Roman Catholics, though the proportion in Staffordshire was smaller than this. Yet the sanction of the established church was continually sought: would-be policemen were advised on recruiting forms to obtain a reference from their local Church of Eng-
land incumbent. Churchmen as referees did not figure very large in either Buckinghamshire or Staffordshire, but all those that did write recommendations were members of the established church.

The overt religiosity of county policemen was designed to be a reflection of a social and religious establishment. Where the religious affiliations of borough policemen entered — and were designed to enter — a public arena, they, as in the counties, reflected the convictions of a policeman's masters. The egregious Mr Murphy believed that half the head constables he met on his Black Country and north-western circuit were papists. (31) Following the spate of his prejudice does reveal one thing: there was a small but significant number of head constables with clear support from local notable and militant Protestants operating in these districts. 'I am sorry to say,' wrote a Church of England incumbent of Wigan in 1868, when the police were accused of permitting

conservative intimidation of liberal voters, 'that 30 policemen were looking on unconcernedly. The head constable is an Orange-man, and 25 of the officers by whom he was surrounded are members of the same faction.' (32) What is interesting here is the clear line of political interest that this observer believed he could trace. In some places use was made of the police in political arenas, and this was particularly well provided for in boroughs, where the administrative relationship between ratepayer, watch committee of the elected town council, and policemen, made political influence of the police easier than it was in the counties.

Matters of geography and discipline, of conscience and belief, were what compounded a policeman's separation and distinction from other men. To the Victorian statistician as well, a policeman was distinct from the general working population. In 1876 the mortality rate for county policemen was nearly half what it was for the general population. It was much higher than this in the boroughs, and after ten years of service the urban policeman's likelihood of dying was about level with that of the general male population. In both county and borough, life expectancy decreased as years of service were clocked up. Policemen were, after all, chosen for those qualities of health and strength that made them such good risks in their first years of service. (33) What policemen believed and often complained of was that they were worked near to death, and then discarded. An eminent Victorian statistician came to the same conclusion: 'a low mortality among the effectives corresponds with a higher mortality of men in the first five years after they are pensioned. The mortality of the pensioned is much higher . . . than it is among the male population of England at the corresponding age.' (34) Out of the thousand pensions that were granted to English and Welsh provincial policemen between the creation of their forces and 1874, only about one in eight was granted for injuries received on duty. (35) Rather, it was 'the inclemency of the weather that tells upon you; you get one cold lodged upon the other until at last it affects the lungs.' (36) Lung diseases and acute rheumatism were the major hazards of the policeman's working life.

A rural constable might think that country service was more tiring — 'it is very different from walking in the streets where you always have clean shoes' — and a policeman who had experience of both rural and urban service might point from the town to the simple rural virtues of fresh air. (37) Whether in county or borough, policemen led a working life that statistically main-tained them in good health and, at the same time, wore them out: 'When a policeman has been a policeman up to the age of 50, he is subsequently very seldom fit for really robust hard night work . . . we find they are generally employed in the stations at some light, special work . . . .' (38)

The pattern of work was absolutely regulated and consistent, wavering neither from day to day, nor week to week. The exten-sive use that policemen made of the thesis that 'we also have mortal souls to save' as they petitioned watch committees for days of rest was the expression of a tactical religiosity, cal-culated to appeal to a churchgoing, ratepaying public.

Before the 1870s police work — length of beat, hours on duty — were not at all standardised. In 1865, Stratford-upon-Avon borough constables worked a fifteen-hour day. They had three-and-a-half hours of breaks during the fifteen, and stretches on duty varied from one-and-a-half hours to five hours. Night duty, which was broken up in a similar way, was followed by a longer rest period than was day duty. Night and day duties were worked by all the constables. (39) In the same year Inspector Williamson of the Northamptonshire constabulary worked from eight hours to thirteen-and-a-half hours a day in one average January week. Occasionally he put in much longer days than this when travelling was involved. (40)

These figures do not outline hours of tramping, but this, with reporting before and after duty and consultations with officers and magistrates, measured the length of a working day, seven days a week. The journals which preserve this information had to be completed in the policeman's own time. In Buckinghamshire in 1859, six hours a day was spent walking, and a general order from that county's chief constable in 1861 shows how an allotted time on patrol could be extended: 'on all future night duty routes the constables must patrol together on meeting at conference points for as long a time . . . as may be found practical . . . being seen together in pairs cannot but have its beneficial effect.' (41) As late as 1867, a borough constable spoke of '98 hours work a week' (42) — fourteen hours a day in a seven-day week. Yet, generally, working hours were regulated earlier in the boroughs than they were in the counties. In a town like Sheffield, which before the act of 1856 had operated two quite separate police forces, one for the night and one for the day, amalgamation of the two meant that there was a ready-made shift system there to be operated by the new force. (43) In the northern counties a system of eight hours duty in every twenty-four was common by the mid-1870s. A turn of duty was longer in the south: 'we work nine hours, but we work at different hours.' (44) Other rural chief constables spoke of nine or ten hours duty being common in the mid-1870s. A good deal of the working day in the counties was spent on the maintenance of its own organisation. In 1865 Inspector Williamson of Northamptonshire was visited by his divisional superintendent three times a day on average, patrolled for about five miles with one or more of his constables, examined their journals once a week and was himself examined by his chief constable once a month. The number of hours patrolling, the length of the working day, did not materially lessen in the twenty years after 1856. But by this time in the boroughs the policeman could anticipate more time off duty than the county constable could. The latter, isolated with a large geographical area under his surveillance, was much more likely to have random demands made on his time.

Policemen from both county and borough complained of 'exercising their wits' to feed their families 'on the paltry sums doled out to them', (45) of never eating meat, of long hours, and of their misery and isolation. Yet none of these complaints was so specific and emotive as the charge of 'uncertainty' and 'change-

ability' that they brought against the pattern of their lives. The
search for certainty will be seen in both the struggle for pension
rights and, through strike action, the pursuit of higher wages.
But the charge of 'changeability' is more difficult to interpret.
A policeman's life, in its unswerving round of duties, not until
late in this period punctuated by days of rest, seemed to offer
a perfect consistency and lack of change. Certainly constables
complained about their movement in an arbitrary fashion from
station to station. But when they said that police life was
'uncertain' they expressed feelings about something deeper than the
nuisance of removal, the image of a poverty-stricken old age, or
fear of assault on the streets.   The permanent policeman was one
who had shown himself ready to pay a high price for some kind of
certainty. What he hoped for, and how he saw what he left, are
really questions that cannot be asked until we know more about the
silent rural labourer in the mid-Victorian years. But it is clear
that some men-turned-policemen did not find whatever it was they
sought. 'It is not the complaint of hardship under the existing
system, but it is the complaint of the uncertainty . . .' (46) said
Constable Chambers of the Hertfordshire to the gentlemen of a
select committee in 1874. James Chambers was a patient and enduring man. Seventeen years a policeman, and no higher than a first-
class constable — 'It has never come to my lot yet; we cannot all
be promoted' — he held his chief constable in awe, and some degree
of fear. (47) He had children; he knew the expense of moving.
But he was not of that substantial majority who had stated their
opinion quite simply, and left. Did James Chambers believe that
were he to die before pension time, and in such circumstances that
his wife did not receive a gratuity, then his children would go to
the workhouse? (It was, after all, pensions that he was being
questioned about.) Did he know that at his death, had he achieved
the estate that would bring a reporter to his graveside (that is,
had he been Sheffield's glamorous and 'well-known detective officer,
Richard Brayshaw'), that his final epitaph would be that 'his
children were all neat and tidy'? (48)

   Mid-Victorian society grew to expect something from men like
James Chambers. Whilst borough watch committees and county chief
constables extracted from a group of working-class men the social
virtues, and the ratepayers who laid out money for the application of these virtues as a means of community control looked on,
none of them had any means of understanding by what struggle and
denial and obeisance, individual men became policemen. By 1880,
when central government devolved more and more duties on the
police without any intermediary of local government, when the
power of the magistrate had declined, when the relationship
between paymaster and policeman had become less personal, when
police forces had become directly involved in a system of punishment, then there was a national police force ready and waiting,
and men like James Chambers had made it so, out of their own
experience.

Chapter 7

SECURITY: THE CAMPAIGN FOR POLICE PENSION RIGHTS

I always.had in my mind the idea of getting a pension and I did
& a very good one. (1)

Permanent policemen sought security from their work. The search
for long-term financial security was partly prompted by the nature
of local police communities, within which individual policemen saw
their advancements and reversals of fortune. Police hierarchies
demanded that men look inwards, rather than to an outside world,
in their search for identity. The organisation that evolved out
of the quest for financial security in old age was directed and
operated by the officer class. Most permanent policemen were in
fact officers, and it is here that the divisionbetween officers
and the rank and file in English local police forces becomes most
apparent. The pension campaign became a national one, and the
officers involved in it turned to central government for support,
whilst the struggle of the rank and file for better pay and work conditions was to remain localised for much longer. The campaign for
pension rights brought the long-term, professional policeman, usually an officer, to public attention, and it is on him that most nineteenth-century discussion and perception of the policeman rests.
This chapter is intended to serve as a preliminary to Chapter 8,
which deals with the broader question of the identity that policemen
in general came to adopt in the years between 1856 and 1880.

A few points of comparison did exist for the policemen who campaigned for pension rights. There was a traditional soldier's
pension, for instance; but a growing sense of corporate identity
among policemen involved a rejection of military precedents. A
more favourite analogy for long-term policemen was between themselves and pensionable civil servants and government clerkdom
in general. (2)

The Police and Constabulary Act of 1840 (3 & 4 Vict. c.88) and
the County and Borough Police Act of 1856 (19 & 20 Vict. c.69) had
made some provision for the superannuation of county policemen, and
an amending act of 1859 (22 & 23 Vict. c.32) extended the possible
provision of a pension to borough policemen as well. By 1860 it
was possible for a policeman retiring with fifteen years' service
to be granted a pension of half pay. More than fifteen years' ser-

vice could bring a pension of up to two-thirds of pay. There was
also provision for granting gratuities to men with less than fifteen
years' service. The wife of a policeman who died in service might
be granted up to one year's pay as long as her husband had been
paying into the superannuation fund for more than three years. All
payments of pensions and gratuities were discretionary — no policeman had a right to them — and were heavily dependent on the head
or chief constable who had to sign the certificate of incapacity
required by law. Some men felt severely cheated, like Sergeant
Curtis of Sheffield:

> we see the advertisements in the bills or newspapers asking for
> men at certain wages and at the same time 'a liberal retiring
> pension will be given after 15 or 20 years' service.' We
> naturally consider that we have a claim upon that when we join,
> and then we find out that we have no claim. (3)

It was not until 1890 that a right to a pension was established, and
pension funds were guaranteed not by local authorities but by central government.

Before the national campaign for pension rights got off the
ground in the 1860s, many local police forces had made provision
for their dependants in case of death. The Widows and Orphans
Fund of the Wiltshire Constabulary serves as a good example of
these. It was established in 1856 by the superintendents of the
county, and the fund was open to all classes at an entry fee of
1s. and contributions of 1d. a week. In the event of death, £10
went to the widow or nearest relative, either in a lump sum or in
weekly instalments settled by the chief constable, who acted as
treasurer and trustee. (4) Many police provident funds like this
one were registered as Friendly Societies. In Sunderland there
was a private burial fund which about half the force belonged to.
(5) In some boroughs provision for dependants before 1859 was
made out of a general prerequisite fund into which all extra police
earnings went. Ye urban policemen especially spoke about the
vagaries of watch committee discretion when it came to paying
out the rates as pensions or gratuities. 'We are under a watch
committee,' said the head constable of Birmingham in 1875,

> they treat it as their money and not as the policeman's money,
> but as if they were doing it out of the ratepayers' pocket.
> When a man comes up for a pension they look at the character
> book and see what family he has and if he has saved a hundred
> or two that would count for a shilling or two less pension;
> they pay a man according to his necessities, and not accord-
> ing to his rights . . . (6)

Above all, borough policemen were sure that they needed to control
their own burial funds.

In both counties and boroughs it was invariably officers who
organised these forms of self-help. The appearance of the 'Police
Service Advertiser' in February 1866 (7) provided many superintendents with the vision of the police forces of England become
one vast Friendly Society: 'there is no society or insurance company of any denomination which has so good an opportunity as we
. . . we have as it were our branches already established', wrote
one of them. (8)

The 'Police Service Advertiser' provided the first means for many

local policemen to gain a national perspective on their work, and
its anonymous letter column was the only place where many county
constables could speak. It published the annual reports of the
inspectors of constabulary, thus giving some policemen their first
opportunity of comparing wage rates across the country. To be
caught reading it in some county forces meant dismissal. The
excitement felt by men writing for the first time for an audience
that could understand is palpable in its first issues. The impact
of that sudden vision of a vast and organised national body of
police never left some of the officer class.

'The many can help the few,' declared 'Verdad', the superintendent who first proposed that a national burial fund be
operated through the 'Police Service Advertiser'. Should a superintendent die, then 2s. paid by every superintendent in England and
Wales would produce £60 for his widow. Sixpence from every inspector and sergeant in the country would raise £50, and 1d. from all
12,000 constables should raise the same amount for a dead brother
of the same rank. The scheme, said 'Verdad', could be worked by
the chief clerk and the superintendents. 'I have not included the
chief constables of the counties,' he continued, 'but it is not
intended [to exclude them] that is if they do not think it dero-
gatory to their position as gentlemen to identify themselves with
those under their orders.' (9)

The first meeting of the Police Mutual Assurance Association
(hereafter PMAA) was held in Windsor, where the 'Police Service
Advertiser' was published, in 1866. Only officers attended, all
of whom came from the south or the Midlands, and those from the
counties felt obliged to tell their audience that they had their
chief constable's permission to attend.

The chief clerk of the Hampshire force, who was present at the
meeting, placed policemen's endeavours in the same rank as the
'provident habits of prudence and forethought of the bulk of the
English industrial classes'. On the part of policemen it was to
be a prudence tactical in expression: 'if we succeed, we shall,
like good citizens, be lightening the burden of the ratepayers.'
(10) 'If they could only get the men of the forces to agree to
the scheme, there could be no doubt as to its successful working.'
By the end of 1867 there were 800 names on the list of those
interested in the scheme, and Superintendent William Young, secretary of the PMAA, believed that once the rules were settled, he
could count on 3,000 subscribers out of a possible 20,000. (11)

The pattern of application for membership in the last quarter
of 1866 showed the influence of the officer class: divisional
superintendents, welfare-conscious deputy and chief constables of
counties, newly wage- and security-conscious head constables of
boroughs, all sent in list of 'interested' men for whom they were
institutionally responsible. William Young was right to be opti-
mistic. Membership of the PMAA grew from 3,000 in 1867 to 5,000
in 1870. By 1877 there were 7,000 members. (12) The number of
members joining from county forces remained steady from year to
year, but the membership of borough constables increased rapidly in
the mid-1870s. A developing level of communications among police
forces demonstrated how much more fragile was a policeman's life
should he work in a borough rather than in a county.

But the PMAA did not provide pensions. What it did was ensure a dependant some security on the death of a breadwinner. It was a flexible system and answered the vagaries of police life far better than did the discretionary system of gratuities operated by county and some borough forces. What is more, the scheme extended to policemen who had already been pensioned off, and also to those retired through ill-health but unpensioned up to a year after their leaving a force, as long as they paid up during that time. In 1867 a widowers' list was started whereby for the payment of 1d. a week a policeman could insure against the death of his wife. By 1869, 2,000 men had started subscribing. (13)

At the national level, the operation of the PMAA had two effects. Annual general meetings held in major provincial cities emphasised a fraternity among policemen that, on certain points, transcended local differences by a thesis holding that policemen themselves formed a community: 'the first meeting of police officers as a Police Meeting on record . . . the whole Police Force are brethren; their interests are one, and as such, they should be united.' (14) Emphasis on the initiative and influence of the officer class in its local organisation was reflected at the national level and in 1870, a 'superior officers' list was established for head, chief and deputy chief constables who wanted to pay a higher subscription. Though it was argued that this would 'tend to bind the superior officers to the interests of the association', rank differences actually became much more emphasised in the organisation. (15)

The PMAA never had a large following; however, its membership figures do roughly represent the number of permanent policemen discussed in chapters 2-5. It was in this way an important means of self-identification for that minority of men who stayed on after the first few years. For the officers who ran it, it was an extremely important means of defining rank differentials in local forces, of delineating responsibility and paternalism. The same kind of paternalism, but expressed by a chief constable, could keep the PMAA out of a county for many years: 'As a general rule they [chief constables] are adverse to this echeme of which their silence is ample proof.' (16) The chief constable of the Isle of Ely refused permission for his men to join on the grounds that the scheme was 'very unfair . . . a man joining at 50 . . . had to pay no more than a man joining at 30.' But the story went round that he had some interest in a local life insurance office. (17) Some policemen objected too, because the scheme was framed 'altogether on the principle of charity'. (18) Others might have done calculations as careful as 'Fourth Class Constable' who wrote in May 1867 that:

if we take the lowest class of pay to constables I find it by the Government Report to be 17s, deduct therefrom 7s for sickness and 5d for superannuation, this will leave the constable 9s 7d to maintain himself in sickness and also his wife and family . . . the Association steps in in the case of an epidemic and helps the poor fellow to his grave . . . (19)

No policeman's family ever received the sums that 'Verdad' predicted. A dependant in 1870 received on average £18. It took about seven weeks to collect and collecting it cost 6s. At every insured death there were about twenty defaulters 'paying later'. (20)

'No,' said one constable in 1867, 'some association or <u>union</u>, having rules to pay the just claims of subscribers . . . is the only one that will ever become popular.' (21)

The campaign conducted by the 'Police Service Advertiser' and the officer class of certain police forces, for the <u>right</u> to a pension, got off the ground in the 1870s. In all counties 6d. a week was deducted from policemen's wages for the superannuation fund, yet no policeman had any claim on this fund as of right. 'It is looked upon by the men more as a tax than a benefit,' said one, (22) though others reported that the more sixpences that were deducted, the less they though about them and the more their sense of outrage abated.

But the sense of outrage was there, particularly among articulate careerist officers who knew precisely what they were seeking in joining a police force. 'I for one', complained 'Verdad' 'joined the service with the idea of making it my profession and had been given to understand . . . that after serving with zeal and fidelity . . . I might look forward to an annual allowance.' (23) He spoke of the way in which his county's police committee stretched and re-interpreted the years of service that gave claim to a pension. Many officers believed with him that the phenomenon of very short-term policemen 'who have failed to obtain other employment and enter the police force as a recourse', was because 'intelligent', 'good class' recruits were driven away by the 'uncertainty of their position and prospects'.

Several borough head constables campaigned for petitions, demanding pensions as a right to be presented to the government inspectors on their next tour of inspection. (24) They found an especially sympathetic advocate in Major General William Cartwright, whose son, the conservative member for Northamptonshire South, introduced a bill dealing with police superannuation into the lower house in 1869. (25) 'We again earnestly impress upon our readers the necessity for combined action,' urged the editor of the 'Police Service Advertiser'. (25) Petitions of a year earlier, drawn up by the <u>Advertiser</u>'s editorial staff, had been presented to the Home Secretary asking that a policeman who had served a certain number of years should have a legal claim to a pension similar to 'a soldier, a Poor Law Board or Revenue officer'. (27) The petitions of 1869 revealed the influence of the PMAA: 'Police Officers now regard the fund as an insuring fund and as such the law ought to declare what sum his family . . . shall be entitled to on his death.' (28) In this year, and for the next twenty, the most overt and public agitation came from borough officers. 'If we were allowed to open our mouths or use our pens . . . we could speak for ourselves,' wrote 'Freedom' from one anonymous county. 'There are no petitions from the county forces. The boroughs it is true can act with a certain amount of freedom. I dare not sign my name to this. It is forbidden to write.' (29)

Sympathetic MPs drafted several police superannuation bills. This attention from central government, and a growing dissatisfaction with the arbitrary ways of local police authorities, turned the aspirations of provincial police officers away from quarter sessions and watch committee and towards Parliament in the years 1868-71. The editor of the 'Police Service Advertiser' urged

his readers to use the divisional organisation to forward their
cause:

> There is a Bill . . . there is the Home Secretary . . . police
> officers can help themselves. MPs are now at home in the coun-
> try and every such home has a constable on the beat, its ser-
> geant of the section, its inspector of the sub-division. Why
> should not an effort be made by one of these . . . to speak to
> the member at home? Let them take a copy of this journal in
> their hands. (30)

The agitation for pension rights reached its peak in the summer
of 1872, when a police conference, attended by over 200 head and
chief constables and several MPs, was convened. They called on
the Home Secretary to make 'the position of a man more certain
. . . the government should be responsible for the payments and
they should not be allowed to depend upon a committee or county
magistrates . . . or anybody else.' (31) All the MPs present considered the police to be 'a very deserving set of man', though one
of them at least, the conservative member for Shrewsbury, certainly
tempered his idea of a just reward to a good policeman with the
hope that legislative ordering of pension funds might relieve his
supporters' ratepaying burden. But it was not just the presence
of gentlemen like these that made the assembled police officers
reject a proposal to form a permanent police committee to represent police views to Parliament. Many officers agreed that such
action would smack of unionism — the fear that policemen might
resort to 'force, and strikes' reverberated from MP to MP during
this meeting. But the officers knew as well that there was
another reason why the proposed standing police committee would
not work: officers could not represent all policemen; 'the interests
of the different classes were quite distinct and different . . .'
The pension struggle was the officers' struggle.

There followed many years of petitions, of hours spent waiting
on Home Secretaries and recruitment of more MPs to the pension
cause. Each deputation, each petition, foundered on the rock of
an existing financial structure which was ossified in borough autonomy. All this effort, fruitless though it was for the next fifteen years, revealed some results of the organisation and self-
help that had accompanied the PMAA and the pension campaign. As
a result of this organisation, police officers became more and
more willing to contemplate the idea of a national police as a
means of gaining superannuation rights. Some chief constables
saw a statutory precedent for a national police already existing:
'we are supervised by the same (government) inspectors, county
and borough, and we are promised one half from the consolidated
fund.' (32) Police officers' mutual and local aid was translated
into a national concern that turned to central government as the
only possible guarantor of rights.

The select committee appointed in 1875 to inquire into police
superannuation was seen by many police officers as an interim
victory. (33) It was the first time in a quarter of a century
that the police had received attention at this level, and the
'Police Guardian' letter column and full reprint of the minutes
of evidence demonstrated the gratification that many permanent
policemen felt. Witnesses before this committee, from govern-

ment inspector to constable, deflected attention away from superannuation as a reward for length of service, towards the more
immediate question of getting and keeping men. The pension schemes
and scales of payment that the committee welcomed from witnesses
placed the question firmly in the here and now, in the context of
the maintenance of superannuation funds by local ratepayers. The
Select Committee exposed the relationship between the police and
local ratepayers. The mayor of Bristol, for example, had

> no doubt that the 2½% [deducted from police wages] is looked upon
> by the men as giving them a direct claim to a pension . . . but
> as a member of the watch committee I do not look upon it in that
> light; I look upon it rather as the property of the ratepayer,
> that their pay is so much, less 2½% . . . (34)

Members of police authorities who gave evidence gave many such
precise descriptions of the relationship between ratepayers and
policemen. That the image of masters and servants was so frequently
evoked was partly a reaction to the trade combination and strike
action on the part of many policemen in urban areas over the past
few years. But in any case, for elected town councillors, 'master
and servant' was a more realistic way of describing the attitude of
the ratepayer to the policeman in the boroughs than it was for
members of county police authorities. Borough ratepayers literally
paid for their police and the management of them by elected officials. In the counties, the police served not the ratepayers, but
unelected masters, the traditional rulers of rural England. (35)
If the pension campaign failed to achieve its ends for so long,
it was not because of the tactics of extreme respectability that
the officer class adopted: a genteel public needed to be con-
vinced that policemen were 'a very deserving set of men'. It
failed because rights and rewards could not be distinguished
or catered for by two sets of masters whose practices of community
government, based as they were on two traditions of local finance
and local representation, were in deep conflict.

Within local forces, the movement maintained the distinction
between officers and men. No committee member was ever of lower
rank than divisional superintendent (most in fact were borough
head constables); none but head and chief constables waited on
Home Secretaries. Commuting of pension rights (an important new
campaigning point added at the planning meeting of 1872) could only
benefit the mobile, careerist officer. Very few policemen gained
pensions, and the vast majority of police recruits never thought
of police work as anything more than a short-term measure. Yet
this officer-conducted campaign played a significant role in the
creation of a distinctly modern image of a policeman. But the constable, in whose name much of this campaigning was done, did not
turn to central government, nor to a respectable public, in order
to gain security. He turned to his local paymasters, and what he
sought was better wages.

Chapter 8

IDENTITY

This chapter involves a discussion of the identity that was
adopted by policemen, by officers but more particularly by the
rank and file, in their local search for improved pay and conditions of work. It is divided into three parts, the first dealing with two periods of police strike activity, one in the early
1850s, the other in the early 1870s. The second part deals with
the growing sense of corporate identity among policemen that the
1870s witnessed. This had much to do with a conscious rejection
of militarism and the development of the idea of police work as
a kind of trade. The third part, 'Good and Faithful Servants',
is a discussion of the emotional impact of an intitutional ideology on individual men.
    When policemen complained about the arbitrary use of the super-
annuation funds and about poor wages, they attacked the financial
autonomy of local police authorities. The editor of the 'Police
Service Advertiser' saw poor pay as 'the evil that like a canker
worm lies at the root of our police administration.' (1) His
newspaper certainly received more correspondence on this topic
than any other, and as with the pension question, the fundamental complaint was about the random nature of local authority
'discretion'. Whilst the same antagonism turned a body of respectable officers to central government as a guarantor of rights,
this kind of relationship was already provided for on the wage
question — at least for the counties — for which the Home Secretary had a statutory obligation to issue pay scales. The 'Police
Service Advertiser' was first published a few weeks after George
Grey's 1866 circular on county pay, and many letters were received
about the machinations of county magistrates: 'Just look at the
various quarter sessions reports,' wrote 'X',
    some chief constables have recommended a substantial increase in
    pay . . . in . . . Devon present pay is deemed to be sufficient
    . . . the justices say they will not increase the pay of
    Superintendents but to meet Sir George will call them by another
    name. One magistrate said . . . the lower class of labourers
    was plentiful in the county, and this is the class from which
    our lower constables are principally supplied. . . . (2)
'X' saw the way ahead:

in England we have 22,561 police officers and men. Let their
voices be raised. Petition and agitate the Inspector Generals,
MPs and the public whose lives and property we protect whilst
they are sleeping andenjoying themselves . . . .
Yet this method did not come easily to the county constable. He was
forced to live in an extreme passivity, and there is no evidence
that any county force ever petitioned a quarter sessions for an
increase in pay. But borough watch committees saw their policemen
as workmen as well as servants and were sometimes, especially in
the early part of this period, willing to accept carefully-worked-
out comparisons with other forces as a basis for pay claims. In
1857 in Middlesbrough (then governed by an improvement commission)
the police force drew up a tabulated comparison of their wages with
those of the Liverpool, Manchester and Hull forces. In response the
watch committee of the commission asked for a comparison of hours
of duty in these towns. The petition was granted within two weeks.
(3) In Sheffield in 1859, the police petitioned for increased pay.
This was not granted, but leave of absence for one day a month with
pay was. (4) All other pay claims made by the Sheffield force during the next 20 years were granted.

(i) POLICEMEN AS WORKING MEN: ON STRIKE

What one policeman euphemistically called 'the police wages movement' of 1872, (5) and what the 'Police Service Advertiser'
labelled a 'natural result of the feeling which has found expression among the working classes of the United Kingdom', (6) contained within it a series of strikes that expressed the bitterest
opposition between men and employers in the boroughs. There had
been strikes before 1872. The first extensively documented one
took place during a long dispute in the Manchester cotton finishing trades, in 1853. (7)
     Some time during May of that year, the men of the Manchester
force petitioned the watch committee for an increase in wages,
amounting to 2s. a week for men, and 3s. a week for officers,
because, as they said, they were 'justly entitled to be placed on
an equality with their brethren in Liverpool'. Having also made
enquiries about wage rates in other boroughs, the watch committee refused to meet the claim. It was incompatible, they said,
with their responsibility towards the ratepayers, and the price
of bread was not particularly high. In any case, the Manchester
police scarcely deserved an increase in pay, for 'superior stations
in other forces are continually being filled up with men from the
Manchester force'. Within a few hours of the issue of this notice,
168 men (out of a force of 435) had filled up and handed in their
month's resignation form. Over the weekend a further 250 men
did the same. Resignations were almost exclusively confined to
the constables. They were harangued by their superintendents
and by the watch committee; though this body was, on the face of
it, sanguine about the prospect of filling 400 vacancies:
     It is well known that every police force is largely supplied
     with men from the agricultural districts, unskilled labourers
     who find police wages a considerable improvement on farm

wages. There will be little difficulty in filling up present vacancies. (8)

The watch committee moved uneasily between the notion of an eternal reservoir of law-keepers whose only qualifications were poverty and passivity, and the notion of police work as a special-ised and skilled trade. Manchester constables saw things more clearly. They know that they were working men and that their needs were related to the exigencies of a wider community. But they knew as well that they were different now. They had done what working people were to be increasingly asked to do — become tem-perate, responsible, forward-looking — and what working people were to be increasingly condemned for not doing. They had been allowed to become good. But the price of bread still mattered:

1d. a loaf dearer than a month past; beef is 8d. a pound; very indifferent vegetables 1s. 8d. a score . . . How far goes 16s. 8d. in a family of 5 or 6 to say nothing of those who are 7 or 8 . . . 4s. for rent and 2s. 6d. for coal . . . some-thing less than 2s. a head to find food and raiment for the family of a police constable, who should appear as respectable members of society . . . . Have we asked more than others? No, nor earlier . . . we feel it now a duty to ourselves . . . we have firmly resolved to leave as a man before any constable shall receive less pay than 20s. a week . . . we know we richly deserve it . . . . You will be somewhat surprised when you are hereby informed that there are plenty of [us] . . . who have not been in a place of worship during service for several years . . . . (9)

Most policemen withdrew their notice, claim unsuccessful, by the end of June, and the local press rejoiced at the triumph of a market economy that vanquished 'extensive combination'. (10) It was a well-publicised dispute in the dyeing, dressing and finishing branch of the cotton trade that propelled 238 policemen again to hand in their notice by 6 July. (11) It is clear that a dyers' protest march through Manchester's main thoroughfare on 4 July accelerated this second spate of police resignations. For some policemen the spectacle of a watch committee alarmed at the possibility of social disorder seemed a more pliable body than before to confront with police 'combination'. The secretary of the dyers union's address to the ratepayers and the gentry of Manchester showed that in the context of urban living men and policemen learned something from each other: 'The object of the men was a legitimate one', said Secretary Tear,

to improve their social condition, as the first step to which, as an absolutely essential one, they asked an increase in wages — they averaged only 15s. a week for the most laborious work, and most of them had to maintain wives and families, so it was impossible they could maintain their position relatively to the other classes of artisans. (12)

The policemen who spoke, although with very similar vocabulary, underlined a policeman's growing notion of a reward due to en-forced respectability. The policeman's protest had to emphasise a responsibility more overt, more of a calculated display than that of the dyers and finishers. No march for the police, but the ostentatiously dignified assembly of 'about 170 of the police

on strike . . . in Stevenson Square, to attend the Cathedral service'. (13) No demand for an 'advance of wages, of 3s., for all'
but a consistent desire to maintain the wage differential between
officer and constable. (14)

Men with many years of working experience behind them before
becoming policemen, cut off from their roots by geography, yet
with the attitudes enforced by rural life become a market commodity in the city, men with wives who shopped and with children
who had not only to be clothed, but as policemen's children, shod
as well, they walked those Manchester streets more profoundly
strangers than did the dressers and dyers who marched there. And
because they understood both the connection of their lives with
urban workers, and their own dislocation more deeply than did the
gentlemen on the watch committee, they were able to put this question to them: 'And will you trust your property to a few novices
just green from the country?' (15)

The striking policemen knew what the outcome would be. The
second, earnest stage of the police strike on 6 July 1853 led to a
rapid breakdown of social discipline in the city. The new police
'blacklegs', 'green from the country' were attacked. Officers not
on strike were assaulted 'by a large gang . . . who during the
attack were continually shouting "Knobsticks" and "Go to it lads,
there's no policemen now".' Shopkeepers barred their windows and
shut up. (16)

The watch committee rapidly decided to give 2s. a week extra
to each member of the force, 'feeling that as they were situated
it was absolutely necessary to make some concession'. In doing so,
they paid full attention to 'the present uneasy feeling among the
operatives of the city'. (17) By the evening of 6 July, all but
fifteen of the striking policemen were back at work. The operative's strike ended, not triumphantly, in November. Within a
month of their return to work, the police had broken up two of
their meetings, arrested two men (on the 'orders' of a share-
holder in a dyeing and dressing manufactury), and some of the detective officers had prepared a comprehensive dossier on what would no
now be called 'the violent element'. (18)

There was one other known strike in 1853. There was agitation
in the City of London and the Metropolitan forces for increased
pay, but they did not strike. Their pay claim of 22 July was
granted in December and backdated to 1 January. (19) The London
press gave the Manchester police strike a fair amount of coverage.
But more important than any influence from police force to police
force across the country was the fact that in both places the roots
of complaint were the same: the price of food, increased rents, and
there was the same pattern of disuasion by the officer class.

It was Hull police who actually struck in 1853. They made
repeated wage claims during the early summer of that year, and
finally struck in July, when thirty of the men resigned and about
fifty refused to do duty and also refused to resign. This was a
display of sophisticated tactics, based not so much on a following
of the Manchester strike, as on a nice reckoning of local circumstances: 'the watch committee have not had a single [applicant] .
. . . labourers not being willing to work 7 days a week for 2s. 6d.
a day.' (20)

Petitions for increases in pay based on comparisons between
similarly situated forces remained a common mode of discussion
between police forces and watch committees during the next twenty
years, and the national and local publication of the inspectors of
constabulary's reports, with their information about rates of pay
across the country, gave this method a force and respectability
that it had lacked before 1857.   The first offensive in 'the police
wages movement' came in Brimingham in 1871. At first it followed a
familiar pattern.   The usual petition, signed by policemen and presented to the watch committee, mentioned 'the high price of Provisions, chiefly meat'. (21)   What was unusual about the petition
was that it made a pleas for increased leisure time and, using
information not found in the reports of the constabulary inspectors,
spoke of 'the discrepancy between London and other large boroughs
as compared with Birmingham in the matter of . . . holidays . . .'.
The petition was successful mainly because the Birmingham police
exercised the discretion that Manchester constables had been
accused of wanting twenty years before: they made their application to the watch committee through the head constable.   Head
Constable Glossop of Birmingham displayed some sympathy for the
position of policemen. Three years later, away from a watch committee that treated policemen's money (the superannuation fund)
'as their money and not as the policeman's money, but as if they
were doing it out of the ratepayers' pocket', he spoke before a
select committee of how 'it requires a peculiar man to be a constable (he mentioned height and a degree of literacy) . . . he must
be a sober man . . . incessant walking and working every day of the
week . . . .' (22)   One effect that 'the police wages movement' did
have, was to make public paymasters aware of the police as possessing a distinct body of skills and virtues.
    The agitation in Birmingham, though, did not receive the national
attention that was given to a concurrent police strike in Newcastle.
There had been a longstanding dispute between the head of the Newcastle City Force and his men.   Much of this conflict was based
on accusations by constables of the arbitrary exercise of power by
a military man.   The police force turned to the watch committee as
their protector, asking that 'the suspensory powers now invested in
the head constable be withdrawn from him and retained in the hands
of your worshipful body'. (23)   Two months later, in November, 87
of the establishment force of 129 had walked out.   As the force was
short by 21 men anyway, the town was left, according to the local
press, in a perilous position. Reports from 'The Times' north-
eastern correspondent placed the police strike in the context of
the Nine Hours Movement and the colliery strike in northeast
Durham. (24)   The policeman's newspaper, respectable now, ('we are
heartily glad that they are not members of the PMAA or it might
have caused immense damage to that institution') chose to present
the conflict as one between the civil nature, learned on a hard
and domestic front, of the good permanent policeman, and the dan-
gerously autocratic tendencies of some ex-soldier head constables. (25)   Yet the editor of the 'Police Service Advertiser'
was forced, by the position that striking policemen took, to use
the language of the market place when condemning strike action.
If 'strikes were an abomination at all times' they were doubly

wrong for policemen, foolish too, 'for the men have no trade to turn to when they strike nor any clubs the funds on which to throw themselves for support'. Yet as we have seen, policemen found it very easy in many parts of the country to return to their old trade; government inspectors and provincial paymasters recognised that many men joined local forces 'intentionally for a short time'. It was implicit by the early 1870s in the columns of the 'Advertiser' that these short-term men who were related by trade and experience and intention to the wider labour market were not really considered policemen at all. The true policeman was the respectable long-term man, most likely to be an officer who contributed his time and his status to the machinations of the PMAA and the superannuation campaign. Yet in provincial towns the activity of policemen in this year forced some watch committees to turn aside their image of their policemen as servants, their pay and pension contributions 'the property of the ratepayers', and face their constables, briefly, as working men, employees.

The Plymouth police petitioned for an increase of wages and a shortening of hours in May 1872 — 'Et tu Brute?' asked the Thunderer — making it clear that 'if their terms are not complied with [they would] tender their resignations and seek other employment at some of the large provincial towns where high wages and short hours are offered'. (26) Within three days agitation had spread to the Devonport police. A local trade conflict (the journeymen shoemakers of Plymouth were seeking an increase in their scale of pay, and the Salcombe shipwrights were on strike this month) sustained this conflict between policemen and watch committees. (27)

None of the action taken by policemen in these years demonstrates anything like a national unionisation of policemen. A threatened strike in Oxford in September 1872, the strike of the Dundee City Force in July 1873, the Dublin Metropolitan Police strike of the same month and the well-publicised case of police constable Goodchild of the London Metropolitan force, victimised for engaging in police unionism, all remained localised affairs. (28) Policemen certainly knew about other police action in other places (the 'Advertiser' gave it extensive coverage, and so did the national press) but what policemen believed they were doing was exerting pressure on local paymasters to reward them in the light of other police pay conditions. Policemen were recruited by watch committees as travellers through provincial pay conditions: employers knew that men joined local forces to escape from the poor wages of a rural hinterland, or as a stop-gap when trade collapsed or went into recession. Membership of a police force, for even a short time, made comparison with police wages around the country a matter of easy discovery. This knowledge was used in pay claim and petition, yet it was the intensely local context of strikes, protest and agitation that sustained policemen's union activities. Goodchild, for instance, seems never to have mentioned provincial police strikes as a motive for action, and the Metropolitan struggle, which he helped initiate, for better pay and working conditions always spoke in local terms. (29) In the early 1870s national combination was still confined to the officer class, which attended PMAA conferences, waited on Home Secretaries with superannuation bills in hand, and collected pennies for dead brethren.

(ii) THE TRADE OF POLICEMAN

In policemen's local struggles, a great deal depended on the dis-
position of the chief officer of police. In the counties, constables complained that there was no appeal at all against a chief
constable's decision to fine, dismiss or order removal. In this
situation the government inspector's routine 'any complaints?' at
annual inspections was, said one West Riding policeman,

> farcical, for the only man who spoke up on this occasion
> was suspended on the spot to the disgust of every police con-
> stable present, and it was actually left to the officer of
> whom he complained whether he should be dismissed or not . . . .
> Policemen are reported by their officers and judged by them
> . . . was anything heard so un-English and unjust . . . . (30)

The dislike felt by many rural policemen for their chief constable was often expressed as a resentment against poor promotional
opportunity. The case of one superintendent of Merthyr Tudfil who
applied for the position of chief constable of Glamorganshire with
20 years' police work behind him in 1867, only to be rejected in
favour of a 'gentleman . . . who was no constable at all and could
not have answered one question on the rudimentary part of a constable's education' aroused great anger on the part of the permanent policemen of England and Wales. (31) But the anger of
officers was not necessarily based on their own experience: most
superintendents and many inspectors had never been constables, but
had been appointed to officer posts. The unfortunate Mr Wrenn of
Merthyr had been astoundingly hopeful even to contemplate becoming
a county chief constable (ten years later the 'Police Guardian' was
still casually pointing out that chief constableships were for
'the friend and gentlemen who happened to enjoy the greatest popu-
larity in the society frequented by justices of the peace' (32);
and the resentment of the officer class turned to the position of
deputy chief constable as the one left within the realm of promotional realism. Deputy chief constableships were technically
supposed to be filled by men who had risen through the ranks.
However, towards the end of the 1860s the practice developed of
appointing military men, 'outsiders' to the office. Protesting
against such appointments, officers were often forced to emphasise
a community of experience among policemen that was not really
based on fact: 'how preposterous it is' wrote 'Justice' in 1867,

> for 'DCCs' [deputy chief constables] . . . to tell the world
> what men could do and the service that men would be . . . .
> Ask 'DCC' if he ever did five years police service as a con-
> stable? If he has he is a model . . . I suppose there is not
> to be found in all England three deputy chief constables
> that have and therefore . . . he . . . cannot say a word to
> ameliorate the condition of the working man . . . . If I stood
> before him, I should at once see before me a man I suppose
> of about 30 who has by good friends, been lifted to a very
> comfortable position and has got as much feeling for the men
> under him as a sweep has for his apprentice. (33)

The 'Police Guardian' mounted a loud campaign against 'militarism' in police forces in the 1870s. This was the period when
large barrack accommodation was built in some northern counties

and boroughs, and when cutlass drill became more approvingly noted
in the government inspectors' reports. There was a respectable
public's unease about these new developments, flamboyantly represented by a letter reprinted in the 'Police Guardian' in 1878:

> I utter the sentiments of hundreds of quiet decent ratepayers
> who . . . indignantly look on whilst the government of this
> fair country is being transferred from its ancient heads to
> an army of mercenaries at five and twenty shillings a week. (34)

Thus the police campaign against militarism, which was really a
protest against poor promotion, was partly wedded to a ratepayers'
protest against the increasing professionalism — which cost money
— of local police forces.

The constable, too, was denied the promotion he believed had
been offered on recruitment. One constable said that this was
because 'the officers who recommend promotion are very illiterate
and continually keep some raw recruit to do some work — as regards
the accounts, etc.' (35) Many long-term police constables believed
that the police service offered, in clear contrast to the contemporary army, rapid promotion through the ranks, with good behaviour
materially rewarded. Constables, like their officers, saw their
disappointments and resentments represented by the ex-army men
who filled the posts of deputy chief constables in the 1870s. The
rank and file came more and more to express this resentment in
terms of their ability to do a specific job of work, rather than by
asserting their right to promotion: 'Would you employ a carpenter
to make [you] a pair of boots, or a blacksmith a pair of trousers?'
asked a constable who signed himself 'Alpha' about another 'military' appointment in 1873. (36)

'Alpha' saw policing as a craft, which he had learned on the
job, rather in the manner of an apprentice. (37) But all professional policemen, not just constables, came to see police work as
a trade during the 1870s. They operated in a social situation
deemed to be 'quiet', in which a soldiery had become less and less
a respectable part of civil life; local and central government had
devolved on to policemen more and more administrative tasks, and
the administrative structure that was built up around the inspection
of weights and measures and common lodging houses demonstrated to
officers that they were a civil body working in a specialised area
of civil government. (38) In the late 1860s a kind of education
as policeman developed, under the encouragement of the government
inspectors (one of the objections to the appointment of that 'gentleman soldier' to the chief constableship of Glamorganshire had been
that he would not be able to 'instruct his force in their <u>legal</u>
liabilities'). (39) Rudimentary grounding in the law was the basis
of these early schemes, though 'reading, writing, dictation, punc-
tuation and arithmetic' was still the bedrock of police night school
education. (40) Internal examinations, again encouraged by the
government inspectors, were established in many forces, and were
peculiarly inward-looking. (41)

In all forces the constables' only constant companion was their
pocket guide. All of them emphasised the civil nature of forces;
the most widely sold emphasised the individual and 'cultivated
intelligence' to be expected of the legally aware police constable.
(42) All underlined the fact that policemen were a class of public

servants. Indeed, it was becoming increasingly difficult in the
1870s to learn of this doctrine elsewhere. Certainly it was not
to be learned from the government inspectors, for the whole import
of their annual visit was increased drill in anticipation of their
arrival, a standing to attention on parade when they had. The
rejection of militarism, which seemed to join officers and men in
the 1870s, was drawn from very different sources. For the constable,
it was a demonstration of his own self-found identity. It was the
place where his virtues, sought and bought by watch and police committee, became to him a commodity, tentatively called a trade, a
skill, but more positively seen as the equipment for a journey, an
ascent. In the boroughs this was expressed urgently in pay claims,
petitions, walk-outs. In the counties, where the most patient
campaign for pension rights was pursued for thirty years, it was
seen in the expression of a belief in a reward on this earth due
to good and faithful servants. In both places the police force
offered an improvement for individuals that the contemporary army
could not offer. Because promises of this betterment and improvement had been made, in police act and superannuation schedule,
and because the lineaments of an ascendable hierarchy had been
laid before them, aspiration was both represented by, and des-
cended from, officers who were resented by the rank and file.
    Policemen had to live up to a high level of expectation. This
expectation came at first from a ratepaying public, later from a
national public awareness of what a policeman ought to be. The
clearest example of high expectation fulfilled that was available
to policemen came from the officer class, and officers were able
to perform so well not only out of their experience as policemen,
but out of their position in a social hierarchy of which police
forces were a constricted reflection. A borough head constable
was in a particularly good position to develop a conventional
analysis of social life. Mid-Victorian society came to enumerate
itself, and the transmission of statistical information from the
provinces to central government, and its return, in government
report, re-published in local papers, played an important role in
this enumeration. But provincial police officers, acting as social
statisticians, played a direct local role in this process. (42)
Reporting on the 'state' of a town to a watch committee involved
taking account of a vast number of seemingly disparate factors:
the number of gas lights in working order, the scavengers' wages,
the incidence of street begging, the numbers in the local tramp
ward, the proportion of those apprehended by the police who could
neither read nor write. Life's drama, the theatre of the streets,
was thus enumerated, made concrete:
    if passengers traversing the Causeways could be induced to keep
    to the right they would pass with much greater comfort, and
    when it is remembered that the average number of persons who
    travel through High Street on a Saturday between 9 o'clock
    in the morning and 10 in the Evening is 58,980 of whom 27,400
    are females it cannot be denied that some such arrangement is
    necessary. 11,000 Carriages, Coaches, Cabs . . . and 1,340
    Carts and Waggons also pass during the same hours . . . . (44)
'Householders generally complain', said the head constable of
Sheffield to the water supply sub-committee of the Town Council in

1864, 'of the inconvenience to which they are subject by reason of
their being able to procure water each alternate day. They have no
suitable vessels in which to store it . . . .' (45) A job of work
defined a sphere of action by a set of finite possibilities. It
was because success could be measured out by things done — inhabitants of lodging houses counted, gas lights reported not
working, piles of rubbish in the street reported to the appropriate sub-committee — that a more general social improvement was
imaginable, and seemed possible. A police force might do great
things:

> it has not yet ever been proved how far it is possible for the
> police force to be made the instrument not only in the pro-
> motion of public health and the prevention of crime, but also
> in promoting the general good of society. (46)

Mr Sadler, the head constable of Stockport, delivered this piece
of evidence to a select committee that was, in 1850, cynical about
the contemporary police recruit being 'of that class having the
education and character generally which would lead them to feel an
inducement to reform'. (47) But Sadler knew, even as early as this,
that work within a stratified and purposeful institution had a
deep and permanent effect on some policemen's minds: 'in exercising his function in the prevention of crime, he is frequently
acting from conscientious motives of what his duty is . . . .' (48)
Twenty years later this connection was easier for many policemen
to perceive, as they had by then been clothed by local and central
government in the capacities of relieving officers, nuisance
inspectors, supervisors of convicts on license and so on. Their
role was wider than that of law enforcer, and as Sadler knew, it
involved some of them as men.

County officers, the divisional superintendents, fought that
same fight for good order, and they too, were acknowledged as
institutional reclaimers in the same way that urban officers often
were. The landscape was different though. County officers who
wrote, and gave their tempered evidence to select committees and
filled in questionnaires from temperance organisations, all clung
particularly to the theory of 'contamination.' This was extended
by some county officers to a condemnation of family association,
and to simple encounters at 'wakes and fairs'. 'I find Statute
Fairs to be one of the greatest evils in existence,' wrote a Midlands superintendent in 1869. 'I have seen married and single conducting themselves with the greatest impropriety, children stopping
all night, drinking and dancing . . . .' (49)

An exegesis on 'contamination' was a public and formal expression of an acceptable social theory. Men like these may perhaps
have written what their audience wanted to hear; it is striking
that none of the anonymous letters to the 'Police Service Advertiser' dealt in this terminology. It is possible to suggest tentatively that underneath such public expression lay a less-accept-
able vision and interpretation of society. This is not to propose
that many county officers patrolled their lonely roads brooding, as
Inspector John Pearman of the Buckinghamshire Constabulary obviously did, on the fact that 'In England 66 persons own two millions
of acres of Land, 100 persons own four millions of acres, 710
persons own one quarter of the whole soil of England and Wales,' and

on how the poor 'must be kept poor or they would not work to keep
the other two fifths in comfort and most of them in pomp and splen-
dour.' John Pearman was an unusual officer, being one of those rare
men who rose through the ranks to the position of inspector, and
to the end of his days he identified himself with the life that he
had left in order to become a policeman. His memoir shows the
radical underside of the conventional and acceptable theory of contamination. John Pearman was an environmentalist, who through
the 250 pages of his memoir struggled to dispose of the idea of
'sin' as explanatory of crime and social discontent: 'the temptation to Break the Law or what is called sin is very great with the
poor. I cannot but think if there is such a thing as sin. The
cause as (sic.) not been the same with the Poor and yet they sin
but very little compared with the Rich.' Pearman had spent long
years as a soldier and a policeman contemplating the differences
between people in a class society: 'Look at the difference in the
start in life our Queen had a noble start and compare that with the
Gutter Children of the earth . . . they surely have nothing to thank
God for,' and he knew it was only his uniform and his luck that
divided him from those he watched with his dour and questioning eye:
    when I look back for only the past two generations of my Family
    what an amount of temptations to have to endure to avoid and
    look at if what our parsons Call sin to gut (sic) a chance to
    live which our Queen and the Lords fare of the best, the poor
    Children of the Carrupt (sic) earth can get for them . . . .(50)
On John Pearman's evidence, Cyril D. Robinson is right when he
claims that in 'labelling the police politically conservative, socio-
logists are confusing the function of the police with the police
themselves.' (51) For this particular county inspector twenty-five
years of policing actually gave him the statistical and sociological evidence with which to elaborate his radicalism. His job
showed him, most intimately, how a class society worked.
    The official and unofficial evidence of county officers, living
many years in the same station house, surrounded as far as they
could see by a 'drunken, fighting, cursing population', (52) shows
that their landscape was different from the one watched by urban
officers. Here was no constant backdrop, measured by its gas
lamps, mapped by the pinpointing of vagrant wards; the grid of
streets made a picture of control. In the country the officer
saw the empty roads, the blank landscape ordered and regulated,
now and then traversed by those walking towards association, punctuated by the sudden meeting, the men gathered in the game preserve for ill purpose, the group walking to the nearest tramp ward,
people making their way to the ale-house, some on their way to the
larger and more corrupting influences of the great county fairs.
    Most country officers who did not remain anonymous, who signed
their names to their opinions, expressed ones that were identical,
like those of Superintendents Wild and Humphries of the Warwickshire constabulary quoted above, to those of their chief constable.
In these cases, the hierarchy's opinion had been made into their
own. None ever saw the enforcement of the law as a solution to
the problems they were asked to contemplate — this for simple
reasons sometimes — 'we should not have cells to hold them' (53) —
but also because the work they did, the statutory expectations

increasingly shown to them, deflected attention from law, to
morality. On the drink question, the one most particularly put to
officers, county superintendents placed much emphasis on education:
'night schools'; 'educate the masses'; 'compulsory education to 13
years'; 'reform the vicious'. They looked to the agents of the
moral society:

> It is all very well thundering in a pulpit to a small apparently
> well-educated congregation, but where are the thousands of
> neglected cases of whom no one in the higher orders cares
> anything about . . . more sympathy among all classes and we
> might expect a better state of morality. (54)

John Pearman believed that the law he had enforced during his
twenty-five years as a policeman was 'artificial law . . . not the
law of God'. 'Looking justice strait (sic.) in the face I cannot
see were it begins or were it ends,' he commented, 'but still I like
Law and have always tried as a Soldier and a Policeman to maintain
it . . . but when we think of God and then our Rulers we look for
the reasons why it is so maintained. . .' (55)

In the late 1860s there was in any case a theory developing
among the officer class that it was not a policeman's place to
comment on the legislative process, nor indeed upon law enforcement. Neutered responsibility set many officers free, and they
grew in confidence of their own situation and the validity of their
own experiences precisely because they were nowhere asked to discuss their own role as enforcers of the law.

Consider for example, William Young, superintendent at Woburn,
Bedfordshire and for twenty years before his death, Secretary of
the PMAA, praised by General Cartwright in his annual report as a
careful statistician, (56) whose frequent and exuberant letters to
the 'Police Service Advertiser' were decorated with quotations from
Shakespeare and Milton and the classics in popular translation.
His unwieldly subordinate clauses were gradually tamed as he came
more and more to grips with a permeating middle-class culture.

The freedom given to some officers to enter a literate, letter-
writing, pontificating world produced in some cases an analysis
of society reduced to banality, a conventional plot. (57) But
from some few officers there were echoes of a social analysis
that was not banal, that transmits faintly evidence of an enduring
belief in the capacities of armies of men to become armies of right.
There are some slight indications of a sub-culture of political
analysis, represented here by policemen, in John Pearman's use of
the figure of Cromwell to represent justice on this earth; (58) in
the frequent use of Miltonic language by policemen, including
superintendent Young, mentioned above; in the name that the officer
who wrote to the 'Police Guardian' in 1875 gave himself when he
protested against a pay increase to municipal officers 'who have
not our hardships to contend with'. He signed himself 'Cromwell',
and thus used the powerful metaphor of an army that had kept its
promises to its recruits. (59)

But what a respectable ratepaying local society expected of its
permanently stationed officers was something far more prosaic than
this. Some officers drew status from membership of teetotal
associations, of the Methodist church, from positions of responsibility in Friendly Societies. The silver teapots, the purses of

sovereigns donated by grateful ratepayers on a superintendent's
retirment, defined quite specifically their status and importance in a local context. (60)

Within this institutionalised morality many constables felt a
keen misery and isolation. Many zealous officers and paternal
chief constables based their expectations of an improved state of
society on the fact that they had taken some drinking, working-
class men, and made them into policemen. A chief constable who
envisioned a rural utopia in which he might one day do his duty
based this vision not only on reading and reflection, and his
acquaintance with improving landlords, but also on what had been
done for his own foot-soldiers in life's battle:

the provision of good comfortable cottages, with gardens close
at hand, prizes for the best cultivated. A reading room with
occasional lectures during the winter . . . a committee room
for coal, clothing and shoe clubs, the committee partly composed of working men. (61)

If the 1860s saw a 'laudable zeal . . . labouring to carry the
light of spiritual law up alleys where law is known chiefly as
the policeman' (62) then the irony was not only that officers left
so much unsaid about the enforcement of law and the control of
men by other men, but that the constable, walking up that alley,
knew not only the weight of that expectation, but also knew most
profoundly where he stood. Constable Green told a gathering of
Birmingham policemen in 1875 how he had met an old friend, 'a
common labourer' one Birmingham Saturday afternoon in a busy
street. 'Getting on middling' he replied to his friend's greet-
ing. They discussed wages and the policeman concluded that he
had the worst deal. The other man came to the same conclusion:

there's good men and there's bad men and great men and little
and all sorts of men, but I would rather be a little dog and
laugh at the Devil than wear the uniform of a policeman. (63)

There was 'laughter and loud applause' from the hall where the
city police were gathered. They recognised their own predicament.

(iii) GOOD AND FAITHFUL SERVANTS

The most ready emotional description that constables attached to
themselves was that of 'servant'. They meant first of all to
describe their loneliness: 'the constable is shut out from many
little pleasures . . . of which every other class of the community
can avail itself'; 'the police constable is always the spectre at
the feast.' (64) Cut off from the 'mirth and harmony' that they
watched, policemen were wakeful whilst others slept. A contemporary literary reference to police work deals with this faithful
service through the silent watches of the night with great perception. One Herefordshire morning in 1873 'between 6 and 7
o'clock', the Reverend Francis Kilvert

rose and opened the window . . . the moon was nearly full and
shining brightly in the West . . . . A slow measured footfall
was pacing down the gravel towards the white gate, the policeman Vincent on guard watching for the man who is supposed to
be lurking about here . . . . The black gate clanged and the

white gate clashed and the postman came up the drive . . . meeting the policeman. Today the policeman went to the Superintendent and laid the case before him and received orders to be
about this house a good deal at night for some time to come. (65)
The good and faithful servant who worked with no interest of ownership in what he protected, so that others might sleep, deserved
some reward.

By the late 1860s the policeman was the target of those organisations that sought to find in this archetype of the respectable
working man both the secular counterpart of the missionary (walking
daily through heathen haunts), and the guard (protecting the respectable from onslaught the refrom). When Detective Officer Richard Brayshaw of Sheffield was buried, his Methodist minister placed a con-
struct on his life familiar to all those who attended police
funerals:

a few words . . . to the deceased's comrades . . . put the question 'Am I ready?' . . . their brother was dead and those who
were now the watchers over public order were about to bury him.
Their temptations were many . . . their influence great. (66)

An appeal could have been made in similar terms to other rigidly
structured work-groups, and many were. But the particular point
of these messages to the police was that they rested on an appeal
to men who had, by joining the police, already been partly saved,
and become the children of God:

You watch for the thief by night, you seek out and bring to
justice the murdered and those who offend against the laws . . . .
Your position at once shows that as far as man can judge your
character is good and you are considered worthy . . . .' (67)

Police life, and the theory of promotion through the ranks indeed
presented the outline of a journey. There were easy similies to
forge between police duty, and an individual soul's exertions.
(68) Too easy sometimes, as when a chief constable translated the
specific matters of daily life — the long tramp through the cold
and wet, the open door of the late ale-house, the offer of a drink
— into an impenetrable definition of the relationships between good
men and an evil society: 'I cannot say what trials they go through
in the way of temptation.' (69)

Yet temperance organisations paid scant attention to the 'gambling fighting drunken policeman' in the mid-nineteenth century.
In the 1830s temperance workers were taking note of payment in
spirits to soldiers and sailors; work for the advancement of
sobriety among railway workers began in the 1840s; the United
Military Temperance Society was formed in 1845; one for Ombibus
Workers in 1854. The National Temperance League devoted much
effort to contacting groups of specialised workers in the 1860s
and 1870s, but does not seem to have contacted the police. (70)
There was indeed some spasmodic organisation among the Metropolitan police, but contemporary comment placed this firmly among
working-class organisation. There seems to have been very little
attempt to appeal to police work and organisation.

Whilst temperance principles provided some officers with specific local identity, it is possible to search the subscription
lists of the United Kingdom Alliance and the Church of England
Temperance Society in this period and only find the name of the man

certain to be found: John Lynn, head constable of Devonport, who fo
for twenty-five years waged a public and private war against the
drink interest of the watch committee and the local bench. (71)
A temperance festival might be held for a borough police force,
as in Leicester in 1875, but reports in the local press show that
it was just a party (without drink) given by local temperance
organisations in much the same manner that borough businessmen paid
for annual Christmas dinners for their police. (72)   Becoming a
permanent policeman — a good man — provided in itself the structure for living a life according to the principles of temperance.

A man being made good by becoming a policeman is the theme of
the only novel of police life that I have found for the second
half of the nineteenth century.   (There are several novels about
detectives — much more romantic figures.)   Unfortunately it was
published by the Religious Tract Society in 1887, and it deals
with the Metropolitan situation. (72)   However, the background
of the granite-faced 'Constable 42Z' does seem authentic.   '42Z'
has been four years in the when the novel opens. He must have
been 19 or 20 when he joined. He is an agricultural labourer's
son, who left home after firing a hayrick at the age of 16. He
got a job on another farm (the long upward climb from perdition
beginning), later became a groom; and arrived in London to join
the Metropolitan police (how useful it would have been had the
the author noticed in a book full of observation what trade he
gave the police clerk). He joins a partly saved but irreligious
man. He is finally saved through good works during a turbulent
police career. But the perfect and natural equation of being
good with being policeman is put into the mouth of Annie, the
slum girl whose delinquent brother he tries to help. He tells
her that, falsely accused, he has had to leave the force, and she
asks 'and are ye bad now?' (74)

Police life, governed as it was by the principles of obedience,
sobriety and decency, was lived within a structure that turned all
hope and aspiration towards itself, and provided the chimera of
salvation in actually being a policeman. Religious tract writers
and funeral orators reckoned that constables saw so much of the
results of profligacy and crime that they would find it easier than
other men to avoid temptation. But some policemen interpreted
their contact with misery quite differently:

The police constable is always the spectre at the feast . . .
he is never wanted where mirth and harmony prevail, unless it is
to keep away discord . . . . His chief occupation is in the
haunts of misery and crime to deal with the most wretched and
criminal of mankind . . . enough to make one feel miserable . . .
we cannot help . . . sympathising with these outcasts as in
most of them there is one redeeming trait in their character
which attracts the pity of the feeling-hearted and makes one
feel that all mankind is akin . . . . (75)

Surrounded by high expectations, and confined by the high hopes
of him as much as by his background, a simple statement about work
by a county constable might take on the language of a patient
religiosity:

we go out at great hazard; we never know what we will have to
contend with; we are single-handed in the country . . . we have

to do battle daily with all the roughs in the neighbourhood . . .
we have to fight the battle at great odds; we have to do the
best we can . . . . (76)

James Chambers was not in daily physical conflict with 'all the
toughs in the neighbourhood', though assaults on the police were a
weekly hazard of life. But he walked alone through the Hertfordshire dusk, and being an isolated policeman in a lonely, 'very
hilly county' took on the quality of a spiritual struggle.

One policeman at least prepared for the same spiritual battle
by taking upon himself the role of a passive comforter:

As round my evening beat I stolled
At the close of a summers day
I for a moment stood to watch
A little lad at play.

As I looked at him, unhappy child
'Many like thee' I thought
'Are growing in sin and ignorance
Uncared for and untaught'.

He goes to speak to the boy;
But when he saw my buttons bright
And ominous coat of blue
Adown the dark and narrow street
Like a frightened bird he flew.

He pities the child, knowing : that he is 'not to blame,' for his
parents, 'Spend in beer and gin/What ought to feed and nourish
thee/And Clothe thy naked skin.'

Though the sight of my blue coat
A terror to some may be
Beneath this coat there beats a heart
That aches for such as thee.

Then as I hurried on my way
(For I must work to time)
I breathed this little fervent prayer
And finished up my rhyme.

O may the efforts meet success
Of those good powers that be
To feed and clothe and EDUCATE
A ragged wretch like thee. (77)

The Prevention of Crimes Acts, dealing as they did with the supervision of convicts on licence by the police, had long placed them
in the ostensible position of reclaimers. (78) Yet what the policemen quoted here indicate is that the impulse to reclamation was just
as much the expression of a development of police forces themselves,
that turned organisational goodness into a separate order — a
reserve of right, propriety and pity. By 1876 it was possible for
an officer to speak quite naturally of the police forces of England
as 'the cloth'. (79)

The rank and file viewed its situation, and its relationship with
other men, passively. Policemen watched, they waited. They did not
believe that they had 'discretionary powers'. The transmission of
the Metropolitan concept of 'discretion' — 'something must neces-

sarily be left to the intelligence and discretion of the individual'
— to the provinces, has been discussed above. (80) But it was
unfortunately necessary for nineteenth-century local government,
unable to exercise a personal supervision of social life, to send
ill-educated body-servants upon the streets to act out a charade
of social relationships. It is therefore no surprise to find
that among policemen, obedience was a far more prized virtue than
was 'intelligence', and that the first lesson impressed upon a
recruit was that he should cultivate an extraordinary passivity
of demeanour, 'never offer himself to be moved in the slightest
degree by language or threats', and should always maintain 'calm-
ness and self-control'. (81) Many constables did not believe that
they had any right to act upon their own individual promptings.
'A man only has to do his duty', said James Chambers of the Hertfordshire constabulary. 'If we see a case we lay it before the
Superintendents who decide whether proceedings are to be taken or
not.' (82) Even in the case of a drunken brawl in the streets at
closing time, men like this believed that the structure of the
police force was a bar to their own individual exertions.
   Police divisions were constructed so that the hierarchy might
supervise the men with ease. The superintendent used the reports
of his inspectors (who in turn perused their sergeants' journals)
to make decisions about the balance between decency and impropriety — or as much as would make a reasonable case — in his
division. 'No police constable can act upon his judgement,' said
the chairman of Lancashire county constabulary committee in 1877.
'He must report to the inspector, and take instructions from
him.' (83)
   Under such institutional restrictions, a policeman could only
do his best, which was to walk around and watch, and wait for
instructions from above. James Chambers's implicit assertion was
that, in representing the law, he was not an individual actor.
He worked within a rigidly defined framework, and because this
framework demanded so much of him, it became the focus of his
aspirations, and provided the dimensions of his belief.

Chapter 9

POSSIBILITIES: THE EXAMPLE OF THE LICENCING LAWS

A central theme of this book, and especially of this second part of it, has been the tension between the intentions of local government in policing matters, and the origins and background of the executive force that was used to implement policy within the localities. This chapter assesses the capacities of policemen within local communities and to do this, new material on the police operation of the licencing laws is introduced in order to show what restrictions were placed upon them. Three dimensions to a policeman's sphere of action have been latent within the preceding discussion: restrictions were placed upon him by the type of hierarchy he operated within, by the kind of law he used, and by the sort of man he was. Issues that have previously implied a similar pattern of capacity and restriction are the Night Poaching Prevention Act, the police operation of the vagrancy laws, and the use of policemen as agents of riot law. These issues are considered briefly again in this chapter, in order to clarify what were the possibilities of police action within mid-nineteenth-century communities.

Preceding chapters have emphasised how dependent the nineteenth-century constable was on the chain of command within his police division, and how this made his individual exertions institutionally impossible. In the counties, the divisional superintendent was often presented by the rank and file as the final power and arbiter; but officers themselves were dependent on the local magistracy, and without day-to-day administrative co-operation, the officers in charge of divisions or subdivisions, were frequently powerless to act, as this icy entry in Inspector Williamson's Northamptonshire police journal shows:

> On duty to Oundle called on the Supt . . . also called at _____
> Smith Esq to get the summonses signed and he refused to see me
> consequently the summonses will have to be signed on some future
> day. (1)

All policemen, officers and rank and file were restricted in this way by the organisation within which they worked.

Other restrictions have been noted in these pages. There were obvious physical limitations on the policemen who acted as agents of riot law: they went on foot, they were not supplied with fire-arms, and in spite of Home Office laudation of the individually

acting policeman in preference to the corporate action of a soldiery, the restrictions of the physical situation of a riot meant
that they could <u>not</u> act individually in putting it down. The
policeman on the beat was a drinking, working-class man, and these
facts placed as much limitation on his activity against drunkenness as did the licencing laws, or the presence of brewers on a
watch committee.

There was another set of restrictions placed on police action
by the legal situation they found themselves in. In general,
nineteenth-century constables knew that legally they stood alone,
and the pattern of arrest that modern commentators have noticed,
their reluctance to approach the respectable, (2) was frequently
a policeman's estimation of his own situation: he knew exactly
where he stood. An individual estimation like this could, for
example on the poaching question, he wedded to the official policy
of a force. In 1862, just after the Night Poaching Prevention
Act came into force, the chief constable of Buckinghamshire
ordered his men to exercise 'extreme caution and discretion' in
apprehending people, only to approach respectable persons if they
felt 'assured in their own minds' that an action could be carried
through. (3) 'I expressly pointed out,' said the chief constable
of Cumberland and Westmorland 'that the police should be very careful never to interfere with anybody whom they knew to be a respectable man . . . .' (4)

The County and Borough Police Act of 1856, and the removal of
treasury aid to the county rates for prosecution costs, made law
enforcement both technically and actually a much more localised
affair in the 1860s than it had been a decade before. The anomalous local results of such a system — the cities without stipen-
daries, the watch committee in one place composed largely of
magistrates, in another without any members of the local bench, the
local unwillingness actually to pay for supporting its police in
court — all this helped raise the cry throughout the 1860s and
1870s for a public prosecutor. (5) In this situation what local
managers of local forces could actually do was give strength to
police action by the local interpretation of administrative law.
Each appointment of a policeman as a poor law relieving officer,
or an inspector of nuisances, or lodging houses, was an attempt
to strengthen the police arm. Policemen were not legally or
individually powerful at all, and the local extension of their
capacities under administrative law was both a way of making them
locally useful and of keeping them in their place. In fact, as we
have seen, this kind of administrative inspectorship was only
bestowed on the officer class.

Some county administrators had felt a disappointment at the
scope and role of the 'new' police after 1856. This was especially apparent in counties that had not taken advantage of previous
permissive legislation and which established paid police forces
for the first time in 1856. County gentlemen, cognisant of the
extensive powers for stopping and searching that the Metropolitan
police possessed, campaigned for an extension of those powers to
county constables. The vehicle of their lobbying was the game
question, though the chief constables were anxious to present
their case as one of law and order:

the law of the land is openly set at defiance by gangs of armed
men who by violence overpower all opposition, and so inflict
a moral injury on the general supremacy of law and order. (7)
They maintained that poachers were frequently professional thieves,
that they congregated in county towns from which they issued forth
to commit their depredations,and that it was impossible to watch
them as they passed through several police jurisdictions. What is
more the law was 'at present insufficient to justify a police officer
stopping and searching persons suspected of carrying stolen property.'

It is clear that several chief constables were personally
involved in the preservation of game: the chief constable of
Staffordshire, for instance, saw one of his main local duties as
dispelling 'the false halo' of poaching, and his superintendents
belonged, with his encouragement, to an Association for the Preservation of Game. (8)   The poached rabbit was certainly the point
of the proposals to effect a change in the law of the late 1850s;
but the rabbit was part of a larger question too. The Night Poaching Prevention Act of 1862 (25 & 26 Vict. c.114) gave provincial
policemen the wide powers to stop and search on suspicion that
county magistrates and chief constables had lobbied for. The constable was meant to be sure in his own mind that the person he
stopped came from land 'where he shall unlawfully have been in
search or pursuit of game'; but search could reveal a turnip as
well as a pigeon, and as the current Home Secretary said, the act
gave the police 'very arbitrary powers'. (9)   The chief constable
of Norfolk understood the new immensity of powers that the Night
Poaching Prevention Act gave his men when he opened his instructions
to the force with the glad cry that 'every constable now has power
to stop and search any person . . . [this is] essentially a police
act . . . .' (10)   The Home Office refused to be 'responsible'
for this order, but it is in fact a description of the way the act
was used in the rural districts of England for the next twenty
years. 'A little against our idea of freedom,' commented government inspector Colonel Cobbe in 1872, 'but otherwise . . . a very
good thing for the police.' (11)

When Colonel Cobbe (ex-chief constable of the West Riding as
well as HMIC) praised the Night Poaching Prevention Act for giving
'a defined action for the police upon the public ways', (12) he
meant that the local powers of local policemen had been extended
by central statute. They had been extended in a way that was precisely useful to the traditional rulers of rural England so,
though the individual powers of constables were legally strengthened, the actual power and ability of policemen was confined
and constructed by the intentions and assumptions of the county
government within which they worked.

In recent years the involvement of police forces in the operation of mid-Victorian licencing laws has been seen as the clearest
example of how local police forces were used to apply a developing
means of social discipline. But there were several tensions involved in their use and operation of these laws. The first varied
from place to place: that many town councils were dominated by
brewers and maltsters and hop merchants was a commonplace of provincial political analysis. Contemporary comment however was far

more revealing of another tension: most policemen were assumed to
have a drinking problem. The 'gambling, fighting, drunken policeman' was the material for comic turns which were to develop into
the burly outline of the Gilbertian sub-plot at the end of the
century. But what jokes and cartoons concerning this figure
demonstrated in the 1860s and 1870s was the relationship between
the invitation that police forces made to working men, offering
them respectability and temperance, and the institutional acknowledgment in dismissal figures that police sobriety was a state
impossible to achieve.

The most important basis for police action on the drink question
in the early part of the period under discussion here was the distinction made in law between the public house and the beer-house.
The licenced victualler was bound of his own authority to keep
good order on his premises, whilst the beer-shop keeper was obliged
by law to close at certain times. Beer-house owners could state,
in their application to the Excise for a licence, which rooms they
wanted the police to enter. The complete administration of the
licencing laws by the police was a development of the 1860s and
1870s, a time when a wide range of administrative and local goven-
ment functions were devolved on local forces. Before this, in the
early 1850s, solutions to the problem of supervising drinking
places were seen to lie in systematic inspection of all public
houses 'as in the case of common lodging houses' or by creating
local bodies of 'watchers'. None of these proposals for supervision was seen necessarily to involve the police. (13)

The legal powers of the police to enter and control licenced
premises developed in the 1860s. This did not take place through
a development of the individual powers of the police (as in the case
of police action against poachers) but rather through increased
magisterial control. In 1865 for example, the granting of beer-
house licences was removed from the Excise, and passed to two
justices sitting in petty sessions. (14) Throughout the 1860s and
1870s there were shifts and changes in police powers, rights to
grant occasional licences, to enter licenced premises at all times,
being successively bestowed on them, and removed from them for
over a decade. (15) None of this licencing legislation could provide that clear definition of 'action . . . upon the public ways',
that the Night Poaching Prevention Act provided.

Police powers in the supervision of much working-class drinking
were, then, severely limited in law in the 1850s and 1860s. In
many places before 1869 parish constables were used to supervise
beer-houses, because until legislation of that year policemen had
few powers in the beer-house, and in terms of public relations the
less time they spent there the better. (16) Often, later systems
of police supervision grew out of those operated by parish constables, (17) and in fact the 1850s saw a growing determination
of police activity under a legally inadequate supervisory system.
By 1856 most county chief constables had instituted some uniform
method of watching beer-houses. In Hampshire in the 1850s constables on night duty were told to watch for drunkards through
the windows or open doors of ale-houses. They were not to go in,
were not to speak to the drinkers. (18) They were to report what
they saw to their superintendent who 'invariably lays an informa-

tion.' Some chief constables thought that the police should not be
placed at 'the disposal' of landlords to call them in when they
'thought fit'. (19)   Police officers in this early period dwelt much
on the idea of making the licence-holder more 'responsible' — in the
same way as the law had made the owners of common lodging houses more
responsible for what went on on their premises — and in Birmingham,
if a policeman saw known criminals in a beer-house on several occasions, then he was instructed to point them out to the landlord.
If seen there again, the landlord was summonsed. (20)

The publication of the newly appointed government inspectors'
reports after 1856 gave a national platform to police officers'
complaints about beer-houses. Official police disapproval of them
grew, not only on the grounds of their harbouring criminals, but in
the context of a growing belief that drunkenness was the basis of
'all general crime'. (21)   The collection, publication and transmission of statistics on licencing and the drink question pushed
head and chief constables into the assertion of criminological
theory.   Many officers were willing, by the late 1860s, to state
that the pattern of working-class life formed the basis for crime
in general.   'It is well known', said one police officer in 1869,
'that drunkenness is the greatest promoter of all the misery and
crime that exists.' 'When the lower classes get intoxicated they
get regardless, and don't think of what they are doing.' Much of
this social diagnosis was conventional in the extreme, delineating
a sad round of cause and effect: 'the liquor traffic causes a
morose, morbid state of mind, immorality, neglect of employment and
pecuniary difficulties: then crime commences.' (22)

'A fiction of superior upper class morality was preserved by a
police force which publicised the intemperance of the poor, while
quietly conducting upper class drunkards to their homes without
taking them to court,' notes Brian Harrison. (23)   Indeed, the
pattern of arrest for drunkenness in the mid-Victorian years can
only be explained in these terms, in terms of class. But the
police were in this way not only agents, but actors as well. Officers held beliefs on the drink question, conventional though they
may have been, of their own volition. That their opinions, like those
recruited by the Convocation of Canterbury in 1869 and quoted
above were both for some officers a mere reiteration of respectable
and magisterial opinion, and for others the point of silent conflict and self-identity before a licencing magistrate with a beer
interest, makes their relationship with their 'drunken, fighting'
constables harder to deal with.   Police constables were invited to
become the archetype of the respectable working man and the loudest
exhortation and example came from their officers. When clergymen
complained to the convocation of Canterbury about police 'corruption' on the drink question they spoke quite specifically of
temptation held out to working men: 'the whole of the evils are
systematically winked at by the police, who say that they had
better not be always interfering . . . .' 'Policemen should not
be left too long on one beat.' 'The late alehouse is an almost
unconquerable snare to the weary policeman . . . .' (24)

In spite of the restrictions imposed by local government, by the
law, and by the background of their own men, some officers believed
by the late 1860s that drunkenness could be eliminated. Their

belief was sustained by an understanding of a social anomaly
that could be discussed in purely physical terms: buildings to
watch, drunkards to summons, a race of beer-houses that could be
made by law to be no more. The Wine and Beerhouses Act of 1869
(32 & 33 Vict. c.27), which passed the licencing of ale-houses to
the justices and required applicants for a licence to be of good
character (in most places good character rested on police evidence),
was welcomed by those police officers in a position to make public
statements on the matter. Yet there were differences in reaction
between county and borough police hierarchies, and they showed up
most clearly where the geographical basis of police distribution
defined the possibilities of police action. A county magistrate
pointed to the difficulties of dealing with 'a man . . . staggering
about the streets on a Saturday night . . . creating a disturbance
. . . [when] you first of all have to find the policeman.' (25)
A magistrate from the West Riding told a select committee of 1877
that it was usual to deal with drunkards by summons in country
places:

> the persons are known in small populations . . . . The police
> constable notices them and reports them to his superior officer
> and the magistrate's clerk issues the summons . . . . In the
> counties the police have already made a selection; they take into
> consideration the person. (26)

It was this witness who pointed out that the magistrate's clerk
received a fee if a case were proved against a summonsed man and
that this had an effect on police operations. Summons was also
a means of police protection in rural areas: 'the police act alone;
they have large areas to protect and it is obviously not desirable
to have them come into contact with a rough, drunken man.' (27) A
borough police frequently did not have the local knowledge that
would have enabled them to follow a practice like this. The head
constable of Birmingham spoke of the impossibility of enforcing
those clauses of the Licencing Act of 1872 (35 & 36 Vict. c.94)
that dealt with drunkenness on the highway: 'the only procedure
by which we can bring the law to bear . . . is by means of summons
. . .'; being bound in this case to know the drunkard's name and
address, the only way to obtain it was for 'a policeman to leave
his beat and follow a drunkard all round the town . . . it is
utterly impossible'. (28) Some borough head constables complained
before 1872 that existing legislation gave

> no direct power to the police to apprehend without a warrant in
> simple cases of drunkenness; it must be (rather) that they find
> him so incapable that it is necessary for his own safety; . . .
> in other cases they cannot apprehend unless drunkenness is
> accompanied by some breach of the peace. (29)

'If persons under the influence of drink go quietly away', said the
head constable of Leeds in 1872, 'the police do not interfere with
them . . . we should not have cells to hold them all . . . .' (30)
In Liverpool in the 1870s a message from the jail that all the cells
were full would be sent out to police stations, and men on the beat
would be told to stop arresting. (31) Liverpool also practised a
system of arrest that could be achieved by summons in rural areas:
every person brought to a police station on a charge of drunkenness
was booked and taken before the magistrates

with this exception.   There is what is called a refused charge
book kept by the bridewell keeper. . . if a man is known to be
a respectable person, if his friends follow him and say 'we will
take care of him' and he does not live far off, he is entered
in that book and not locked up . . . . (32)
Borough policemen looked for another kind of control similar to that
involved in the rural summons when they urged that the definition
of 'habitual drunkard' be established in law. The head constables
of Leeds and Sheffield for example wanted a third conviction for
drunkenness to carry an automatic sentence of three months. (33)

The Intoxicating Spirits Licencing Act of 1872 (35 & 36 Vict. c.
94) marked a clear change in police operations because it made
closing hours compulsory. The penalty for being found on licenced
premises after hours was a fine of up to £2, and if the apprehended
refused to reveal his name and address the constable could arrest.
It was in this way that the legal onus for good order passed from
the licencee to the drinker. This power to enter licenced premises
was again removed in 1874; (34) but it did not signify for police
action so much as the tendency of licencing legislation after this
date to push the drinker on to the street, where police powers were
wide and efficient.

What officers dwelt on above all else when they were asked for
their comments on drunkenness and the law was the material provision
for good order: small police forces spread over large areas; police
hierarchies that rendered individual policemen powerless on the
streets; too few cells; not enough lock-ups. Within this set of
geographical and material considerations, a legal enactment that
provided for immediate differences in the appearance of the streets
was an important factor in shaping officers' theories about the
limits and possibilities of their action. Many officers, like the
head constable of Preston, praised the Licencing Act of 1872
because it cleared the streets by midnight. (35) It was not that
it decreased drunkenness, explained the head constable of Liverpool, but it gave the city the benefit of a few hours more public
order each day. (36) The act coerced the working-class drunkard
off the streets, said the head constable of Birmingham, in evidence
of wonderful explicitness:

I will not say that there was less drunkenness, because one does
not know where the people went to, but as regards that which I
was responsible for, viz.: the peace and quiet and safety of
the town, the order of the streets was perfectly marvellous
. . . . Of course it was immaterial to me where they rolled
themselves . . . . (37)

The street, the highway, the public place, was the policeman's
arena of action. In many urban areas the rate of assault on policemen increased in the late 1860s and early 1870s. (38) After 1869
police supervision of drinking was legally provided for in a way
that had not been the case before the acts of 1869 and 1872. Legislation turned large numbers of ale- and public-house customers on
to the streets at specific times. Whilst police authorities, magistrates and chief constables knew that it was not advisable to have
policemen come into contact with these customers, and whilst in
rural areas, by local knowledge and summons, it was often possible
to avoid contact, it was frequently unavoidable in urban areas. It

was not the mere fact of police presence that provoked assault, but rather the extension of specific police capacities under law that did so.

By the early 1880s, then, there had developed in most provincial places a fairly regular system of inspecting licenced premises. This systematisation was attributed by many officers to the increased powers of surveillance given to them by the acts of 1872 and 1874. In Liverpool in 1876 six inspectors and six constables did no duty other than that connected with public houses. Eight of this group of personnel entered pubs constantly, reported on information laid against houses and communicated with the head constable every day. (39) In Preston two plain-clothes officers were detailed off to visit the pubs every Sunday. (40) In the counties detailing of men for permanent pub duty was seen as a geographical impossibility, a waste of manpower. 'What is more, our system of constabulary makes the superintendent wholly responsible for everything in his district,' said a rural magistrate in 1877. 'No police constable can act upon his judgement; he must report to his inspector and take instructions from him.' (41) A borough policeman's 'discretion' in drunkenness cases was really a reflection of the closeness of his officers. In the late 1860s and 1870s the supervision of public houses became part of a police system. The surveillance of drinkers and drinking places was not an inherent part of police action; it developed rather out of the growing context of administrative policing, of the inspection and regulation that was discussed in the first part of this book.

Most borough authorities believed that the legislation of the early 1870s had led to 'increased vigilance' on the part of the police, that 'simple drunkenness' had become more noticed by patrolling policemen, that the streets were quieter and that licence-holders were more inclined to obey the law. Yet it was still a common complaint towards the end of the decade that

the police are rather desirous of not seeing [drunkards] than of seeing them . . . they are very willing to take a favourable view of a man's conduct . . . . I think the natural tendency is that in a small place like ours the police act more from their general knowledge than from [instruction]. (42)

The 'small place' in question here was Norwich, and the head constable mentioned obliquely one item of the constable's general knowledge: 'we have two brewers I think, on the watch committee . . . the difficulty of getting convictions . . . .' (43) Looking at the policeman on the beat, the contemporary commentator noted that his 'discretion' was bound precisely to this sort of organisational necessity.

The public attention that was devoted to the drink question in the mid-Victorian years served an important function for policemen in that it set their local actions in a broader, national framework:

Certainly there cannot be a doubt that the great amount of public attention which has been drawn to this question of drinking has had for several years an effect on the actions of the police; because even though the constable who actually arrests has not had his mind so much influenced by it, yet he is under the orders of sergeants and superintendents whose minds have been influenced by public opinion . . . and they in turn act under general instructions from the centre. (44)

'It was immaterial to me where they rolled themselves . . . .' For the policemen who operated central statute there were important legacies of perception about their own role, and at this level one of the most important effects of the licencing legislation of the 1870s was that it defined a sphere of action that was centred on the street and public places. As with the Night Poaching Prevention Act and the use of the police in the supervision of the vagrant poor, (45) it reinforced a police perception of people on the move as suspect and potentially criminal.

Chapter 10

CONCLUSION

The second part of this book has dealt with the movement of people
from one situation to another, and with the changes involved in
the making of policemen out of working men. We do not know, and
possibly will never be able to discover how mid-nineteenth-century
rural workers understood their situation, and it is for this reason
that the evidence of those who left, escaped, and who were made
vocal by the pressure of new circumstances is important. The words
of policemen, puzzled by their new situation and made aware of the
possibilities of written communication by the demands of their new
job, have been used in these pages partly to reveal an understanding of a situation wider than the job of policing. The working-
class men who became nineteenth-century policemen had a value
placed on their past experience by a governing class that was rare
in the mid-Victorian years. They were recruited from rural areas
not only because they would — at least for a while — accept low
wages, but because their experience, and the social beliefs wrought
by that experience, could be made good use of. But how that rural
labourer saw the land, the landscape, the fields and woods and
hamlets, is a harder matter to discuss. There are centuries of
people whose ways of seeing we do not know. (1) Become policeman,
the rural worker had to watch the landscape still. Detection, as
police work, was an art confined to a few urban centres; in the
counties, long-term, responsible constables were put into disguise
and sent out to the pubs and fairs to find out what they could.
John Pearman was sent out several times in his first years of
service; he saw it as a reward for good work and a stage in his
upward climb to promotion: 'I dressed ragged and had a small
Parcel of writing Paper to sell and some times I beg (sic.) but
was 3 weeks before I could get a Clew (sic.) . . . .' (2) Understood in its modern sense, detective work could not become a
widely used police method until some primitive forensic science
established itself, and the novelty of taking plaster casts of
burglar's footprints became dispersed throughout general police
work. The detective policeman of the mid-nineteenth century
operated by talking and listening, and by acting on information
received. City streets, public houses, the broken stair of the
common lodging house, offered opportunity for the pursuit and

capture of sudden offence. (3) Yet still the pattern of most police
work was watching. By walking around and watching, policemen saw
not only changes in the rural landscape, but also in the landscape
of the city street. Watching, they observed the stranger's face,
the familiar meeting at the unfamiliar time of day, the break in
the pattern. With permission received, the cause of the anomaly
might be investigated. Watching for change, the break in the
pattern, may have been the rural labourer's way of seeing, and it
may be that this attribute was used, though unknowingly, by police
authorities.

Yet it was the law that formalised a policeman's understanding
of the possibilities of his action. He had been recruited in
country and city as a servant of property, paid for by those who
owned it. He had been allowed to be successful if in possession
of the complete understanding of ownership and power that being
a rural labourer bestowed. Nevertheless, it was statute law that
came to define a policeman's capabilities. That route, from an
understanding of class relations, a placing of people in relation
to what they owned and what they lacked, to a series of legislative
enactments, needs tracing. Its beginnings are hard to find, for
the understanding was implicit, the connection made so prosaically
every time a watch committee met, or a chief constable cast his
eye over a roomful of applicants for the county constabulary.
Legislation of the 1870s and 1880s strengthened the individual
policeman's capacities, and at the same time severed the force he
worked in from local governments. This legislative change reflected changes within local forces, and within individual policemen's consciousness, that were themselves the product of institu-
tionalising the class attitudes that made men successful policemen.

Legal commentators began to write about the police in the 1880s.
Noticing, as the historian must, the absence of comment on, and
theorising about, police matters since the days of Bentham, their
analyses attempted to account for some half-century of silence.
The inherent difficulty of these contemporary analyses was that
such commentators attempted whilst defining 'police', also to
define a 'policeman'. Legally, the argument went, a system of
'police' was an administrative system that included neither
making the law, nor the law itself; 'police' was the instrument
by which 'conformity to the rules of the commonwealth was
obtained'. (4) Given this context, any analysis was bound to
render policemen shadowy and passive, and readers were given no
way of dealing with the social reality that made policemen agents
of local government and, increasingly, of central statute. Thus
the very contradictions involved in this sort of exegesis were
not only left undiscussed, but in the wooden figure of the eternal
policeman were actually turned into a positive definition of his
capacities. Every policeman, asserted J. E. Davies, legal advisor
to the Metropolitan police, county magistrate and chairman of
quarter sessions, stood in the position of a servant of the crown.
It was from his oath to his sovereign that he derived his powers:

> police constables . . . [have] been expressly invested with
> the powers and duties of the old parish constables . . . the
> possession of them is so essential that however they may be
> supplemented by modern legislation without them no police
> force could exist for a day. (5)

There were particular reasons why, in the 1880s, analysis was made
in this way, and policemen's capacities seen as lying in the abstract delegation of abstract powers by an abstract crown to the
changeless figure of 'the policeman'. These pages have noted the
way in which permanent policemen and officers came to define themselves in the 1870s, not as autonomous individuals, nor as agents
of local government, but as members of a nation-wide community.
The tendency was confirmed in legislation that made 'the police'
a general administrative agency, again in the 1870s. There was
also an increased financial supervision over local forces exercised from the centre and dating from the mid-1870s, and 1880
marked the beginning of an era in which the structure of the
government areas that had shaped local police forces underwent
drastic change. (6)

The legislation that used the police as a general administrative
agency in the 1870s did so because they were a convenient, pre-
existing executive force to be found in all areas. This kind of
administrative convenience marks the legislation of the 1870s off
from the Summary Jurisdiction Act of 1879 (42 & 43 Vict. c. 49),
which was the first measure to outline a nation-wide and system-
atised police procedure in the disciplining of social life.
Extended police powers within the community were provided for in
two ways under this statute of 1879. The first, local police
forces already had some experience in: in the case of default,
fines and all payments of money were to be extracted by distress,
'the warrant of distress . . . exercised by . . . a constable'.
Publicity-conscious officers had never been very happy about this
aspect of their duty, for the local execution of law, especially
rate law, had forced it on them at a much earlier period. The
head constable of Sheffield made the same point again and again
over twenty years to the Home Secretary and watch committee: that
serving warrants of distress only made public a long-standing
source for police unpopularity. In Sheffield in the 1860s he
said that his men often went their own way in the matter and,

deeming it inexpedient to seize the little furniture possessed
made a return 'nulla bona' . . . . The police are bound to
execute all the warrants directed to them and it must and
indeed does rest with the magistrates and the overseers to
see that commitments are not issued against Persons who from
their poverty . . . are improper objects to send to prison. (7)

Yet the Summary Jurisdiction Act of 1879 formalised this process
and gave it national criminal law status. One contemporary commentator thought that it cast upon the police 'the duties of
bailiffs'. (8) But it was not just that an act of Parliament
provided for unpopular police action in this way; it also provided a method of police working, an involvement in a system-
atised and logical process of legal discipline that had not previously been the province of the police, when their work and
their capacities had been fragmented by a hierarchical chain of
command, and when final power had rested with a magistrate. Now,
after 1880,

after the accused has been convicted and punished by the fine
imposed . . . some public officer will watch the happening of
the default of payment, then apply for a warrant of distress

. . . the same public officer would have to issue and serve summonses, and bring evidence of means and ability to pay. (9)
Some contemporary commentators believed that because of their background and status, and the widespread unpopularity that the 'role
of bailiff' placed upon them, policemen were incapable of under-
taking this work, and that 'a new class of executive officers must
discharge this duty'. (10)

The Summary Jurisdiction Act also enabled the police, at the discretion of a magistrate, to whip juvenile offenders over the age
of 7. For the first time, then, police forces were involved in a
wholesale system of watch, apprehension, trial and <u>punishment.</u> The
area of social concern that enabled some policemen in two decades
past to cross the barrier of passivity and afford some sympathy
because 'they were not to blame,' ended finally with the symbol of
fear and authority, birch rod in hand, waiting in a private place.
Working-class literature became more explicit about the relationship between people and police towards the end of the nineteenth
century. Being beaten by a policeman counted as a common memory,
as indeed it still does among older people today. (11)

The law defined a policeman's capacities and outlined the ways
in which he, as part of an organisation, related to a community.
Yet his self-estimation of his capacities derived not only from
this source but also his position in a class society, from the
propulsion of his own experience, from knowing in many different
ways where he stood in relationship to other men, both his peers
and his masters. The most dominant feature of his self-consciousness before the 1880s was that which arose from administration and
local government taking men's lives, and using them. Masters and
men were often quite explicit about what it was that was used.
'Marked Respect must be shown at all times to the Magistrates,'
ordered the new chief constable of Buckinghamshire in April 1857,
'and they will be saluted in the usual manner . . . .' He did
not need to tell his band of rural workers clothed as policemen
what that manner was. (12) 'My Nature', observed John Pearman
on his retirement, 'was not to take pleasure. But to watch the
way and doings of Mankind and to learn if possiable (sic) what
he as (sic) to live for.' He understood how his interest in the
workings of society had become part of his capacity as a policeman: 'I cannot say much for the Policeman's life he must be a
special man and Look after other men's faults and shut his eyes
to all virtues.' (13)

With experience and understanding used in this way, some
policemen were placed in a position of deep conflict. The law
called them individuals; but the organisation within which they
worked told them that they could never act as such. Central
government eschewed force as a means of maintaining law and
order, but a policeman could only stop a riot by acting as a
soldier. More and more people might be admitted to a spurious
kind of citizenship, and the symbol of this might be a policeman,
a representative of the law, but for all that, just a man dressed
in blue; yet by recruiting only men who could be called servants,
a traditional form of relationship was maintained and even strengthened in the mid-nineteenth century.

Nineteenth-century police constables were not asked to do any-

thing that working people in general were not asked to do, though
pressures for policemen came a little earlier. They were asked not
to drink, and to develop and maintain a regulated pattern of life
and work. They were asked to keep their children clean and ordered,
their wives off the labour market, to worship God and practise a
regulated domestic economy. As for all working people, promises
were held out, and small material rewards offered. All working
people had to fight against tremendous odds, and were never given
the means to do so. The reward offered to a policeman was more
precise, the road narrower, the end laid down in pay scale and
government circulars on superannuation. That his disappointment
might be keener resulted in a state of mind that many long-term
constables faced with puzzlement. Most men indeed would 'rather
be a little dog and laugh at the devil than wear the uniform of a
policeman'. Most recruits left. Nearly 48,000 men joined county
forces alone between 1839 and 1874. Over 24,000 of them resigned
and 12,000 were dismissed. (14)
    Those who stayed, and became permanent policemen, were put in a
position which a history that deals in terms of either simple conflict or simple transmission will find difficult to deal with. In
the police and constabulary records of the English provinces lies
important evidence not only of individual working lives, but of the
means by which several thousand mid-Victorian working-class men
played a positive and active part in a social process that, as
part of a wider pattern of legal and social discipline, was finally
to contract working people to the state, and make them participants
in the restrictions placed upon them. And informing this change,
this metamorphosis of men into policemen, is the faint but per-
sistent echo of a much older social ideal: the possibility of
belonging, of being part of the commonweal. The argument here
has been that magistrates and urban police authorities used this
ideal too — from a vastly different perspective it was also theirs
— in recruiting policy, in making county police forces comprehensible replicas of the militia for example, or city policemen the
body servants of the ratepayers. But of course they did not mean
by admittance to the commonweal what those policemen who signed
themselves 'Justice' and 'Cromwell' meant. They sought to resurrect
an ordered and harmonious village community in which everyone knew
his place.
    This unacknowledged reciprocity has served several purposes. It
forms the basis of the shadowy policeman of the legal textbooks,
the essays on the constitution of the late nineteenth century;
and it has in this way left modern policemen bound to write a
police history that can nowhere deal with the relationship of
policemen to historical reality. Yet mid-Victorian commentators
who spoke of the police outside the confines of constitutional
commentry did understand something of this reciprocity, and what
it meant to men caught between the experience that made them policemen and the institutional need to deny that experience. A chief
constable described police practice in controlling beer-houses.
In his plain evidence he outlined the dramatic enactment of the
policeman's tension: constables on night duty were told to watch
for drunkards through the open doors of beer-houses. They must
not go in, must not speak to the drinkers. A familiar life was

thus staged, made theatrical. (15)   Police Constable Kirkland of
Chesterfield, appearing for the defence of a man accused of trade
outrage in 1862, swearing that he could not be the one, he was not
in Sheffield that night, he, Kirkland had seen him in Chesterfield
'very drunk,' leaning up against a fence in the company of a
woman: 'I did not call him by name, but told him he had had enough
and had better go home.' (16)   It was on the drink question that
Victorian commentators evaded in hilarity the tension of a social
relationship.   Provincial papers reported almost daily cases of
assault on the police; they reported as well the irresistible
knock-about farce of the men in blue.   Constables were being sworn
in in Huddersfield in 1856, the chairman of the bench enjoining
them to look out for Sunday gambling in beer-houses. A furore from
the public gallery: policemen are too-frequent visitors to beer-
houses to be of any use in surveilling them.   Why, a year ago two
of them 'had been looking over the beer houses and it was a very
cold night so they called at the Wagon and Horses and had three-
pennyworth each.'   They took one man into custody and the county
police officer who met them on the way to the lock-up said they
were both 'worse drunk than their prisoner'.   Laughter in the
house. (17)   The compulsive comedy of this made for a style of
journalism that staged the event in staccato style, a foretaste of
the relentless two-four rhythm of the late-nineteenth-century music
hall celebration of big feet and funny hats.   Policemen could be
laughed at because as working men it seemed that they had sought
entry to a wider sphere, and had tried to become among those who
govern and manage.   The gap between aspiration and reality was
evident — and funny — as maidservants aping their mistresses were
deemed funny by 'Punch' cartoonists. (18)   A wedding feast at the
Rose Inn in Thurgoland, Lancashire: several times during his
stretch on night duty Constable Wilson of the county constabulary
looks in on the party.   At 1.30 in the morning there is riotous
betting that the bridegroom is still capable of dancing a reel,
the prize is more to drink and there's a whip-round to provide it.
Constable Wilson, stepping over that theatrical door frame, makes
his contribution, and soon, having had a couple, tries to sing a
song 'but stuck in the middle of the first verse'.   He leaves the
party and — this is the subject of the court case brought by the
policeman — 'is attacked outside by [the bridegroom] who threw him
down, bit a piece out of his finger and only released him after the
truncheon had been freely used.'   What private quarrel or public
antagonism was here exposed was as obviously unclear to the magistrate trying the case as it must be to us.   But he, on hearing
that Wilson had told one of the witnesses for the defence to
'say as little about the affair as possible,' dismissed the case
and left the policeman to the mercies of his chief constable. (19)
     The Birmingham labourer described above, (21) who stopped to
talk to his old friend the policeman, knew quite well, in the
common currency of theatrical imagery that propelled vernacular
commentry on the police, that the little dog did not bark at the
devil any more; Toby barked at the policeman. (21)   And the
respectable might watch this by-play among the working classes
in the way that they might watch rustics tumble and jest.   Still
excluded from the commonweal, their conflict was only a sub-plot.

'The Guards, the Guards are coming,' wrote a local poet in a Huddersfield paper in 1856, seeing a come-uppance for the city constable in the discharge of soldiers from the Crimea:
    A week and we shall find
    His nose put not less out of joint
    Than our larder where he dined.
    Cousins from the Crimea
    With his rights will interfere.

    But there is vengeance in his hand
    So do not deem him weak
    There's many a soldier will be watched
    And brought before the beak.
    And of his rivals he will try
    To keep our kitchens clear. (22)
The counterpoint to this condescending eye cast at a comedy
among the domestics was not only the fierce assault in midnight
city street, but the search, by the respectable, for the image
of the good and docile and comprehensible servant in the working-
class policeman. Good and docile, the riotous assembly of the
beer-house and the policeman's stumbling might be swiftly translated to a scene of pathos, his exclusion might be recognised:
'a policeman dare not go into a public house; he is surrounded by
enemies and people are only too glad to "put a knife into him
. . .".' (23) That a reality could be found beneath the image,
that many policemen did find in policing a patient religiosity,
a usable idea of service, is one of the reasons why an understanding of nineteenth-century policing and policemen can lead to
an analysis of stoicism as a means of self-assertion, and self-
identification, and sometimes, of defiance. After Swing we are
faces with forty years of silence from the rural labourer. To
listen to the evidence of some who left, who got by by doing what
was expected of them, is important. For generations, English
villages yielded up their men to fight for those who owned the
land those men worked. Pressed into the navy, or taking the king's
shilling, they provided that long tradition of leaving, and
returning, of linking through experience smaller and larger communities. It is cheap to say that they fought for ideas and ideals
that they did not understand or hold to. Some few nineteenth-
century working-class men found a personal salvation in becoming
policemen. They were not recruited unknowingly; their understanding
of their situation was what was bought and paid for by their
masters. What this knowledge and understanding consisted of, on
the part of policemen and masters, was that in the mid-nineteenth
century policemen were not important. Governmental structures and
class relations and police hierarchies rendered policemen agents
rather than actors. Yet it was these conditions that provided
policemen with the means to a self-consciousness that, with legal,
constitutional and governmental changes, made the English police a
separate and relatively autonomous force as the 1880s passed.
They entered an area of public action and became important in a
way that was not the case in the mid-Victorian years.

NOTES

PREFACE

1 Maureen Cain, Trends in the Sociology of Police Work, 'International Journal of the Sociology of the Law', vol. 7 (1979), pp. 143-67.

2 Cyril D. Robinson, Ideology as History: A Look at the Way in Which Some English Police Historians Look at the Police, 'Police Studies', vol. 2, no. 2 (Summer 1979), pp. 35-49.

3 On the question of modern police professionalism, see Maureen Cain, Police Professionalism: Its Meaning and Consequence, 'Anglo-American Law Review', vol. 1, no. 2 (1972), pp. 217-31, and Robert Reiner, 'The Blue Coated Worker' (Cambridge University Press, Cambridge, 1978), pp. 168-218. On the control of the police, see Maureen Cain, 'Society and the Policeman's Role' (Routledge & Kegan Paul, London, 1973), pp. 223-40, and Reiner, 'Blue Coated Worker', pp. 219-27. On working-class policemen in a modern class society, see Robert Reiner, The Police in the Class Structure, 'British Journal of Law and Society, vol. 5, no. 2 (Winter 1978), pp. 166-84; The Police, Class and Politics, 'Marxism Today', vol. 22, no. 3 (March 1978), pp. 69-80. For a recent historical account of this question, dealing mainly with the context of the USA, see Cyril D. Robinson, The De-Radicalisation of the Policeman: A Historical Analysis, 'Crime and Delinquency', vol. 24 (April 1978), pp. 129-51.

4 Jacques Donzelot, 'The Policing of Families' (Pantheon, New York, 1979), pp. 139-264. Stuart Hall et al., 'Policing the Crisis' (Macmillan, London, 1978), pp. 57-77, pp. 120-38.

5 Carolyn Pilling, The Police in the English Local Community, 1856-1880 (University of Cambridge, M. litt thesis, 1975).

6 Victor Bailey (ed.), 'Policing and Punishment in Nineteenth Century Britain' (Croom Helm, London, 1981), pp. 15, 24, 33, 74-5, 81, 86, 88-9.

7 Bailey, op. cit., p. 15.

INTRODUCTION

1 The only contemporary work of police history that deals with
  provincial forces as well as that of the Metropolis, was
  written, and recently revised (1979) by a former Home Office
  official: T. A. Critchley, 'A History of Police in England and
  Wales, 900-1966' (Constable, London, 1967). For a discussion
  of police history, see Cyril D. Robinson, Ideology as History:
  A Look at the Way Some English Police Historians Look at the
  Police, 'Police Studies', vol. 2, no. 2 (Summer 1979), pp.
  35-49. For historical accounts of policing that do <u>not</u> take
  the Metropolitan force as a starting point see Victor Bailey
  (ed.), 'Policing and Punishment in Nineteenth Century Britain'
  (Croom Helm, London, 1981).
2 J. M. Hart, The Reform of the Borough Police, 1835-1856, 'English
  Historical Review', vol. 70 (1955), p. 411. J. M. Hart, The
  County and Borough Police Act, 1856, 'Public Administration',
  vol. 34 (1956), p. 405. Henry Parris, The Home Office and the
  Provincial Police, 1856-1870, 'Public Law', vol. xx (1961),
  p. 230.
3 There are about a hundred of these local force histories, and a
  full collection is held in the Police College Library at Bramshill. Those that have been specifically used for this study are
  listed in the Bibliography.
4 There is a striking contrast where between nineteenth century,
  and modern British police forces, which are 'unique (among organisations) in that the elite is generated internally'. Robert
  Renier, The Police in the Class Structure, 'British Journal of
  Law and Society', vol. 5, no. 2 (Winter, 1978) p. 171.
5 Parris, Home Office and Police, p. 230. Sidney Webb, 'Grants
  in Aid' (Longman Green, London, 1920), pp. 19-20. J. Watson
  Grice, 'National and Local Finance', (P. S. King & Son, London,
  1910), pp. 37-41; 64-5.
6 Hart, County and Borough Police Act, p. 410. Parris, Home
  Office and Police, p. 246f.
7 PP 1867-7, xxxix, p. 634.
8 For a recent account of this 'escape from class' through policing in the modern American context, see Cyril D. Robinson,
  The De-Radicalisation of the Policeman: A Historical Analysis,
  'Crime and Delinquency', vol. 24 (April 1978, pp. 150-1.
9 Charles Reith, 'A New Study of Police History' (Oliver & Boyd,
  Edinburgh, 1956), pp. 21-4, and chapter 9.
10 Charles Reith, 'The Police Idea' (Oxford University Press,
  London, 1938); 'Police Principles and the Problem of War'
  (Oxford University Press, London, 1940); 'The British Police
  and the Democratic Ideal' (Oxford University Press, London,
  1943); 'A Short History of the British Police' (Oxford University Press, London, 1948); 'The Blind Eye of History' (Faber
  & Faber, London, 1952); 'A New Study of Police History'
  (Oliver & Boyd, Edinburgh, 1956).
11 David Philips, 'Crime and Authority in Victorian England' (Croom
  Helm, London, 1977), p. 88. See Robinson, Ideology as History,
  pp. 35-49 for an account of teleological police history, and
  for a biography of Charles Reith (p. 48).

12 James McClure, 'Spike Island: Portrait of a British Police
   Force' (Macmillan, London, 1980), p. 9. Sir Robert Mark,
   'Policing a Perplexed Society' (George Allen & Unwin, London,
   1977), p. 12.
13 Reith, 'A New Study', p. 140; 'British Police', p. 37.
14 Belle Brittan (Hiram Fuller), 'Sparks from a Locomotive (Derby
   & Jackson, New York, 1859), pp. 25-6.
15 W. E. Davies, Police, 'Encyclopaedia Brittanica', 9th Edition,
   1875-1889. F. W. Maitland, 'Justice and Police' (Macmillan,
   London, 1885), pp. 105-6. A Barrister and Chairman of Quarter
   Sessions, 'Police Handbook' (Worcester, 1869).
16 Returns Relating to theMetropolitan Police, PP. 1830, xxiii,
   pp. 409-18. Reith, 'A New Study', pp. 133-42.
17 Most provincial police force regulations seem to have been
   direct copies of the Metropolitan rule book.
18 See below, pp. 148-50.
19 This book does not deal with the policing of Welsh communities,
   though the legislation under consideration in the first part
   of this book applied to England and Wales.
20 For Kilvert's evidence, see below, p. 143-4. Charles Dickens,
   The Detective Police, and On Duty with Inspector Field, in
   'The Uncommercial Traveller' (Penguin, Harmondsworth, 1964).
   Flora Thompson, 'Lark Rise to Candleford' (Oxford University
   Press, London, 1965), p. 553.
21 Geoffrey Best, 'Mid-Victorian Britain' (Weidenfeld & Nicholson,
   London, 1971); see plates 2, 10 and 20.
22 David J. Bordua (ed.), 'The Police: Six Sociological Essays'
   (Wiley, New York, 1967), p. vii.
23 Maureen Cain, 'Society and the Policeman's Role' (Routledge &
   Kegan Paul, London, 1973), pp. 238-40, 243.
24 Maitland, 'Justice and Police', p. 105.
25 Davies, Police. For earlier theories of policing see Jeremy
   Bentham, 'Idea of a Proposed All Comprehensive Body of Law'
   (J. M. M'Creery, London, 1822). J. Bowring, 'Works of Jeremy
   Bentham', 3 vols. (W. Tait, Edinburgh, 1843), vol. 3, p. 169.
   Jacques Donzelot, 'The Policing of Families' (Random House,
   New York, 1979), pp. 6-7.
26 Edwin Chadwick, On A Preventative Police (extracted from 'The
   London Review' and privately printed, London, 1829). PP 1839,
   xix, pp. 149-59; PP 1852-3, xxxvi, p. 260. S. E. Finer, 'The
   Life and Times of Sir Edwin Chadwick' (Methuen, London, 1952),
   pp. 15-17, 29-31.
27 Gareth Stedman Jones, 'Outcast London' (Clarendon Press, London,
   1971, p. 131. Robinson, De-Radicalisation of the Policeman,
   p. 134.

CHAPTER 1 — GOVERNMENT AND POLICING

1 There are several classic accounts of the developing statutory
  context to police activity. S. and B. Webb, 'The Parish and
  the County' (Longman's Green, London, 1906) pp. 15-32. Redlich
  and Hirst, 'Local Government in England', (Macmillan, London,
  1903) vol. 1, pp. 170-1; vol. 2, pp. 302-12. H. B. Simpson,

The Office of Constable, 'English Historical Review', vol. 10,
(1895), p. 625. T. A. Critchley, 'A History of Police in
England and Wales' (Constable, London, 1967), chapters 1-4.
All these accounts have concentrated on the legal provision for
peace officers, indicating no other framework than this for
police activity within Victorian communities.

2 Of the 147 English boroughs that were, just before 1856, managing their own police under the Municipal Corporations Act of
1835, 33 had had some primitive form of police before 1835.
These bodies of police acted concurrently with the constables
appointed by the parish — or the burgesses, or the borough
justices, or the court leet. J. R. S. Somers Vine, 'English
Municipal Institutions, 1835-1879', (Waterlow and Sons, London,
1879) pp. 185-91.

3 Thirteen English boroughs had moved not one inch from their
pre-1835 position by 1856. J. M. Hart, Reform of the Borough
Police, 'English Historical Review', vol. 70, (1955), p. 14.
PRO, HO 45, 65/3.

4 PP 1839, xix, pp. 155-65.

5 PP 1852-3, xxxvi, p. 5.

6 Full information on all men appointed under these acts was to be
sent both to individual justices throughout the county, and to
quarter sessions. Where a paid county police officer existed,
control of the parish constables was given to him.

7 'Buckinghamshire Advertiser', 10 January, 1857. By the early
1850s the 13 English administrative counties that used the
superintending system employed between them 118 superintendents
and 74 paid constables in charge of lock-ups. PP 1852-3,
lxxvii, p. 511f.

8 Critchley, 'History of Police', pp. 60-1.

9 Report of Kent General Quarter Sessions, 20 August 1840, in
'Maidstone Gazette', 25 August 1840.

10 Crichley, 'History of Police', p. 61. There is a better account
in Webb, 'Parish and County', pp. 604-5.

11 As ubiquitous as the Vagrancy Act of 1824 (see p. 56) this
act gave local police forces wide powers for action against all
manner of social anomaly. A quarter of a century after the act
was passed a witness before a royal commission on contagious
diseases recommended that in default of other legislation, the
vagrancy acts and the relevant sections of the Town Police
Clauses Act to be used to control street soliciting. PP 1871,
xix, pp. 15, 432.

12 There were 146 boroughs with their own police powers in 1866.
Of these there were 88 where the Public Health Act, Local
Government Act or both, were in force. PP 67-8, lviii,
pp. 789f.

13 PP 1867, lix, pp. 141f.

14 See note 12. There were 54 corporations with their own police
becoming Boards of Health, 1848-1857, and 34 from 1858-1866.
PP 1857 (Session 2) xli, pp. 3f., PP 1867 lix,
pp. 141f.

15 David Philips, 'Crime and Authority in Victorian England' (Croom
Helm, London, 1977), p. 83.

16 J. M. Hart, The Reform of the Borough Police, p. 421 and note

1.   Charles Reith, 'Police Principles and the Problem of War' (Oxford University Press, London, 1940) p. 55.

17 Charles Reith, 'A New Study of Police History' (Oliver & Boyd, Edinburgh, 1956), pp. 133, 139, 200. 'British Police and the Democratic Ideal' (Oxford University Press, London, 1943), p. 37.

18 Report of Kent General Quarter Sessions, 9 March, 20 August, 1840, in 'Maidstone Gazette', 10 March, 25 August, 1840. See also PP 1852-3, xxxvi, pp. 21, 220.

19 PP 1852-3, xxxvi, p. 55. 'The Times', 15 October 1850.

20 PP 1852-53, xxxvi, p. 76.

21 Burnett Tabrum, 'A Short History of the Essex Constabulary' (Essex County Chronicle, Chelmsford, 1911).

22 Kent General Quarter Sessions, 20 August 1840 reported in 'Maidstone Gazette', 25 August 1840. Kent General Quarter Sessions, 9 March 1840, reported in 'Maidstone Gazette', 10 March 1840.

23 When Buckinghamshire magistrates came to implement the compulsory police act of 1856 they were quite specific about their fears: 'it unecessarily severed the police from the magistracy by breaking up the present petty sessional divisions.' Bucks. Epiphany Quarter Sessions, 5 January 1857, reported in 'Buckinghamshire Advertiser', 10 January 1857.

24 PP 1841, i, (59) (369); PP 1842, iii, (209) (247) (432); PP 1844 i, (488); PP 1850, v, (142)·, PP 1852, iii, (188) (345).

25 The superintending constable owed something to an English understanding of the Royal Irish Constabulary's chief constables — without the latters' judicial powers. Galen Broeker, 'Rural Disorder and Police Reform in Ireland' (Routledge & Kegan Paul, London, 1970), p. 220.

26 Kent General Quarter Sessions, 20 August 1840, reported in 'Maidstone Gazette', 24 August 1840; Kent General Quarter Sessions, 28 June 1849, reported in the 'Maidstone Gazette', 3 July 1849.

27 Hansard, Third Series, 120, p. 963.

28 PRO HO 65/66; HO 45 OS 6810, 6811.

29 Philips, 'Crime and Authority', p. 22.

30 The chairman of Kent quarter sessions consulted one of the commissioners of Metropolitan police on the appropriate salary for a superintending constable, and one 'between that paid to sergeants and inspectors in the Metropolitan force' was recommended. Kent General Quarter Sessions, 12 September 1850, reported in 'Maidstone Gazette', 24 September 1850.

The previous police experience of the 16 superintending constables appointed in Buckinghamshire between 1850 and 1856 breaks down like this:

Bucks. Superintending Constables, 1850-1856;			16
Former service in county police forces:	13	other:	6
Essex	3	RIC	1
Surrey	2	City of London	1
Herefordshire	2	Men formerly in charge	
Cambridgeshire	1	of Bucks. lock-ups:	4
Northamptonshire	1		

Lancashire	1
Huntingdonshire	1
Denbighshire	2

Source: Buckinghamshire Record Office, Quarter Sessions Volumes, 4 October 1851; 3 January 1854.

31 PP 1852-3 xxxvi, p. 127. Kent General Quarter Sessions, 23 June 1853, reported in 'South Eastern Gazette', 28 June 1853.

32 Kent General Quarter Sessions, 23 June 1853, reported in 'South Eastern Gazette', 28 June 1853. The three years that remained before compulsory policing witnessed a growing conflict between petty sessions and quarter sessions in this county. The main argument was over the development of the constabulary committee of quarter sessions into a kind of county police authority. The right of the petty session to do what it wanted with its own superintendent was asserted in a fight for lock-ups and station houses refused by a retrenching quarter sessions.

33 PP 1852-3, xxxvi, pp. 101-2, p. 162.

34 This was a long-enduring perception of the head constable's role. PP 1898, xxxv, p. 79.

35 PP 1852-3, xxxvi, pp. 119, 104.

36 Hansard, Third Series, 140, pp. 2128-9.

37 PP 1875, xiii, p. 533. E. Hardy, 'How to Repel Invasion: the Rural Police of England an Auxiliary to Rifle Corps' (R. Hardwicke, London, 1859), contains much evidence of John MacHardy's influence, and in 1857 Buckinghamshire magistrates spoke of him as one whose 'opinion was received with the greatest deference by Government'. 'Buckinghamshire Advertiser', 10 January 1857.

38 'I had been eight years inspecting commander of the Coast Guard in different parts of England . . . which I deemed my apprenticeship qualifying me for the chief constableship,' said MacHardy, PP 1852-3, xxxvi, p. 50. He had been much influenced by the ideas of Captain Willis Bowles, Comptroller General of the Coast Guard during the 1830s. Bowles had presented his scheme for turning paid policemen into excise men to the constabulary commissioners in 1839. Chadwick absorbed Bowles's ideas into his own definition of the complete Benthamite policeman, PP 1839, xix, p. 164. MacHardy in his turn presented Chadwick's ideas to the select committee of 1853. For a description of the changing conflict between local and central financing of police forces, see S. E. Finer, 'The Life and Times of Sir Edwin Chadwick' (Methuen, London, 1952), pp. 164-80.

39 Edward M. Spiers, 'The Army and Society' (Longmans, London, 1980), pp. 162-3.

40 PP 1852-3, xxxvi, pp. 50-1. 'The Times', 24 April 1852. Centurion, 'A Few Words on the Militaroy Organisation of Great Britain' (James Ridgeway, London, 1860).

41 Broeker, 'Rural Disorder', p. 143.

42 PP 1852-3, xxxvi, pp. 132, 22.

43 Home Office Circular, 28 March 1855, quoted in Hansard, Third Series, 140, p. 2130.

44 'The Times', 25 March, 5 November 1853.

45 PP 1852-3, xxxvi, p. 102.

46 'The Times', 31 March 1853.

47 Hansard, Third Series, 119, pp. 1226-7.
48 Hugh Cunningham, 'The Volunteer Force' (Croom Helm, London, 1975) pp. 5-13.
49 Ibid., pp. 5-6.
50 Hansard, Third Series, 120, pp. 120, 278.
51 Hansard, Third Series, 122, p. 714. J.W.C, 'The Militia as an Army of Reserve' (Thomas Hatchard, London, 1856).
52 'The Times', Leader, 13 March 1855; 14 April 1854. 'Northampton Herald', 22 April 1854. James Hawker, 'James Hawker's Journal: A Victorian Poacher' (Oxford University Press, London, 1961), p. 3.
53 See pp. 68-79.
54 Hansard, Third Series, 122, p. 2120.
55 Hansard, Third Series, 141, p. 391. 'The Times', 21 August 1856. 'I fear the setting free of so many men who have been made familiar with blood and crime in their military life'; a Buckinghamshire magistrate addressing Epiphany Quarter Sessions, reported in the 'Buckinghamshire Advertiser', 10 January 1857.
56 'The Times', 24 April 1854.
57 Hansard, Third Series, 140, p. 2120.
58 'It would appear from a perusal of the bill . . . that . . . the magistrates were considered to be incompetent, or not of sufficient character.' 'It cast a slur upon the county gentlemen,' Hansard, Third Series, 106, pp. 133, 146.
59 See the evidence of Joseph Sadler, head constable of Stockport, PP 1850, xiii, p. 190.
60 PP 1854, v, p. 467, s. 2-11.
61 'South Eastern Gazette', Leader, 19 February 1856.
62 Philips, 'Crime and Authority', p. 61.
63 Police were finally able to vote at Parliamentary elections in 1887 under 50 & 51 Vict. c.9 and at rural sanitary and school board and other local elections in 1893 (56 & 57 Vict. c.6).
64 Half the municipal corporations in England joined forces to fight the 'subversion of the rights and privileges of popular government'. Cambridge Borough Records, Town Council Minute Book, 15 June 1854; 15 February 1856. Hansard, Third Series, 141, p. 1580. The Local Government Act of 1880 (51 & 52 Vict. c.41) finally provided for the compulsory consolidation of boroughs with populations of under 10,000.
65 'The Times', 18 January 1856.
66 Henry Parris, The Home Office and the Provincial Police, 1856-1870, 'Public Law' (1961), p. 235.
67 See PRO, HO 65/6, out-letters to Kent police committee, May 1859-February 1865, approving plans for the building of improvement of 13 lock-ups and station houses. The Home Office was not a remote rubber stamp; a positive interest was taken in minute details, shown in letters to the county surveyor and the clerk of the peace, dated 5 May, 27 May, 11 June 1863.
68 PRO, HO 65/3, out-letter to Leicester watch committee, 14 August 1857:
    Sir George Grey thinks that the allowance of gratuities by individuals to policemen paid by salary for the discharge of their duty, is open to objection, and is not fair to

those persons unwilling or unable to pay . . . but whose
property is equally entitled with that of others . . . to
protection . . . by a police paid by a general rate.
The same point was made to Reading watch committee in September.

69 Or it may be the case that they were no longer preserved. Home
Office material was frequently 'weeded', and a single document
on an issue that may have prompted a wide correspondence at
the time preserved for reference purposes.

70 PRO, HO 45 65/3, 16 April, 24 April, 1857.

71 PRO HO 65/3, 27 May, 5 June, 20 June, 27 June, 8 July, 2
November 1859. In this last letter which was in reply to a Mr
Baxter of Norwich who had complained to the Home Secretary about
being locked in the cells all night on a false charge of drunkenness, the reply was curt: 'Complaint must be made to the watch
committee. The secretary of state cannot interfere.' But in
June that year George Grey had welcomed correspondence from Hull
on the watch committee's failure to direct its police on the
occasion of a dock fire, though he emphasised that he had 'no
power in such cases.'

72 See below, pp. 44-5.

73 Parris, Home Office and Police, p. 236.

74 PRO, HO 45 OS 7933, 23-5. This relationship, with all its con-
fusions as well as its positive expressions of policy, is well
summarised in a correspondence between the chief constable of
Suffolk and the Home Office. The Home Secretary had expressed
disapproval of the county police patrolling armed with cutlasses
(he knew as well as the Permanent Under Secretary who minuted
the correspondence thus that 'the cutlasses (were) required for
the protection of game'). The chief constable said that 'the
magistrates in general concur that the police ought to be armed,
in which opinion I fully concur . . . but am I to consider your
letter an order?' In response, the Under Secretary of State
just copied out again the relevant portion of his first letter,
and added that there was nothing to prevent 'the police going
armed with the sanction of the justices'. PRO, HO 45 OS 7487.

75 PRO HO 65/3, out-letter dated 7 October 1856. Hansard, Third
Series, 161, p. 1487.

76 PRO, HO 45 OS 6811. 'This gentleman has very grand ideas,'
minuted George Lewis, the then Home Secretary. 'I wish these
chief constables would think more of their staves and less of
their rifles.'

77 Hansard, Third Series, 215, pp. 974-5.

78 National Association for the Promotion of Social Science, 'Transactions', 1875, pp. 321-3. H. A. Bruce speaks here as Lord
Aberdare.

79 Hansard, Third Series, 168, p. 705.

80 PRO, HO 45 OS 7210. Late in 1861 the Home Office received a
spate of petitions from the chief constables of England and
Wales dealing with the same question. The best supported petition, signed by 33 chief constables, asked that the provisions
of a Metropolitan police act that enabled the police to remove
on suspicion 'anything stolen or unlawfully obtained' (2 & 3
Vict. c.47) be extended to the counties. These desires were
codified into a bill: PP 1862, iv, p. 195.

81 Hansard, Third Series, 168, p. 377, p. 580.
82 'Law Times', 29 May 1858, p. 129. PRO HO 45 OS 6647.
83 In Middlesbrough in 1858, a watch committee member was approached
   in the street on the subject of property being stolen from a
   local school, classes being disrupted and police inaction in the
   matter. The complaint formed the basis of a watch committee
   meeting. 'Stockton and Hartlepool Mercury', 17 April 1858.
   The practice is to be seen in other towns: 'Dr Ransom attended
   the meeting and complained of a large bell being thrown at his
   door.' Cambridge Borough Records, Watch Committee Minute Books,
   13 December 1869. The watch committee and its police function
   were seen as one. For the same perception of a town council's
   sanitary powers see E. P. Hennock, Composition of Borough Councils, in Urban History Group, 'The Study of Urban History'
   (Edward Arnold, London, 1968), p. 317.
84 'Cambridge Independent', 7 July 1860.
85 POR HO 45 OS 8323.
86 Horatio Waddington was Permanent Under Secretary at the Home
   Office until his death in 1867. He had the same background in
   professional rural administration that many Home Secretaries
   possessed: he was Recorder of Warwick and Lichfield. Henry
   Parris, 'Constitutional Bureaucracy' (George Allen & Unwin,
   London, 1969), p. 139.
87 Parris, Home Office and Police, p. 235. PRO HO 45 OS 6811.
88 POR HO 45 OS 6810; HO 65/6, out-letter to the chief constable
   of Norfolk: 'providing there is no objection on the part of the
   county authorities, the Secretary of State approves the chief
   constable commanding a force of Volunteers.'
89 PRO HO 45 OS 8110.
90 PRO HO 45 OS 6965.
91 Hansard, Third Series, 68, p. 705.
92 PRO HO 45 OS 7319. Local newspaper cuttings sent to the Home
   Office show that Lincoln's small police force was known by
   name, and their individuality was contrasted with the army-
   like appearance of the county police in the borough.
93 The parliamentary expression of this distinction, and its ex-
   position in the light of current events, is to be found in
   Hansard, Third Series, 185, p. 930. In spite of this careful
   distinction, the Home Office allowed the constitutional impact
   of 'insurrection' to colour local dealings with 'mere riot'.
   There were members of the RIC drafted to Manchester during the
   Fenian disturbances of 1868. One of them, Chief Constable
   Welby, was briefed to investigate the connections between
   Murphyism and Fenianism. He was in direct communication with
   the Home Secretary. PRO, HO 45 OS 7991/48/59.
94 PRO HO 45 OS 8060. This reiteration of an impossible position in
   the Law Officers' opinion (no. 160) struck the Home Secretary
   as being of such clarity that he wanted it issued as a general
   instruction to the police. He was dissuaded by his permanent
   staff.
95 William Murphy's lectures caused a constitutional furore. There
   is a file four inches thick on the more spectacular of his
   activities in the Public Record Office (PRO, HO 45 OS 7991)
   and he occupies dozens of pages in Hansard. Son of Michael

Murphy, master of the National School, Castle Conyers, County
Limerick, he was born on 1 August 1834. He seceded with his
family from the Roman Catholic church (there was a rumour that
his father was stoned in the village street for his action).
Murphy became a scripture reader for the Irish Society and
worked as a cobbler in Dublin. He started lecturing against
the Catholic church in 1863. He died in Birmingham in 1872
from injuries received whilst lecturing in Cumberland. F.
Boase, 'Modern English Biography', supplement, 1908. His
headquarters were in Birmingham, where a 'permanent tent' was
erected. He had strong connections with the Protestant
Electoral Union and the Protestant Evangelical Mission. It's
fairly clear that he received financial support from the
Birkenhead Orangemen. His 'Confessional Unmasked', on the
salacious theme of which he based most of his lectures, was
ruled obscene. For a recent description of Murphyism in the
context of Fenianism, see Patrick Quinlivan and Paul Rose,
'The Fenians in England 1865-1872' (John Caulder, London, 1982),
pp. 33-42.

96 PRO HO 45 OS 7991/26.
97 The yeomanry were only infrequently used by magistrates as a
peace-keeping force in the second half of the nineteenth century. They had earned themselves considerable unpopularity
in the 1840s; see F. C. Mather, 'Public Order in the Age of
the Chartists' (Manchester University Press, Manchester,
1959), pp. 147-8. The Yeomanry had been armed landowners in
defence of their property. See Alan Silver, The Demand for
Order in Civil Societies, in David J. Bordua (ed.), 'The
Police: Six Sociological Essays' (John Wiley, New York, 1967),
pp. 10-12. After the 1850s the Volunteer movement attempted
to harness the defensive energies of the middle classes, and
they were used consistently during the Murphy Riots. Cunningham, 'Volunteer Force', p. 11.
98 PRO HO 45 OS 7991/30; 7991/20/25. See Silver, The demand for
Order, p. 10. In some places, where special constables were
used in the Fenian disturbances or during the Murphy Riots,
they were afterwards formed into proper auxiliary forces with
distinguishing badges and books of instruction. S. P. Thompson, 'Maintaining the Queen's Peace' (Birkenhead, 1958).
99 'The Times', 8 June 1866.
100 'The Times', 10 June 1868.
101 'Manchester Guardian', 28 January 1868. PRO, HO 45 OS 7991/16.
102 'Manchester Guardian', 15 February 1868.
103 As for example in Warrington: 'Manchester Guardian', 17 February 1868.
104 As for example in Wolverhampton in February 1867, when the
lecture hall sheltering Murphy was surrounded by police and
special constables: 'A rush at the door was defeated and
bludgeons taken from the Irish.' The town was cleared within three hours. In Oldham a year later, the protestant
crowd arrived at the Catholic chapel to find it surrounded
by 'a body of police and 300 Irishmen . . . and . . . seeing
the state of affairs, retired'. In Preston in the following
June two dozen policemen attempted to disperse a crowd

estimated to be 2,000-3,000 strong. Failing to do this they set to guarding the Irish quarter of the town from attack. Soon the crowd 'dispersed in frustration.' 'The Times', 25 February 1867; 'Manchester Guardian', 15 February 1868; 6 June 1868.

105 'The Times', 19 June 1867.
106 'Manchester Guardian', 25 April 1868.
107 'Manchester Guardian', 1 May 1868.
108 'Manchester Guardian', 1, 2 September 1868. 'The Times', 7, 8 September 1868.
109 Geoffrey Best, 'Mid-Victorian Britain' (Weidenfield & Nicholson, London, 1971), p. 270.
110 'Manchester Guardian', 2 September 1868.
111 PRO HO OS 7991/26. 'Manchester Guardian', 16 May 1868.
112 PRO HO 45 OS 7991/10. Letters from the mayor of Birmingham dated 18, 19, 20 June 1867. It wasn't until 1886 that people who suffered damage at the hands of rioters had a legal right to compensation from the local police authority. See the Riot Damages Act 1886 (49 £ 40 Vict. c.38)
113 'The Times', 21 June 1867. PRO HO 45 OS 7991/35.
114 PRO HO 45 OS 7991/10. 'The Times', 27 June 1867.
115 'The Times', 27 July 1867.
116 'Manchester Guardian', 12, 17 February 1868. PRO HO 45 OS 7991/59. 'The Times', 17 June 1869; PRO HO 45 OS 7991/63.
117 'The Times', 3 November 1868.
118 J. Anderson MacLaren, The Police Authorities of the United Kingdom: Their Constitution, Revenue and Responsibility at Law, 'Judicial Review', vol. 22 (1910).
119 Hansard, Third Series, 305, p. 2003.
120 Hansard, ibid.; Hansard, Third Series, 303, p. 1317: the law under which provincial towns had to operate until 1882 demanded that they sought compensation from the ancient and defunct figure of the Hundred Chief Constable.
121 Hansard, Third Series, 303, pp. 1317-18.
122 Northamptonshire County Record Office, Cartwright Papers, C(A) 53/173, Memoir of Ensign Busby of the 61st. 'Police Guardian', 27 June 1873.
123 Captain Woodford, former chief constable of Lancashire HMIC for the northern region from 1856-1868, was the nephew of Sir John George Woodford of Keswick, veteran of the Peninsula War and accolite of Sir John Moore. He belonged to the same generation of administrative reformer as Cartwright. Sir John George Woodford, 'Remarks on Military Flogging', 1835; J. Fisher Crossthwaite, 'A Brief Memoir of Major General Sir John George Woodford' (privately printed, London, 1881). Moore's Moral Training and Military Training probably did impress themselves on the provincial police forces of mid-Victorian England, but the route was more circuitous and more firmly based in provincial experience that the idea of a simple dissemination of a Metropolitan model suggests. See Introduction, pp. 4-5.
124 Northamptonshire County Record Office, Cartwright Papers, C(A) 55/12, 13, 15, 16.
125 'Police Guardian', 27 June 1873.

126 Hart, County and Borough Police Act, p. 412.
127 Cartwright knew a great deal about the Essex constabulary, and at one stage, in the 1840s, applied to be chief constable of that county: Northamptonshire County record Office, Cartwright Papers, C(A) 53/179, 180, 183.
128 Buckinghamshire Record Office, Quarter Sessions Records, Epiphany QS, 5 January 1857. 'Buckinghamshire Advertiser', 10 January 1857. Buckinghamshire Record Office, Quarter Sessions Volumes, Report of the Police Committee to QS, 5 January 1857. PP 1857-8, xlvii, p. 662. Hughenden Manor, Disraeli Papers, B/xxi/P299, letter dated 15 December 1856.

In some counties the adoption of the Essex model did not have to depend on the blandishments of any government inspector. Reports of the Kent police committee show, for example, that Essex was continually referred to and communicated with in the winter of 1856-7 without any outside pressure. Kent General Quarter Sessions, Report of the Police Committee, 3 December 1856, 14 April 1857, reported in 'South Eastern Gazette', 9 December 1856, 21 April 1857.

129 Hughendon Manor, Disraeli Papers, B/xxi/P298, letter dated 1 November 1856.
130 'Buckinghamshire Herald', 24 January 1857.
131 PP 1852-3, xxxvi, p. 260.
132 PP 1871, xxviii, p. 349, p. 350. PP 1865, xlv, p. 468.
133 PP 1867, xxxvi, p. 525. PP 1868-9, xxxl, p. 12.
134 PP 1881, li, pp. 9-10.
135 PP 1861, lii, p. 6; PP 1862, xlv, p. 438.
136 PP 1857-8, xlvii, p. 646.
137 PP 1857-8, xlvii, p. 664; PP 1861, lii, p. 660; PP 1862, xlv, p. 440; PP 1868-9, xxxi, p. 13.
138 In his first report to the Home Office, he spoke of the 'great and inevitable changes' that took place in a man's life when he became a policeman.
139 'Police Guardian', 13 June 1873.
140 At the end of his first year of inspection, he told the Home Office that in the county constabularies was a force 'not only sufficient for the protection of property and the prevention of crime, but (also) . . . for a good constitutional force which . . . might be rapidly mustered upon an emergency for the preservation of the peace in any part of the district.' PP 1857-8, xlvii, p. 668. See also PP 1861, lii, pp. 660-1.
141 PP 1861, lii, p. 646.
142 PP 1871, xxviii, pp. 349-50.
143 PP 1872, xxx, p. 7; PP 1877, xlii, p. 115.
144 Hart, County and Borough Police Act, p. 407. Eric Midwinter, 'Social Administration in Lancashire, 1830-1860' (Manchester University Press, Manchester, 1969), p. 173.
145 Huddersfield Improvement Commissioners gave an increase of pay to their police in August 1856 on the grounds that 'the new police act would soon come into force and if they did not raise the wages, the men would probably better themselves.' Huddersfield Improvement Commissioners Meeting, 6 August 1856, reported in the 'Huddersfield Examiner', 9 August 1856. For the same reaction to legislation in Middlesbrough, see

'Stockton and Hartlepool Mercury', 16 August 1856.   Three
months before the government inspector reached them, Sheffield watch committee reorganised its force and recommended
to the town council that 'the resolution of 1844 prohibiting
any member of the police force from . . . being engaged in
any trade or business . . . be strictly enforced.'   Sheffield
Borough Records, Watch Committee Minutes (written), 31
December 1856; 15 January 1856.

146   Middlesbrough Town Council Meeting, 18 November 1856,
reported in the 'Stockton and Hartlepool Mercury', 20 November 1856.

147   PP 1871, xxviii, pp. 349-50.   PRO HO 45 OS 7488.

148   Hansard Third Series, 141, p. 1580.   Cambridge Borough
Records, Town Council Records, Council Minute Book, 15 June
1854; 15 February 1856.   PP 1860, lvii, p. 531; PP 1876,
xxxiv, p. 5.

149   In Cambridge for instance, 'the regular plan in selecting the
(watch) committee . . . was to retain those who had attended
the largest number of times and strike off those who had
attended the fewest so as to infuse a little fresh blood.'
'Cambridge Chronicle', 10 November 1855.   For a similar system in Huddersfield see 'Huddersfield Examiner', 4 October
1856.

150   Cambridge Borough Records, Town Council Records, Council
Minute Book, 1850-1880.   Sheffield Borough Records, Watch
Committee Minute Books, (printed and written), 1850-80.

151   Municipal Corporations Act, 1835 (5 & 6 Will. IV, c.88 s.76).
J. Anderson MacLaren, 'The Police Authorities of the United
Kingdom: their constitution, revenue and responsibility at
law, 'Judicial Review', (vol. 22) (1910), p. 46.

152   Cambridge Borough Records, Watch Committee Minutes, 13 December 1869.

153   'Cambridge Chronicle', 20 September 1856; 26 August 1871.

154   'Cambridge Chronicle', 20 September 1856.

155   Cambridge Licencing Sessions, 24 August 1870, reported in
'Cambridge Chronicle', 27 August 1870: 'two applications for
renewal of licences were held over until the hearing by the
watch committee was completed.'

156   'Cambridge Independent', 13 November 1875.   Magistrates accounted for one fifth to one third of watch committee members between 1856 and 1880.

157   Cambridge Borough Records, Town Council Records, Minute
Books, 29 May 1879.   Stanley Waller, 'Cuffs and Handcuffs'
(Rochdale, 1957).

158   PP 1867, xxxii, p. 405.   Sheffield Borough Records, Newspaper Cuttings Relating to Sheffield, vol. ii, p. 1; Watch
Committee Minutes (written), 22, 29 March, 5, 12 April,
10 May 1860.   S. Pollard, 'Sheffield Outrages', 1971, p. viii.

159   There was criticism in the local press of the secrecy of watch
committee proceedings and the arbitrary way it spent the
rates.   'Sheffield Independent', 8 November 1862; 10 November
1865.   PP 1863, 1, pp. 256-7.

160   'Sheffield Daily Telegraph', 14 February 1867.

161   The particular way that Cambridge watch committee dealt with

licencing offences endured so long precisely because it fitted
into a pre-existing judicial practice. This was not the case
with attempts to make policemen truant officers of school
boards, which was briefly attempted in some areas in the 1870s.
PP 1882, xxxiii, p. 31.

162 Silver, The Demand for Order, p. 21 for the expectations
raised by sanitary policing. See Sheffield Borough Records,
Watch Committee Minute Books (written), for the appointment of
a sub-committee to inquire into street begging, 14 December
1854; for the report of the committee on common lodging houses,
9 October 1856; for the rationalisation of the lodging-house
inspection scheme, 23 August 1860. On the head constable's
work for the Children's Employment Commission (1862), 15 December 1865; for his appointment as borough surveyor, 29 November
1860. This energetic moral and social statistician was cele-
brated by Charles Reade in 'Put Yourself in His Place' (1870).

163 'Sheffield Independent', 8 November 1862. 'If all the details
which had been discussed by the watch committee were to be
gone into again by the whole council, it would be better not
to have a committee but for the council to resolve itself
into one.' Meeting of Hartlepool Town Council, reported in
the 'Stockton and Hartlepool Mercury', 14 June 1857.

164 But this financial autonomy has not been found in Birmingham,
for example. See Barbar Weinberger, 'The Police and the Public
in Mid-Nineteenth Century Warwickshire, in Victor Bailey (ed.),
'Policing and Punishment in Nineteenth Century Britain'
(Croom Helm, London, 1981), p. 79.

165 When it was proposed to amalgamate Hartlepool's force with that
of County Durham a central objection raised at the town council
meeting was the loss it would mean to local businessmen. An
alderman pacified an agitated clothier: 'with regard to the
clothing of the police . . . the supply for the county should be
thrown open to Hartlepool tradesmen.' Town Council Meeting,
1 November 1859, reported in the 'Stockton and Hartlepool Mercury', 5 November 1859.

166 The Homd Office had to remind the chief constable of Kent of
this point when he wanted to appoint Volunteers as Additional
Constables. PRO HO 65/6, out-letter dated 3 March 1858.

167 Northamptonshire Quarter Sessions, 4 July 1855, reported in
the 'Northamptonshire Mercury', 7 July 1855. 'One inspector
and 24 constables are maintained at the expense of the Mersey
Dock and Harbour Boards and Companies for dock duty, and two
are employed by Messrs. Laird at their works.' A detective
sergeant was employed by the Macclesfield Silk Association.
PP 1868-9, xxxi, pp. 82-3. Eton college kept and paid for a
permanently stationed member of the Buckinghamshire constabulary. Buckinghamshire Record Office, Constabulary
Records, Register of Members of the Force, passim. There
was an 'additional' at Messrs Bagnall, Golds Heath, Staffordshire from 1863 to 1882, and another at the Moat Colliery,
Tipton, from 1863 to 1876. Staffordshire Record Office,
Constabulary Records, 'Register of Members of the Force',
passim.

168 Meeting of Middlesbrough Town Council, 14 December 1858,

reported in the 'Stockton and Hartlepool Mercury', 18 December 1858.

169   'Cambridge Independent', 7 July 1860, where the local press made no distinction between the head constable and the watch committee.

170   Meeting of Huddersfield Improvement Commissioners, 6 June 1855, reported in the 'Huddersfield Examiner', 9 June 1855. 'Huddersfield Examiner', 7 November 1857. Anderson Maclaren, Police Authorities of the United Kingdom, p. 46.

171   Buckinghamshire Record Office, Quarter Sessions Volumes, Midsummer QS, 1850; Michaelmas QS, 1856.

172   The average length of service of county chief constables appointed after 1856 was 24 years. Six of them served for over 30 years, and two of them for over 40 years.

173   Staffordshire Record Office, Quarter Sessions Records, QS Bundles, Q AC P.11, Applications for the Position of Chief Constable. Major Congreve got the job.

174   Staffordshire Quarter Sessions, 2 July 1866, reported in the 'Staffordshire Advertiser', 7 July 1866. Kent Quarter Sessions police committee consisted of the Lord Lieutenant, the Earl of Romsey, the two chairmen of quarter sessions for the east and west divisions of the county, and one magistrate from each petty sessional division. Kent General Quarter Sessions, 13 January 1857, reported in the 'South Eastern Gazette', 20 January 1857.

175   Home Office out-letter dated 27 January 1873, quoted in the 'Police Guardian', 25 April 1873.

176   Buckinghamshire Advertiser, 7 February 1857.

177   Buckinghamshire Record Office, Quarter Sessions Records, QS Rolls, 17 February 1857. Carrington Papers, D/CN/CI a, letter dated 1 July 1857.

178   The same change was seen in Northumberland in 1869, in the East Riding in 1872, and in Staffordshire in 1867. In Staffordshire ex-members of the Royal Irish Constabulary had been relied upon for chief constables since the creation of the force in 1842. In Warwickshire in 1876 J. H. Kinchant of Park Hall, Shropshire, justice of the peace and sometime sheriff took the place of Mr Isaac, formerly of the Metropolitan police. John Bateman, 'Great Landowners of Great Britain' (Harrison, London, 1878).

179   It was through the exercise of this autonomy that many magistrates learned that chief constables were 'a dangerous set of men'. Hansard, Third Series, 215, pp. 974-5. PRO HO 45 OS 6811.

180   Kent General Quarter Sessions, 14 April, 29 October 1857, reported in the 'South Eastern Gazette', 21 April, 3 November 1857: 'The chief constable said that he had the authority of the Government Inspector for stating the hats of the force were "rubbish".'

181   Some county magistrates obviously did believe that the 'new' compulsory police was intended as a substitute for the magistracy, on the model of the RIC. Kent General Quarter Sessions, 9 December 1856, reported in the 'South Eastern Gazette', 23 December 1856.

182 Buckinghamshire Record Office, Quarter Sessions Records, QS
     Rolls, 17 February 1857.
183 The routine of county administration demanded a close relation-
     ship between magistrates and policemen. Many magistrates found
     that the new county constabulary was unwilling to perform the
     work of the old parish constables. This body of men, in recent
     years reviled as 'live lumber', and 'perfectly useless',
     enjoyed a new flowering of status in the years after 1856.
     Tensions between magistrates and the new police hierarchy
     were frequently to do with the execution of warrants: 'Are
     the police not under the orders of the magistrates at all
     times? Are they not bound to serve summonses and execute
     warrants? A few days past I put an affiliation order in the
     hands of the police constable, but he said he was under the
     orders of the superintendents not to serve them' 'South
     Eastern Gazette', 20 April 1856. The chief constable of
     Somerset ordered his men not to serve summonses for payment
     of land and assessed taxes as the parish constables had
     formerly done. PRO, HO 45 OS 7361.
184 Median figures compiled from the reports of HMIC, PP 1859
     (Session I), xxii, p. 339; PP 1868-9, xxxi, p. 2; PP 1878-9,
     xxxiii, p. 1.
185 Non-perambulatory policeman represented 7% of Buckingham-
     shire's force, 8% of Leicestershire's force, and 7% of War-
     wickshire's force in 1868. See also Marquis of Anglesey
     (ed.), 'Sergeant Pearman's Memoirs' (Jonahan Cape, London,
     1968), p. 119.
186 County representative sitting on the Select Committee on
     Habitual Drunkards, PP 1872, ix, p. 488.
187 In County Durham in 1877, there was a policeman to 'every
     considerable village;' they were not attached to 'very small
     villages . . . one policeman to two or three villages per-
     haps, in the country parts.' PP 1877, xi, p. 667.
188 A town or village that might be called a communications
     centre can be defined like this: on a main road, or a canal;
     no more than two miles by road from a railway halt; possess-
     ing a post office. Using this rough description then, it is
     clear that the police were dispersed to make use of this
     system of communications:
     Leicestershire, 1868

| Villages with police: | 67 | Without police: | 224 |
| Communications centres: | 31 | Communications centres: | 19 |

     Source: 'Police and Constabulary Almanac', 1868; White,
     'Directory . . . of Leicestershire', 1863, 1877.

189 19 & 20 Vict. c.69 s.8.
190 PP 1875, xiii, p. 457. 'The effect has been in a great many
     cases to deter fair traders from bringing their weights and
     measures to be adjusted, owing to their apprehension that
     they might be summoned for having them incorrect.' Hansard,
     Third Series, 216, p. 1085.
191 Northamptonshire Record Office, Police Journals, ML 202-12,
     Journal of Inspector George Williamson, entry for 5 April
     1866.

192   PP 1857-8, xxviii, pp. 239-240; PP 1847-8, liii, p. 249.

193   See above, pp. 15-16.

194   PRO HO 45 OS 7933/23-25.

195   PP 1866, xxiv, p. 87; PP 1868-9, xiii, p. 27, p. 94, p. 229;
       PP 1871 vii, p. 689.

196   'The police fancied it was their duty not to afford assistance
       to the trader but rather to detect anything they could by way
       of irregularity.' Hansard, Third Series, 216, p. 1085.

197   PRO HO Circulars No. 86740, 6 September 1870; No. 16414a,
       13 December 1873.

198   Buckinghamshire Record Office, Constabulary Records, letter
       from Sir Harry Verney to the chief constable, dated 29 Novem-
       ber 1871.

199   A precedent had been set for this police autonomy by their
       activity during the cattle plague of the mid-1860s. They had
       then been directed by the Privy Council, completely by-passing
       the traditional adminstrative channels of the county. PP
       1867, xxxvi, p. 423, p. 585.

200   The Old Metal Dealers Act of 1861 (24 & 25 Vict. c.110) marked
       the beginning of this process. It affected very few county
       constabularies, but its requirements that local police forces
       keep a register of convictions under it not only set the pat-
       tern for later enactments, but also taught local forces about
       the power inherent in statistical surveillance.

201   Sratford Borough Records, Police Books B1, Superintendent's
       Report Book, 1876, Report to the Watch Committee dated 7
       November 1876.

202   Police Expenses Act, 1874 (37 & 38 Vict. c.58).

203   The Local Government Act of 1888 did not completely sever the
       magistrate's administrative from his judicial function, for
       management of the county police was passed over to a board
       that was only half composed of elected ratepayers — the other
       half were magistrates. However, this change did provide a way
       of analysing the declining powers of justices in police mat-
       ters. Redlich and Hirst, 'Local Government', vol. ii, pp.
       71-2.

204   Jacques Donzelot, 'The Policing of Families', 1979, pp. 6-7.
       pp. 23-5. F. W. Maitland, 'Justice and Police', 1885, p. 115.

205   'The Times', 14 January, 22, 29 February, 14, 20, 21, 22
       March, 18 April, 21, 22 May, 27 June, 12 July, 7 August, 21
       November, 20 December, 1980; 21 January, 13, 23 February, 1981.
       'New Statesman', 13 February, 1981. Sections 3 and 4 of the
       Vagrancy Act were regarded in October 1982: 30 & 31 Eliz. II,
       c.48, s.70 (Criminal Justice Act, 1982).

206   PP 1872, ix, p. 550: the head constables of Leeds and Sheffield
       both suggested that a man should be committed to prison for
       three months of his third conviction — 'And so on, through the
       rest of his life? — 'If he continued the drunkenness.' — 'You
       would incarcerate him for life?' — 'I should say that he would
       incarcerate himself.'

207   See PP 1861, vii, pp. 187-8 regarding 17 & 18 Vict. c.86 and
       20 & 21 Vict. c.48 which extended the term vagrant to destitute
       children. Vagrancy Amendment Acts, 1868 and 1872 (31 & 32
       Vict. c.52; 36 & 37 Vict. c.38).

208 Northamptonshire Quarter Sessions, 9 April 1856, reported in
     the 'Northants Mercury', 12 April 1856.
209 See above, p. 25. 19 & 20 Vict. c.69, Preamble.
210 Northamptonshire County Records, Poor Law records, Brackley
     Union, PL/47; PL1/1, out-letters, Brackley Board of Guardians,
     15 June 1835, Minute Book, 1, 22 July 1835.
211 Northamptonshire County Records, Ppor Law Records, Brackley
     Union, PL1/3; PL1/4, Brackley Board of Guardians Minute Book,
     24 February 1841, 9 October 1844. The Brackley Plan of
     Parochial Watch is described in a letter to the 'Northants.
     Herald', 4 February 1836.
212 Northamptonshire County Records, Poor Law Records, Brackley
     Union, PL1/47; PL1/4; out-letters, Brackley Board of Guardians,
     30 March 1841; Brackley Board of Guardians Minute Book, 13
     March 1844, 1 May 1844, 22 May 1844, 18 September 1844.
213 'Until some regular system is adopted (and) indiscriminate
     relief witheld . . . the drone will live upon the bee and
     mendicancy will thrive.' PP 1867-8, xxxvi, pp. 7-8; PP 1868-9,
     xxxi, pp. 8-9. 'Transactions' of the National Association for
     the Promotion of Social Science, 1867, pp. 232 f.
214 PP 1867, xxxvi, pp. 422-3; PP 1866 xxxiv, p. 636, p. 653.
     Ticket-of-way No. 353 was issued in the name of Harry Smith
     'labourer', 'and wife', at Stow in the Wold Union, and left
     behind in Stratford police station in 1882, as they made
     their way through Warwickshire to Birmingham. They spent 28
     hours in Stow detained by the worktask and were supplied with
     2 lb of bread by Sergeant Packer at the police station in
     Moreton-in-the-Marsh. Harry Smith was described in great
     detail on his pass. Stratford Borough Records, Police Books,
     unclassified material.
215 PP 1866, xxxiv, pp. 6-8.
216 PP 1866, xxxv, p. 638.
217 PP 1876, xxxv, p. 7.
218 PP 1867-8, xxxvi, p. 7.
219 PP 1866, xxxiv, pp. 6-8.
220 See also PP 1866, xxxv, p. 636, p. 653.
221 PP 1906, ciii, p. 124.
222 K. B. Smellie, 'A History of Local Government' (George Allen
     & Unwin, London, 1946), pp. 66-7.
223 Hansard, Third Series, 49, p. 1385: 'rates should be collected
     in parishes and townships so as to adopt the expense to the
     actual wants of districts. Some parishes do not require
     police . . . hard to make them pay for the wants of others.'
224 Smellie, 'Local Government', p. 66.
225 Webb, 'Parish and County, p. 4, pp. 40-1.
226 Smellie, 'Local Government', p. 67.
227 PP 1834, xvi, p. 239.
228 PP 1834, xvi, p. 239.
229 PP 1852-3, xxxvi, p. 200.
230 See above, p. 27.
231 Hansard, Third Series, 140, p. 2115, p. 2116. See also PP
     1852-3, xxxvi, p. 65, p. 68, p. 69.
232 Philips, 'Crime and Authority', p. 241.
233 The Night Poaching Prevention Act was in fact a substitute for

a much more sweeping piece of legislation proposed in the early
1860s that offered greatly increased powers to policemen to
arrest on suspicion. It was also proposed in this bill to
give powers of arrest to property owners and their servants.
PP 1862, iv, p. 195. This bill got no further than its first
reading, but many of its clauses were incorporated into the
Night Poaching Prevention Act. PRO HO 45 OS 7210.

PART TWO   MEN AND POLICEMEN

1   PP 1867, xxxii, p. 821. 'Sheffield Independent', 17, 19
    February 1859.

    Watch Committee Membership in Sheffield, 1854-81

	Individual members:	75
	%	No.
Iron and steel interest		
Merchant manufacturers	7	(5)
Specialised manufacturers	25	(19)
Other interest		
Manufacturers in other metals	8	(6)
Manufacturers (non-metal)	4	(3)
Merchants (non-metal)	13	(10)
Shopkeepers	11	(8)
Publicans	4	(3)
Brewers	3	(2)
Corn merchants	3	(2)
Pawnbrokers	4	(3)
Solicitors	4	(3)
Auctioneers	2	(1)
Managers	3	(2)
Physicians	7	(5)
'Gent.'/unknown	3	(2)

    Source: Sheffield Borough Records, Watch Committee Minutes,
    (written), 1856-67. 'Business Directory of Sheffield', 1862.
    W. White, 'General Directory . . . of the Borough of Sheffield',
    1864; 'General and Commercial Directory of Sheffield', 1871.

2   PP 1867, xxxii, pp. 821-825, and directories listed above.

CHAPTER 2 — MAKING A COUNTY FORCE

1   For a description of the county of Staffordshire from the point
    of view of policing it, see David Philips, 'Crime and Authority
    in Victorian England' (Croom Helm, London, 1977), p. 170.
2   Many county constabulary records are still held by the police
    force of that area.
3   Most county police registers would seem to contain the more
    limited information of the Staffordshire records. Borough

police records are usually harder to trace than those of the
county forces.
4   Philips, 'Crime and Authority', p. 77.
5   PP 1875, xiii, p. 447.
6   For a description of the superintending system, see above
pp. 19-21.
7   T. A. Critchley, 'A History of the Police in England and
Wales 900-1966' (Constable, London, 1967), p. 145.
8   PP 1875, xiii, p. 456. Neil Osborn, 'The Story of the Hertfordshire Constabulary' (Letchworth, 1969), p. 43.
9   PP 1875, xiii, p. 499.
10   S. Pearson, 'The Lincolnshire Constabulary' (Lincoln, 1957)
p. 8.
11   By 1880 the police clerk of Staffordshire was entering more men
as 'agricultural labourers'. A change in self-perception was
taking place at the time due to the work of the Agricultural
Labourers Union. Seé W. Hasbach, 'A History of the English
Agricultural Labourer' (P. S. King, London, 1908), pp. 253-4.
Hasbach noted that in the 1860s, 'the number of persons
describing themselves merely as "labourers" (had) increased.'
12   The total here is greater than the number of recruits because
some men had more than one period of public service behind
them. In this year of formation Buckinghamshire employed
proportionately twice as many men who had had previous public
service as did Staffordshire in 1856. The gentry were thicker
on the ground in Buckinghamshire, and the village labourer from
that county did not escape the Militia fervour of the mid-1850s
as his counterpart in Staffordshire seems to have done. Throughout the next thirty years men with previous public service
formed a much smaller percentage of recruits in Staffordshire.
13   Philips, 'Crime and Authority', p. 170.
14   The high proportion of Irish-born recruits to the Staffordshire
force in the 18 0s had certainly dropped by 1856. Philips,
'Crime and Authority', p. 73.
15   Sheffield Borough Records, Town Council Minutes (printed) 10
February, 1875.
16   Until 1867 all of Staffordshire's chief constables were former
members of the RIC.
17   I am grateful to John Wilson, formerly of the Politics Department, the University of Edinburgh, for giving me enough information by name and birthplace to decide whether or not these
Irish recruits were Roman Catholics.

CHAPTER 3 — ORIGINS

1   PP 1877, xv, p. 152.
2   John Pearman, Memos. of Late Sergeant John Pearman of H. Mgt.
3rd Kings own Light Dragoons, pp. 189-91. This document is
still in the private possession of the Pearman family. Part
of it was published in 1968: Marquess of Anglesey, 'Sergeant
Pearman's Memoirs' (Jonathan Cape, London, 1968). Much of
John Pearman's reflection on his life as worker, soldier and
policeman was omitted in this edition on the grounds that it

was rambling, 'radical', and that 'in old age Pearman became excessively class conscious.' Anglesey, 'Sergeant Pearman', pp. 14, 17, 64, 131. References here are to the original document, and John Pearman's spelling and syntax is preserved. However, where a transcript is available in the published selection from the memoir, then that is also indicated. Some of the commentry on a working life here reproduced can be found in Anglesey, 'Sergeant Pearman', pp. 127-9. John Pearman had not served in the Crimea before joining the Buckinghamshire Constabulary, but worked as Riding Master at Sandhurst. His family believe that he had been promised a commission after the war and when it was not forthcoming he bought himself out. See Anglesey, 'Sergeant Pearman', pp. 116-17.

3 PP 1864, xxxv, pp. 600-29. 90% of Bradford's force were married in 1863, 77% of Liverpool's (and this a borough that maintained large barracks for single men), 88% of Nottingham's and 66% of Bristol's.

4 See above, p. 70, and note.

5 There is some evidence that many more agricultural labourers applied to be policemen than were accepted: 'Scores of (them) apply who can't even write their names', said Superintendent Leaper of the Lincolnshire Constabulary in 1867. PP 1867-8, xvii, p. 307. See also PP 1868-9, xiii, p. 110, 146.

6 PP 1875, xiii, p. 499.

7 PP 1875, xiii, pp. 535-6, 540, 441.

8 PP 1875, xiii, p. 540.

9 PP 1875, xiii, p. 441.

10 F. G. Heath, 'The English Peasantry' (F. Warne, London, 1874) p. 153.

11 PP 1875, xiii, p. 499.

12 The relative gentleness with which such 'respectable' recruits were treated does not support the view that police authorities recognised that 'the use of social and economic superiors as police exacerbated rather than mollified class violence'. Alan Silver, The Demand for Order in Civil Society, in David J. Bordua, 'The Police: Six Sociological Essays' (Wiley, New York, 1967), p. 10. But recruits like these were rare.

13 George Ewart Evans, 'Where Beards Wag All' (Faber, London, 1970), pp. 235-6.

14 PP 1875, xiii, p. 505.

15 Many chief constables who saw in their army of drilled and smartened farm labourers the vision of an army of right, had learned their vision from the provincial rhetoric with which magistrates accepted or rejected paid police forces in the 1830s and 1840s. See above, pp. 18-19. See Robert Reiner, 'The Blue Coated Worker' (Cambridge University Press, Cambridge, 1978), p. 6 on 'the conservative perspective which regards a military model as the most suitable for the police . . .'

CHAPTER 4 — BECOMING A POLICEMAN

1 In these calculations the formula 'allowed to resign' has been
   counted as a dismissal. Being allowed to resign meant that a
   policeman could legally seek employment in another county force.
   Being dismissed meant that future employment in the counties
   (though not the boroughs) was barred to him. 'Allowed to
   resign' meant that, as with dismissal, a police authority was
   dissatisfied with a man.
2 PP 1875, xiii, p. 433.
3 It was not until 1876 that a government inspector found a formula for this common practice: 'many men enter the police force
   intentionally for a short time because they cannot at the
   moment obtain other occupation.' PP 1877, xlii, p. 208.
   Before this, conventional wisdom among the inspectorate had had
   it that low wages and uncertain pensions were responsible for
   high turnover.
4 Head constables of Chester and Sheffield, PP 1875, xiii, pp.
   453, 441.
5 Sheffield Borough Records, Watch Committee Minutes (printed),
   head constable's report, 10 February 1875.
6 R. D. Storch, The Policeman as Domestic Missionary: Urban
   Discipline and Domestic Culture in Northern England, 1850-1880,
   'Journal of Social History', vol. 4 (Summer 1976), p. 487.
7 PP 1875, xiii, p. 554.
8 Three of them are unaccounted for in the Staffordshire records.
9 Northamptonshire Records Office, Miscellaneous Records, Police
   Journals, ML202-12.
10 Northamptonshire Quarter Sessions, 2 July 1856, reported in the
   'Northamptonshire Mercury', 5 July 1856.
11 PP 1867-8, xvii, p. 307.
12 Stratford Borough Records, Police Records, Police Books D,
   Police Officers' Report Book, November 1865-December 1866.
13 Gilbert Turrall had previously worked in Kent in its superintending constable system. His early start at the career
   of policeman suggests that he was one of the yeoman policemen
   the chief constables complained were rare in the second half
   of the century. Kent General Quarter Sessions, 9, 29 October
   1857, reported in the 'South Eastern Gazette', 3 November 1857.
   Cambridge Borough Records, Watch Committee Records, Minute
   Books, passim.
14 'Sheffield Daily Telegraph', 19 March 1862.
15 PP 1867, xxxii, pp. 827-8.

CHAPTER 5 — A POLICEMAN'S LIFE

1 This was particularly the practice of very large forces, like
   those of Liverpool, Birmingham and Manchester.
3 Jabez Webb represents the ideal-type of nineteenth-century
   policeman. He was a former farm labourer, a native of Buckinghamshire.
3 PP 1867-8, xxxvi, p. 9.
4 By the time John Pearman could drink openly in a public house,

he was an inspector and had been two years stationed at Eton.
In 1866 one of his children caught scarlet fever and he was
asked by the Master of Eton to remove himself and his family
until the infectious stage was over. He could not find any-
one willing to transport them: 'they said no one would ride
in it after us and the students was to come back in two days
Mr F. Bunce of the Turks Head Eton see how I was fixed when
(I) . . . went to the bar to have some Gin . . .' John
Pearman, Memos. of John Pearman, pp. 158, 218. Marquess of
Anglesey, 'Sergeant Pearman's Memoirs' (Jonathan Cape, London,
1968), pp. 125-7.

5   As were agricultural labourers in many parts of the country.
    PP 1868-9, 1, pp. 37-9, 241, 296. 'On duty to Titmarsh
    making inquiry whether Constable Ball is in debt and I find
    that he is.' Northamptonshire Record Office, Miscellaneous
    Records, Police Journals, M 202-12, Journal of Inspector
    Williamson, 5 December 1866.
6   Meeting of the Huddersfield Improvement Commissioners, 6 June
    1855, reported in the 'Huddersfield Examiner', 9 June 1855.
7   'Police Guardian', 29 October 1875.
8   Cambridge Borough Records, Watch Committee Records, Minutes,
    29 September 1869.
9   PP 1875, xiii, p. 553.
10 Policemen did use the railway police as a point of comparison
    in other matters: 'the Manchester, Sheffield and Lincs. Rail-
    way Co. has granted the privilege of a day of rest to its police.'
    'Police Service Advertiser', 13 October 1866; letter from '1st
    Class Constable'. On railway workers' pensions, see Frank
    McKenna, 'The Railway Workers' (Faber, London, 1980), p. 43;
    Philip S. Bagwell, 'The Railwaymen: The History of the National
    Union of Railwaymen' (George Allen & Unwin, London, 1963),
    pp. 61, 76, 597; P. H. J. H. Gosden, 'Friendly Societies in
    England 1815-1875' (Manchester University Press, Manchester,
    1961), pp. 87-8.
11 'Police Service Advertiser', 27 April 1867.
12 PP 1875, xiii, p. 499 and p. 432.
13 John Pearman, Memos . . ., p. 157. Anglesey, 'Sergeant Pear-
    man', p. 120.
14 PP 1866, lviii, p. 585f.
15 PP 1875, xiii, p. 432.
16 'Police Service Advertiser', 17 April, 1866; letter from 'A
    Constable'.
17 'Police Service Advertiser', 7 April 1866.
18 PP 1875, xiii, p. 426.
19 PP 1875, xiii, p. 447.
20 PP 1875, xiii, p. 423.
21 'Police Service Advertiser', 27 April 1867; letter from 'A
    Police Constable and One that Feels a Smart'.
22 'Police Service Advertiser', 11 May 1867; letter from 'D.C.C'.
23 'Police Guardian', 29 October 1875.
24 John Pearman, Memos . . . ., p. 189.
25 'Huddersfield Examiner', 7 November 1857.
26 'Whenever policemen get five or six miles from Huddersfield they
    are no longer policemen . . . when they went to Sessions and

Assizes they considered it a holiday and they were not altogether on duty.' 'Huddersfield Examiner', 7 November 1857.

CHAPTER 6 — 'AN ENTIRELY NEW SITUATION'

1 The head constable of Birmigham, speaking in 1875, PP 1875,
  xiii, p. 426. 'Rules and Regulations of the Derbyshire
  Constabulary', 1857.
2 'Police Service Advertiser', 27 April 1867.
3 'Police Service Advertiser', 11 May 1867.
4 Ibid.
5 'Police Service Advertiser', 27 April 1867.
6 John Pearman, Memos. of John Pearman, p. 208.
7 ' . . . the children was always clean and fit to be seen';
  Pearman, Memos . . ., p. 210.
8 'Police Service Advertiser', 16 January 1869; letter from 'A
  Constable's Grateful But Invalid Wife'.
9 'Police Service Advertiser', 14 April 1869, and following
  issues.
10 'Professionalism for the police has meant the attempt to completely extirpate their ties to working class communities,'
   Cyril D. Robinson, The De-Radicalisation of the Policeman:
   A Historical Analysis, 'Crime and Delinquency', vol. 24
   (April 1978), p. 151.
11 At an earlier date, before barrack accommodation was built,
   it was usual to put constables into lodgings for their training
   period: the plan 'that candidates on joining should remain a
   month or more at headquarters to receive instruction . . . has
   never really been carried out . . . all the candidates are
   obliged to lodge about the town . . . very detrimental to good
   order and regularity,' Northamptonshire Quarter Sessions, 2
   January 1856, reported in the 'Northamptonshire Mercury',
   5 January 1856.
12 PP 1875, xiii, p. 432.
13 'Police Service Advertiser', 5 March 1866.
14 Cambridge Borough Records, Watch Committee Records, Minutes,
   passim.
15 William Plomer (ed.), 'Kilvert's Diaries, 1870-1879', 3 vols,
   1938-42. See entries for 25, 29 June 1871. Information on
   wives' earnings as auxiliary policemen is to be found in the
   annual reports of Her Majesty's Inspectors of Constabulary.
16 Flora Thompson, 'Lark Rise to Candleford' (Oxford University
   Press, London, 1965), p. 553.
17 'White Rose: Journal of the West Riding Constabulary' (16),
   1956. This particular General Order was issued in 1892.
18 PP 1875, xiii, p. 491. Inspector Hartley of the Sunderland
   Borough Police, whose words these are, left county employment for this very reason.
19 John Pearman, Memos . . ., pp. 153-8. Marquess of Anglesey,
   'Sergeant Pearman's Memoirs', 1968, pp. 119-21. Buckinghamshire Record Office, Constabulary Records, Register of Members of the Force, 1857-.
20 Before divisional systems of working were established, the

chain of command between a central police office and a patrolling policeman might become very stretched, even in a small
place. Living on a town beat was designed to make communication between policeman and officer easier.

21 Buckinghamshire Record Office, Constabulary Records, General
Order Book, Order dated 12 December 1857.

22 Days of rest that were instituted before this were negotiated
locally, and granted as a concession.

23 R. D. Storch, The Policeman as Domestic Missionary: Urban
Discipline and Domestic Culture in Northern England, 1850-
1880, 'Journal of Social History', vol. 4 (Summer 1976),
p. 481.

24 It was in any case officers who were detailed off to attend
fetes and feasts, at least in the counties. Northamptonshire
Record Office, Miscellaneous Records, Police Journals, ML
202-12, Journal of Inspector George Williamson, entry for
4 June 1866: '10 p.m.-2.30 a.m., Patrolled the neighbourhood
of Thrapston and Islip and attended to a club feast at Islip
all passed off quiet . . . .'

25 Buckinghamshire Record Office, Constabulary Records, General
Order Book, General Order, March 1857.

26 Inspector Manging, 'The First Hundred Years of the North
Riding of Yorkshire Constabulary' (Northallerton, 1956).

27 Ian A. Watt, 'A History of the Hampshire and Isle of White
Constabulary, 1839-1966' (Winchester, 1967).

28 Northamptonshire Record Office, Miscellaneous Records, Police
Journals, ML 202-12, Journal of Inspector George Williamson;
the entry for 1 July 1866 records chapel attendance.

29 'Police Service Advertiser', 29 December 1866. Major Cart-
wright, who played an important role in the opening of this
orphanage, was a staunch member of the Northamptonshire
Society for the Promotion of Education in Accordance with the
Principles of the Established Church. 'Police Guardian', 27
June 1873.

30 Staffordshire Record Office, Quarter Sessions Records, Quarter
Sessions Bundle QAC P.11, Applications for the Position of
Chief Constable.

31 PRO HO 45 OS 7991/29, telegram from Murphy to Home Secretary,
24 April 1868: 'cannot get protection from Popish Superintendent. Will not let police do duty.'

32 'The Times', 28 November, 11 December 1868.

33 Sick policemen were usually swiftly dismissed: 'if they have
a slow disease they are discharged under 15 years . . .',
that is, without a pension, but perhaps with a gratuity. PP
1877, xv, p. 132.

34 PP 1877, xv, p. 141.

35 PP 1877, xv, p. 153.

36 PP 1875, xiii, p. 478. Constable James Chambers of the Hertfordshire Constabulary is speaking here.

37 PP 1875, xiii, p. 478, p. 491.

38 PP 1875, xiii, p. 498.

39 Stratford Borough Records, Police Records, Police Books, B1,
Superintendent's Report Book.

40 Northamptonshire Record Office, Miscellaneous Records, Police

Journals, ML 202-12, Journal of Inspector Williamson. One of his constables found it a long working day: 'met Cons. Ball found him fast asleep at the point and snoring his lamp stood by his side and after standing by him for some few minutes I picked up his lamp and brought it home with me he knowing nothing about it'; entry for 23 January 1866.

41 Buckinghamshire Record Office, Constabulary Records, General Order Book, 22 February 1859, 8 October 1861.

42 'Police Service Advertiser', 27 April 1867.

43 Sheffield Borough Records, Watch Committee Minutes (written), 20 December 1855. PP 1876 xxxiv, p. 116f.

44 PP 1875, xiii, p. 478.

45 'Police Service Advertiser', 17 March 1866.

46 PP 1875, xiii, p. 477.

47 The Hertfordshire constabulary had the reputation of being a little odd. The chief constable selected all his men from the county and frowned upon their leaving: 'we have never had a constable leave our force to join another . . . Colonel Robertson selects them all . . . the men do not leave two in a year . . . I fancy the chief constable would not like the men to leave his force.' PP 1875, xiii, p. 456, evidence of Superintendent George Cockeridge of the Hertfordshire Constabulary.

48 'Sheffield Daily Telegraph', 1 March 1867.

CHAPTER 7 — SECURITY: THE CAMPAIGN FOR POLICE PENSION RIGHTS

1 John Pearman, Memos . . . Late Sergeant Pearman, p. 208. John Pearman's receipt of a good pension is confirmed in Buckinghamshire Record Office, Constabulary Records, 'Register of Members of the Force'. John Pearman was 38 when he joined the Buckinghamshire Constabulary in 1857, considerably older than the average recruit. He had a motive that was not considered usual among younger, temporary policemen. See above, pp. 110-11.

2 'Police Service Advertiser', 6 October 1866. Policemen drew surprisingly few analogies between their position and that of certain groups of pensioned railway servants.

3 PP 1875, xiii, p. 553.

4 'Police Service Advertiser', 19 May 1866; letter from 'No Name', 9 June 1866.

5 PP 1875, xiii, p. 491.

6 PP 1875, xiii, p. 427.

7 'The Police Service Advertiser: Journal for the Police and Constabulary Services of Great Britain and the Colonies' was published weekly at Windsor, Berkshire, by Thomas Fell Molyneux. It became the 'Police Guardian' in 1873. It was first intended to be a professional journal serving the interests of prison wardens, chaplains and directors of industrial schools. Its domestic news was slanted towards the more sensational court cases, and it provided information on new statutes and gave notice of the circuit of judges. In its correspondence column it provided a forum for all levels of complaint about police life. Its editor was a fervent supporter of super-

annuation campaigns. By the 1870s it was almost an institution, and in May 1869 the chief constable of Gloucestershire wrote to the editor asking if his journal might help in the detection of crime — by describing for instance the way in which 'notorious' burglars operated. In the 1870s it started to publish more law cases, and offered the advice of a barrister to correspondents. Molyneux was interviewed by the elect committee on Police Superannuation, PP 1875, xiii, p. 459.

8   'Police Service Advertiser' 12 May 1866; letter from 'Verdad'.
9   Ibid.
10 'Police Service Advertiser', 19 May 1866.
11 'Police Service Advertiser', 18 August 1866.
12 'Police Service Advertiser', 2, 18 March, 24 April, 14 May, 8 June, 13, 27 July, 13 August, 14 September, 1867; 2 January, 19 June, 1869; 21 June 1870. Figures for all transactions of the PMAA, 1867-77, are given in the 'Police Guardian', 22 June 1877.

Members of the PMAA, 1867-77:

	Counties	Boroughs	TOTAL
29 September 1867	2,152	962	3,114
30 June 1870	3,470	1,916	5,386
30 June 1877	3,871	3,179	7,050

13 'Police Service Advertiser' 21 August 1867; 19 June 1869.
14 'Police Service Advertiser', 7 September 1867.
15 'Police Service Advertiser', 19 August 1870, 28 October 1870.
16 'Police Service Advertiser', 6 October 1866.
17 'Police Guardian', 23 February 1877.
18 'Police Service Advertiser', 6 October 1866.
19 'Police Service Advertiser', 4 May 1867; letter from 'Fourth Class Constable'.
20 'Police Service Advertiser', 1 July 1870.
21 'Police Service Advertiser', 9 March 1867.
22 PP 1875, xiii, p. 410.
23 'Police Service Advertiser', 24 February 1866; letter from 'Verdad'.
24 'Police Service Advertiser', 17 April 1866; letter from 'Borough H.C.'.
25 'Police Service Advertiser', 22 May 1869.
26 'Police Service Advertiser', 29 May 1869; leading article.
27 'Police Service Advertiser', ibid.
28 'Police Service Advertiser', 19 June 1869; from the Petition of the Wakefield Borough Police to the Home Secretary.
29 'Police Service Advertiser' 26 June 1869; letter from 'Freedom.'
30 'Police Service Advertiser', 14 April 1871; leading article.
31 'Police Service Advertiser', 2 August 1872.
32 The government grant in aid of police expenses was increased from a quarter to a half under the Police Expenses Act of 1874 (37 & 38 Vict. c.58), 'Police Guardian', 2 April 1875.
33 The excited correspondence that accompanied the 'Guardian''s publication of the minutes of evidence (in every detail — a far better record than the PP series) demonstrated the gratification that policemen felt.

34 PP 1875, xiii, p. 499.
35 The liberal MP for York and the government inspector for the northern region agreed that they both knew 'enough of rate-payers to be aware that payment to the police is not the most popular thing in the world, especially in the agricultural districts.' PP 1875, xiii, p. 389.

CHAPTER 8 — IDENTITY

1 'Police Service Advertiser', 7 April 1866.
2 'Police Service Advertiser', 14 April 1866; letter from 'X'.
3 Middlesbrough Town Council Meetings, 9 June, 11 August 1857, reported in the 'Stockton and Hartlepool Mercury', 14 June, 15 August 1857.
4 Sheffield Borough Records, Watch Committee Minutes (written), 15 December 1859.
5 'Police Service Advertiser', 9 February 1872.
6 'Police Service Advertiser', 12 January 1872; leading article.
7 I am grateful to V. A. C. Gatrell of Caius College, Cambridge for drawing my attention to this strike. It is likely that there were other earlier, untraced ones. Charles Reith lists the London strike of 1872 as the first, and policemen using him as their exemplar in writing their own history, have repeated this. Charles Reith, 'A New Study of Police History (Oliver & Boyd, Edinburgh 1956), p. 275.
8 'Manchester Guardian', 4, 11 June 1853.
9 'Manchester Guardian', 11 June 1853. The police issued this notice to 'The Gentry, Trades and Ratepayers in General of this City of Manchester'.
10 'Manchester Guardian', 18 June 1853.
11 'Manchester Guardian', 11 May, 11 June, 2, 6 July 1853.
12 'Manchester Guardian', 6 July 1853.
13 Ibid.
14 'Manchester Guardian', 4 June 1853.
15 'Manchester Guardian', 11 June 1853.
16 'Manchester Guardian', 6 July 1853.
17
18 'Manchester Guardian', 3, 10 August 1853.
19 'The Times', 23, 29 July, 12 August, 23 December 1853.
20 'The Times', 25 July 1853.
21 'Police Service Advertiser', 2 June 1871.
22 PP 1875, xiii, pp. 426, 428.
23 'Newcastle Chronicle', 23 September 1871.
24 'The Times', 11, 13 November 1871.
25 'Police Service Advertiser', 17 November 1871.
26 'The Times', 13, 21 May 1872. 'Western Morning News', 17 May 1872.
27 Provincial correspondents to the London press always placed police strikes in the context of local labour disputes.
28 Royden Harrison, 'Before the Socialists' (Routledge & Kegan Paul, London, 1965), pp. 241-2; 'Police Tyranny' (G. Osborne, London, 1885); 'The Revolution in the Police and the Coming Revolution in the Army' (London 1872 (?)).

29   Neither   'Revolution in the Police' (which speaks of the
     Metropolitan agitation as a contemporary struggle) nor
     'Police Tyrrany' (which documented the continuing efforts to
     obtain justice for Goodchild) mentioned provincial circum-
     stances. This Metropolitan perspective and contemporary
     understanding has dictated modern work on police unionism.
     Robert Reiner calls this Metropolitan action of 1872 'the
     first recorded instance of collective action by policemen'.
     Robert Reiner, 'The Blue Coated Worker: A Sociological Study
     of Police Unionism' (Cambridge University Press, Cambridge,
     1978), p. 19.
30   'Police Service Advertiser', 7 April 1867.
31   'Police Service Advertiser', 13 April 1867: 'The principle
     that involved the rejection of Mr Wrenn logically involved
     the election of Lord Tredegar's son-in-law.'
32   'Police Guardian', 30 March 1877.
33   'Police Service Advertiser', 11 May 1867; letter from
     'Justice'.
34   Correspondent 'Expertus' to the 'Chester Courant', quoted
     approvingly in the 'Police Guardian, 18 February 1876. For
     a police assertion of anti-militarism see '"Policeman Y", His
     Songs and Ballads on War and the Military' (London, 1872 (?)).
     This painfully colloquial set of ditties was probably not
     written by a policeman.
35   'Police Service Advertiser', 24 August 1867.
36   'Police Guardian', 6 June 1873; letter from 'Alpha'.
37   See Maureen Cain, Police Professionalism: Its Meaning and
     Consequence, 'Anglo-American Law Review', vol. 1, no. 2
     (1972), p. 221, for modern theories of policing as a craft
     or trade.
38   The 'Police Service Advertiser' did not just consist of 'a
     series of letters written by malcontents', as the chief con-
     stable of Surrey labelled it. It provided a free and much-
     needed legal service, especially for those officers engaged
     in the new field of administrative law: 'I have been employed
     as Inspector of Nuisances for the last three years, but I am
     not satisfied with the remuneration I receive . . . I shall be
     glad if some of your readers will . . . inform me what is the
     general rate . . . and . . . what is the latest law book on
     the subject.' 'Police Service Advertiser', 18 May 1867.
39   'Police Service Advertiser', 13 April 1867.
40   'Police Service Advertiser', 10 March 1866.
41   One chief constable remarked that no one who wasn't a police-
     man could pass a police exam, but then everyone who was,
     could. Dorset Constabulary (Inspector J. Gray), 'The Dorset-
     shire Constabulary 1856-1956' (Dorchester (?), 1956).
42   Pocket guides were guides to the law, and particularly to a
     policeman's own sphere of action. After 1856, many newly
     established forces reprinted the guides of the older forces
     established after 1839. Many of these had been written in
     the light of the first instructions issued to the Metropolitan
     police in 1829. See, for example, A Barrister and Chairman
     of Quarter Sessions, 'Police Hand Book' (Worcester, 1869).
     The most commonly used handbook was that of chief constable

Bicknell of Lincolnshire. It had gone through seven editions
by 1883. P. B. Bicknell, 'The Police Manual' (Shaw & Sons,
London, 1877).

43 The most consistent use of police officers as information-
gatherers was by the Convocation of Canterbury in 1869, when
the Lower House produced a report on intemperance that consisted almost entirely of police information and opinion.
'Report by the Committee on Intemperance for the Lower House
of the Convocation of the Province of Canterbury', 1869.
Police officers were used as information-gatherers and statisticians by the Childrens' Employment Commission (1862), and
for many other locally sitting Parliamentary commissions of
inquiry. They also collected information for the Poor Law
Board. All this was an extension of their normal function
within local communities: J. H. Bingham, 'The Period of the
Sheffield School Board, 1870-1903 (J. W. Northend, Sheffield,
1949), p. 62. 'The chief constable was approached and arrangements were made for the police to undertake the preparing of a
census of children. This was completed for £34.14.0d.'

44 Sheffield Borough Records, Watch Committee Minutes (written),
head constable's report to the watch committee, 5 July 1860.

45 Meeting of the Sheffield Borough Council Water Supply Sub-
Committee, 5 December 1864, reported in the 'Sheffield Daily
Telegraph', 6 December 1864.

46 Evidence of Mr Sadler, head constable of Stockport, to the
Select Committee on County Rates, PP 1850, xiii, pp. 199-200.

47 PP 1850, xiii, p. 199.

48 There is a good account of Sadler's life and work in A Magistrate, 'Public Instruction and Moral Improvement' (privately
printed, London, 1846). Head Constable Jackson of Sheffield
also caught the mid-Victorian imagination. See above, p.
178.

49 'Committee on Intemperance . . . Canterbury', (1869), pp.
45-6: 'In several instances I have known young men who in the
morning having received their yearly wages have gone to the
Statutes and been robbed and cheated of the whole . . . this
has caused them to run away and connect themselves with bad
company and eventually become thieves themselves.'

50 John Pearman, Memos . . ., pp. 163, 188-9, 239-40.

51 Cyril D. Robinson, The De-Radicalisation of the Policeman:
A Historical Analysis, 'Crime and Delinquency', vol. 24
(April 1978, p. 149.

52 'Committee on Intemperance . . . Canterbury' (1869), pp. 45-6.
Both the superintendents whose words are used here had spent
over half their police career in the Warwickshire force living
in the same station houses. 'Police and Constabulary Almanac
and Guide' 1858-69.

53 PP 1872, ix, p. 577. The head constable of Leeds was talking
here about arresting drunks.

54 'Report on Intemperence . . . Canterbury', 1869, pp. 135, 153.

55 John Pearman, Memos . . ., pp. 163, 238, 245.

56 PP 1862, xlv, pp. 446-7. 'On my inspection I found a police
statistical table at Woburn made by that able superintendent
. . . Mr Young . . . proves him to be an officer not only

conversant with his divisional duties, but with the internal
working of the whole force . . . .' No greater praise than
this, and from Major Cartwright too. William Young was a
famous man.

57 One anonymous superintendent told the Convocation of Canterbury about the working man from a 'good' home who married a
field girl who couldn't cook or clean. 'Is it much to be
wondered that he goes to the pub? Once there, who will say
where it will end . . .?' A woman should make a home for her
family 'instead of toiling all day in the fields, which is not
her place . . . .' This conventional plot was delivered up
on numerous occasions by policemen giving evidence to select
committees, and was used by Richard Jeffries in 'The Toilers
of the Field' (Longmans, Green, London, 1894), 'A True Tale',
pp. 259f.

58 John Pearman, Memos . . . ., pp. 194, 197.

59 'Police Guardian', 7 May 1875; letter from 'Cromwell'. See also
John Vincent, 'The Formation of the Liberal Party', (Constable,
London, 1966) pp. xxxix-xxx.

60 This material reward to life's long upward journey is to be
found recorded in the provincial press and the pages of temperance histories. See the life of Obed Caygill in P. T.
Winskill, 'The Temperance Movement and its Workers' (4 vols)
(Blackie, London, 1892), vol. 2, p. 45. See 'Police Service
Advertiser', 24 August 1867; letter from 'A PC from Wales'.
John Pearman, Memos . . . ., pp. 158-9: 'I was 17 years and
9 months stationed at Eton College and on my retirement Presented me with a Testimonal (sic.) in Velom (sic.) with the
words — To John Pearman of Eton We the Inhabitants of Eton
desire to convey to you on your retirement as Inspector of
Police for the past 18 years Our appreciation of the faithful
manner you fulfilled that office and beg your acceptance of
the accompanying Purse of money.'

61 'Report on Intemperance . . . Canterbury', 1869, p. 143.

62 George Eliot, 'Daniel Deronda', (Penguin, Harmondsworth,
1967), pp. 666-7.

63 'Police Guardian', 29 October 1875.

64 'Police Service Adviser', 24 February 1866; 'Police Guardian,
24 November 1876; 'Lamentation from Helmet'.

65 William Plomer (ed.), 'Kilvert's Diaries, 1870-1879' (3 vols)
(Jonathan Cape, London, 1938-1942); entry for 17 January 1873.

66 'Sheffield Daily Telegraph', 1 March 1867.

67 'Policeman! A Tract' (William MacIntosh, London, no date,
but almost certainly 1868), p. 5.

68 'Policeman!', pp. 5, 17-18.

69 PP 1877, xi, p. 61.

70 Dawson Burns, 'Temperance History', 2 vols (National Temperance
Publication Depot, London, 1889-1891), vol. 1, pp. 77, 244,
260; vol. 2, pp. 11, 51.

71 Church of England Temperance Society, Annual Subscription List,
1884. United Kingdom Alliance, reports for 1858-9, 1863-4,
1868-9, 1884-8. Winskill, 'Temperance Movement', vol. 3,
p. 45. PP 1852-3, xxxvii.

72 The earliest police temperance pledge card that has come to

light is of the 1880s, and the earliest surviving <u>record</u> of temperance organisation within a police force is in Northumberland County record Office, dated by the county archivist Mr R. M. Gard as 'not earlier than 1902 . . .'

73 'E.A.B.D' (E. A. Bland), 'Constable 42Z' (Religious Tract Society, London, 1887).

74 Bland, '42Z', p. 80.

75 'Police Guardian', 24 November 1876; 'Lamentation from Helmet'. The modern reader will find it easy to see that guilt was what propelled the misery of which policemen spoke so eloquently. Relationships with children ('for they are not to blame') occasioned it most overtly. See pp. 312-13', The City Arab'. See also Alexander Clark, 'Reminiscences of a Police Officer in the Granite City Thirty Years Since' (Aberdeen, 1873). This book was popular among policemen because it explored so well their own tension and misery: 'queer and disagreeable duties to perform. One of the most repulsive to my feelings was the apprehending of younsters in the time of frost for raising slides. The young rogues seemed so happy and full of enjoyment . . .' (p. 66) See also p. 33. How clearly Alexander Clark or the pseudonymous 'Helmet' actually felt guilty it is difficult to say. But in the 1870s the idea of 'duty' and its unfortunate necessity was readily available for use and it possibly compounded their sense of impotence.

76 PP 1875, xiii, p. 479.

77 The City Arab: A Policeman's Passing Thought, 'Police Guardian' 12 November 1875. The 'Advertiser' started to publish police poetry in 1872. Most of it dealt in the conventional currency of mid-Victorian parlour poetry; see for example 'W.G.B', 'Work No Degradation', 'Police Service Advertiser', 6 June 1872.

78 See Part One, pp. 62-3, and National Association for the Promotion of Social Science, 'Transactions', 1862, p. 510, and 1880, pp. 340-3 for some account of treatment received by ticket-of-leave men at the hands of the police.

79 'Police Guardian', 24 November 1876.

80 Any set of rules that followed the Metropolitan Rule Book used this formula. See above, p. 6, and pp. 18-30, xxiii, pp. 409-18 for an account of the Metropolitan police regulations of 1829.

81 'Rules and Regulations of the Oxfordshire Constabulary'; Buckinghamshire Record Office, Constabulary Records, unclassified material.

82 PP 1875, xiii, p. 479.

83 PP 1877, xi, pp. 427-8. That a borough policeman might seem to act individually and quickly in the case of street disorder for example, was really a reflection of the fact that in the small geographical unit of a town, his officers were likely to be closer, and the distance between him and the police office less.

CHAPTER 9 — POSSIBILITIES: THE EXAMPLE OF THE LICENCING LAWS

1 Northamptonshire Record Office, Miscellaneous Records, Police Journals, ML 202-12, Journal of Inspector George Williamson,

entry for 10 October 1866. The next day he was able to report
that he had 'called on the Revd. G. H. Capron at 9.15 a.m. and
got three summonses signed'.

2   Brian Harrison, 'Drink and the Victorians' (Faber & Faber,
London, 1971), pp. 889-90.

3   Buckinghamshire Record Office, Constabulary Records, General
Order Book, 2 September 1862.

4   PP 1872, x, p. 59.

5   Local solutions were a reflection of a national need. Middlesbrough watch committee permanently employed an attorney to act
in cases of assault on the police. Middlesbrough Town Council
Meeting, 10 January 1860, reported in the 'Stockton and Hartlepool Mercury', 14 January 1860. For Sheffield's attempt to get
a stipendary magistrate, Sheffield Borough Records, Town Council Minutes (printed), Report of the Stipendary Magistrate's
Committee, 13 January 1870.

6   PRO HO 45 OS 7210; PP 1862, iv, p. 195.

7   PRO HO 45 OS 7210/3.

8   PRO HO 45 OS 7210, letter from Walter Riddell county court
judge to Home Secretary. Staffordshire Record Office, Constabulary Records, Chief Constable's Reports, 27 June 1863.
For a similar arrangement in the West Riding, latters between
the chief constable and Lord Wharnecliffe, Sheffield Central
Library, Wharnecliffe Ms. Wh. M.418. Small ratepayers frequently made the charge that county police forces were used by
the landowning magistracy in the preservation of game. 'Cambridge Chronicle', 7 March 1857: 'the superintendent lives in
a retired situation in the fields, more like a preserver of
game than an officer of county police . . . .'

9   Hansard, Third Series, 168, p. 706. Ten years did not alter
George Grey's opinion: the decision to search rested 'entirely
with the policeman . . . and a policeman is often very imagina-
tive when it suits his purpose . . . the (Night Poaching Prevention) Act gave the policeman the power of imagination.' PP
1872, x, pp. 172-3. James Hawker, 'James Hawker's Journal:
A Victorian Poacher' (Oxford University Press, London, 1961),
p. 35. See also Joseph Arch's understanding of a policeman's
imagination, PP 1873, xiii, p. 384.

10   General Order, 12 August 1862, reprinted in PP 1872, x, pp.
22 f. PRO HO 45 OS 7210/13.

11   PP 1872, x, p. 76.

12   PP 1872, x, p. 75.

13   PP 1854, xiv, p. 256.

14   The Public House Closing Act, 1865 (28 & 29 Vict. c. 77).

15   The frequent changes in police power that the legislation of
the 1860s outlined actually curtailed police activity rather
than extended it. See the Public House Closing Acts of 1865
and 1866 (27 & 28 Vict. c. 64; 28 & 29 Vict. c.77) and the
Wine and Beerhouses Acts of 1869 and 1870 (32 & 33 Vict. c.27;
33 & 34 Vict. c.29).

16   'A policeman dare not go into a public house; he is surrounded
by enemies and people are only too glad to "put a knife into
him" . . . .' PP 1877, xi, p. 639.

17   In Northamptonshire the rate levied for paying parish con-

stables was greater where there were pubs or beer-houses. There were proposals to continue using them in this capacity as late as 1856. Northamptonshire Quarter Sessions, 11 April 1856, reported in the 'Northamptonshire Herald', 12 April 1856. For police systems growing out of supervision by parochial constables, see PP 1852-3, xxxvii, pp. 391-2.

18 PP 1852-3, xxxvii, p. 64.
19 PP 1852-3, xxxvii, p. 392.
20 PP 1852-3, xxxvii, p. 573.
21 'Report on Intemperance . . . Canterbury', 1869, p. 75.
22 'Report on Intemperance . . . Canterbury', 1869, pp. 75, 766, 78, 83.
23 Harrison, 'Drink and the Victorians', 1971, p. 889.
24 'Report on Intemperance . . . Canterbury', 1869, pp. 53-5.
25 PP 1872, ix, p. 488.
26 PP 1877, xi, p. 137.
27 PP 1877, xi, p. 139.
28 PP 1877, xi, pp. 199-200.
29 PP 1872, ix, p. 547.
30 PP 1872, ix, p. 577.
31 PP 1877, xi, p. 468.
32 PP 1877, xi, pp. 13, 468.
33 PP 1872, ix, pp. 491, 550.
34 Under the Licencing Act, 1874 (37 & 38 Vict. c.49).
35 PP 1877 xi, p. 436.
36 PP 1877, xi, p. 13.
37 PP 1877, xi, p. 203.
38 R. D. Storch, The Policeman as Domestic Missionary: Urban Discipline and Domestic Culture in Northern England, 1850-1880, 'Journal of Social History', vol. 4 (Summer 1976), pp. 504-8.
39 PP 1877, xi, p. 12.
40 PP 1877, xi, pp. 436, 487, 468. 'The Temperance Record', 18 December 1875 reported that five police inspectors of public houses had just been appointed in Birmingham.
41 PP 1877, xi, p. 130.
42 PP 1877, xi, p. 444.
43 PP 1877, xi, p. 383.
44 PP 1877, xi, p. 124. There is some evidence that temperance organisations, so uninterested in the constable on the beat in the 1860s, gave some attention to officers in the 1870s. The vigilance committees that were established in various provincial towns to aid the police in the prosecution of licencing offenders (when the local watch committee would not support its officers) usually restricted aid to the officer class. See a report of the Nottingham Templars and Teetotalers Vigilance Committee in the 'Cambridge Independent', 31 August 1871, and the work of the Bristol Vigilance Committee in PP 1877, xi, pp. 529, 537.
45 See Part One, pp. 56-9.

CHAPTER 10 — CONCLUSION

1 Raymond Williams, 'The Country and the City', (Paladin, St Albans, 1975), p. 151.

2 John Pearman, Memos. Late Sergeant Pearman, pp. 153, 157. Northamptonshire Record Office, Miscellaneous Records, Police Journals, ML 202-12, Journal of Inspector George Williamson, entry for 16 May 1866: 'In company with Supt Chambers Malsey and Const. Arnold in plain clothes making inquiry respecting a gipsy in the name of Herm who was wanted for stealing two horses from Radnorshire.'

3 Alexander Clark spoke of the thrill of detection being like that of hunting or fishing: 'neither however partakes of the same intensity of feeling which a detective feels in following up a criminal action . . . To my mind the difference seems to lie in the fact that in compassing the irrational you have an inferior adversary to deal with, while in hunting the human you are coping with your equal.' Alexander Clark, 'Reminiscences of a Detective Officer in the Granite City Thirty Years Since' (Aberdeen, 1873), p. 38. Under Scottish procedure a detective had a much wider sphere of action than he did in England: Thomas P. McNaught, 'The Recollections of a Glasgow Detective Officer (Simpkin & Marshall, London, 1887), pp. 11-12.

4 'Encyclopaedia Brittanica', 9th Edition, 1875-89, 'Police' (J. E. Davies).

5 'Brittanica', 'Police'. F. W. Maitland, 'Justice and Police' (Macmillan, London, 1885), chapter xi.

6 The process has been dealt with in more detail in the first part of this book. The government grant in aid of police expenses was increased in 1874 under the Police Expenses Act (37 & 38 Vict. c.58).

7 Sheffield Borough Records, Watch Committee Minutes (written), 10 April 1862. PP 1875, xxxiv, p. 127.

8 National Association for the Promotion of Social Science, 'Transactions', 1880, p. 327.

9 'Transactions', p. 340.

10 'Transactions', pp. 343, 353-4.

11 Robert Roberts, 'The Classic Slum' (Manchester University Press, Manchester, 1971), pp. 28-9. Graham Greene, 'The Confidential Agent' (Penguin, Harmondsworth, 1963).

12 Buckinghamshire County Record Office, Constabulary Records, General Order Book, 29 April 1857. Because Captain Carter did not need to be explicit it makes it difficult to know whether the salute was military or the cap touched in deference to ones betters. Probably the latter.

13 John Pearman, Memos . . . ., pp. 189, 192.

14 PP 1877, xv, pp. 85-9.

15 PP 1852-3, xxxvi, p. 64.

16 'Sheffield Daily Telegraph', 20 March 1862.

17 'Huddersfield Examiner', 19 April 1856.

18 Christopher Pulling, 'Mr Punch and the Police' (Butterworth, London, 1964).

19 'Sheffield Independent', 18 April 1867, Wedding Feast at Thurgoland: A Musical Policeman. This Fred Karno comedy has

proved irresistible to one modern commentator too, and this
comic turn from Eric Midwinter's 'Social Administration in
Lancashire' is based directly on the perceptions of the watch
committee clerk who recorded constable Dobson's aberrations
in the 1840s:

> he cheated on prison expenses; he spent his duty in bed when
> disorder was such that the militia was called out; he re-
> fused to wear his uniform; he drank excessively; he slept
> in front of the police station fire when he should have been
> on his beat; and when roused, he 'made water upon the floor
> and against the desk' . . . . (159-60).

20 See page 143.
21 George Speaight, 'Mr Punch: A History' (Studio Vista, London,
   1970), pp. 133, 138; 88-9.
22 'Huddersfield Examiner', 5 July, 1856.
23 PP 1877, xi, p. 639.

BIBLIOGRAPHY AND SOURCES

(i)   PUBLIC RECORD OFFICE MATERIAL

Home Office Records
HO 45   Material preserved as reference.
HO 63   Police returns.
HO 65   Correspondence with the provinces on police matters;
        out-letters.

(ii) COUNTY RECORD OFFICE MATERIAL

1 Buckinghamshire County Record Office
   Quarter Sessions Records, Volumes, 1839-80.
   Quarter Sessions Records, Rolls, 1839-45.
   Quarter Sessions Records, Bundles, 1856-80.
   The chief constable's reports to Quarter Sessions are found here
   Constabulary Records, Constabulary Committee Minute Books,
   1852-6.
   Constabulary Records, Register of Members of the Force,
   1857-80.
   Constabulary Records, General Order Books, 1857-80.
   Constabulary Records, unclassified letters.
   Family Papers, Carrington Papers, D/CN/CIa.
2 Northamptonshire County Record Office
   Poor Law Records, Brackley Board of Guardians, Minute
   Book, PL1/1; PL1/3; PL1/4.
   Poor Law Records, Brackley Board of Guardians, out-letters,
   PL1/47, PL1/48.
   Quarter Sessions Records, Miscellaneous, Mis. QS 331 Box
   no. X6788.
   Miscellaneous Records, Police Journals, ML 202-12, Journal
   of Inspector George Williamson.
   Family Papers, Cartwright Papers C(A) 14, C(A) 53/24, C(A)
   53/173, C(A) 53/180, C(A) 53/183, C(A) 55/12, C(A) 55/13,
   C(A) 55/15, C(A) 55/16, C(A) 55/17, C(A) 55/18, ZA 4692.
3 Staffordshire County Record Office
   Administrative Records, Applications for the Office of
   Chief Constable, 1857, 1866.

Administrative Records, Petitions to Quarter Sessions
Concerning the Constabulary.
Constabulary Records, Quarter Sessions Orders to the
Police.
Constabulary Records, Descriptive Register, 1842-63.
Constabulary Records, Return of Members of the Force,
1863-80.
Constabulary Records, Chief Constable's Reports to
Quarter Sessions, 1859-80.

(iii) BOROUGH RECORD OFFICE MATERIAL

1 Cambridge Borough Records, Town Council Minutes Volumes,
   1850-80.
   Cambridge Borough Records, Watch Committee Minutes Volumes,
   July 1869-May 1871.
   Cambridge Borough Records, Licencing Books, 1872-.
   Cambridge Borough Records, Corporation Rentals Books,
   1847, 1861, 1870, 1878.
   Cambridge Borough Records, Police Records, Rule Books,
   1842, 1857.
2 Sheffield Borough Records, Town Council Minutes Volumes,
   1850-. (printed).
   Sheffield Borough Records, Watch Committee Minutes
   Volumes, 1850-, (written).
   Sheffield Borough Records, Newspaper Cuttings Relating
   to Sheffield, Vols 1 and 2.
   Sheffield Central Library, Wharncliffe Ms. Wh. M 418
   (1868, A-Gra).
3 Stratford Borough Records, Police Records, Police Books
   D, Police Officers' Report Book, November 1865-December
   1866; Police Books B1, Superintendent's Report Book,
   February 1863-May 1889.

(iv) PRIVATE PAPERS

1 Disraeli Papers, The National Trust, Hughenden Manor,
   Letters, B/xxi/P/298-9.
2 John Pearman, Memos. of Late Sergeant John Pearman of
   Her Mgt 3rd or King's Own Light Dragoons.
   Privately owned document, 268pp.

(v) NEWSPAPERS

'Buckinghamshire Advertiser'
'Buckinghamshire Record'
'Cambridge Chronicle'
'Cambridge Independent'
'Huddersfield Chronicle'
'Huddersfield Examiner'
'Kent Herald'

'Law Times'
'Maidstone Gazette'
'Maidstone Journal'
'Manchester Guardian'
'Newcastle Chronicle'
'Northamptonshire Herald'
'Northamptonshire Mercury'
'Police Guardian' (1873-.)
'Police Service Advertiser' (1866-72)
'Sheffield Daily Telegraph'
'Sheffield Independent'
'South Eastern Gazette'
'Staffordshire Advertiser'
'Stockton and Hartlepool Mercury and Middlesbrough Gazette'
'The Times'
'Western Morning News'

(vi)   MISCELLANEOUS PRINTED MATERIAL

Annual Reports of the Church of England Temperance Society.
Annual Reports of the United Kingdom Alliance
'Police and Constabulary Almanac and Guide', published
annually, Manchester, 1858- .
'Report by the Committee on Intemperance for the Lower House
of the Convocation of the Province of Canterbury', 1869.
The National Association for the Promotion of Social Science,
'Transactions', 1857-80.

(vii)   DIRECTORIES

1 Local directories
   'Directory of Buckinghamshire', Mosson & Craven, 1853.
   'Directory of Buckinghamshire', Kelly Ω Co., 1864.
   'Directory of Buckinghamshire, Cambridgeshire and Hert-
   fordshire', Cassey & Co., 1865.
   'Royal County Directory of Buckinghamshire, Berkshire
   and Oxfordshire', Harrods, 1876.
   'Post Office Directory of Cambridgeshire, Norfolk, and
   Suffolk', Kelly & Co., 1846.
   'Post Office Directory of Cambridgeshire', Kelly & Co.,
   1864.
   'The Cambridge Directory', 1866.
   'Street and General Directory of Cambridge', 1875, 1878.
   'History Gazetteer and Directory of Leicestershire',
   William White, Sheffield, 1863, 1877.
   'Business Directory of Sheffield', J. S. C. Morris, 1862.
   'General Directory and Topography of the Borough of
   Sheffield', William White, Sheffield, 1864.
   'General and Commercial Directory of Sheffield',
   William White, Sheffield, 1871- .
   'History, Gazetteer and Directory of the County of
   Staffordshire', William White, Sheffield, 1851.

'Post Office Directory of Birmingham, with . . . Stafford-shire', Kelly & Co., 1854- .

2   Subject directories
Frederick Boase, 'Modern English Biography', 1892; supple-ment, 1908.
J. B. Burke, 'Landed Gentry', 1850- .
J. B. Burke, 'Peerage', 1850- .
Crockford, 'Clerical Directory', 1860- .
C. R. and R. P. Dodd, 'The Parliamentary Pocket Companion'.
R. P. Dodd, 'The Peerage, Baronetage, and Knightage of Great Britain'.
E. Walford, 'The County Families of the United Kingdom'.

(viii) PARLIAMENTARY PAPERS SERIES

Returns Relating to the Metropolitan Police	PP 1830, xxiii
Report of the Select Committee on Metropolitan Police and Crime	PP 1834, xvi
Report of the Constabulary Commissioners	PP 1839, xix
Bill, for the Payment of Parish Constables	PP 1841, i
Bill, for the Payment of Parish Constables	PP 1842, iii
Bill, for the Payment of Parish Constables	PP 1844, i
Bill, for the Payment of Parish Constables	PP 1850, v
Bill, for the Payment of Parish Constables	PP 1852, iii
Returns Relative to the Poor Law	PP 1847-8, liii
Report of the Select Committee on the County Rates and Expenditure Bill	PP 1850, xiii
Report of the Select Committee on Police	PP 1852-3, xxxvi
Returns Relating to Superintending Con-stables	PP 1852-3, lxxvii
Bill to Render More Effective the Police	PP 1854, v
Report of the Select Committee on Public Houses	PP 1854, xiv
Return from all local Boards of Health acting under the Public Health or Local Government Acts	PP 1857 (Sess. 2), xli
Returns Relating to the Poor Laws	PP 1857-8, xxviii
Report of HMIC for 1857	PP 1857-8, xlvii
Report of HMIC for 1858	PP 1859 (Sess. 1), xxii
Report of HMIC for 1859	PP 1860 lvii
Return Relating to the Wages of Agricultural Labourers	PP 1861, l
Report of the Select Committee on the Education of Destitute Children	PP 1861, vii
Report of HMIC for 1860	PP 1861, lii
Bill, to Amend the Law for Rendering more Effectual the Police	PP 1862, iv

Report of HMIC for 1861	PP 1862, xlv
Report of HMIC for 1862	PP 1863, l
Return Relating to the Police Forces of England	PP 1864, xxxv
Children's Employment Commissioners (Fifth Report)	PP 1866, xxiv
Report of HMIC for 1865	PP 1866, xxxiv
18th Annual Report of the Poor Law Board	PP 1866, xxxv
Return of Salaries and Allowances Paid to the Rural Police	PP 1866, lviii
Report of an Inquiry into Acts of Intimidation etc. . . by Trade Unionists in Sheffield	PP 1867, xxxii
Report of HMIC for 1866	PP 1867, xxxvi
Return of all districts where the Public Health Act (1848) or the Local Government Act (1858) are in Force	PP 1867, lix
Employment of Women and Children in Agriculture, (First Report of Commissioners)	PP 1867-8, xvii
Report by Examiners into Acts of Intimidation etc. . . by Trade Unionists in Manchester	PP 1867-8, xxxix
Report of HMIC for 1868	PP 1867-8, xxxvi
Return of Local Boards in England . . . Acting under the Public Health or Local Government Acts	PP 1867-8, lviii
Return of the Weekly Earnings of Agricultural Labourers	PP 1868-9, l
Employment of Women and Children in Agriculture (Second Report of Commissioners)	PP 1868-9, xiii
Report of HMIC for 1869	PP 1868-9, xxxi
Report of the Select Committee on the Protection of Infant Life	PP 1871, vii
Report of HMIC for 1870	PP 1871, xxviii
Report of Royal Commission on Contagious Diseases	PP 1871, xix
Report of the Select Committee on Habitual Drunkards	PP 1872, ix
Report on the Game Laws of the United Kingdom	PP 1872, x
Report of HMIC for 1871	PP 1872, xxx
Report on the Game Laws of the United Kingdom	PP 1873, xiii
Report of the Select Committee on Police Superannuation Funds	PP 1875, xiii
Report of HMIC for 1875	PP 1876, xxxiv
Report of the Select Committee on Intemperance	PP 1877, xi
Report of the Select Committee on Police Superannuation Funds	PP 1877, xv
Report of HMIC for 1876	PP 1877, xlii

Report of HMIC for 1879	PP 1878-9, xxxiii
Report of HMIC for 1880	PP 1881, li
Report of HMIC for 1881	PP 1882, xxxiii

(ix)   BOOKS AND ARTICLES

ANGLESEY, MARQUESS OF, 'Sergeant Pearman's Memoirs' (Jonathan Cape, London, 1968).

BAGWELL, PHILIP S., 'The Railwaymen: The History of the National Union of Railwaymen' (George Allen & Unwin, London, 1963).

BAILEY, VICTOR (ed.), 'Policing and Punishment in Nineteenth Century Britain' (Croom Helm, London, 1981).

A BARRISTER, and CHAIRMAN OF QUARTER SESSIONS','Police Handbook' (Worcester, 1869).

BATEMAN, JOHN, 'Great Landowners of Great Britain' (Harrison, London, 1878).

BELLE BRITTAN (HIRAM FULLER), 'Sparks from a Locomotive' (Derby & Jackson, New York, 1859).

BENTHAM, JEREMY, 'Idea of a Proposed All Comprehensive Body of Law' (J. M. M'Creery, London, 1822).

BEST, GEOFFREY, 'Mid-Victorian Britain, 1851-1875' (Weidenfeld & Nicolson, London, 1971).

BICKNELL, P. B. 'The New Police Manual' (Shaw & Sons, London, 1877).

BINGHAM, J. H. 'The Period of the Sheffield School Board, 1870-1903' (J. W. Northend, Sheffield, 1949).

'E.A.B.D' (E. A. BLAND), 'Constable 42Z' (The Religious Tract Society, London, 1887).

BORDUA, DAVID J., 'The Police: Six Sociological Essays' (Wiley, New York, 1967).

BOWRING, J. 'Works of Jeremy Bentham', 3 vols (W. Tait, Edinburgh, 1843).

BROEKER, GALEN, 'Rural Disorder and Police Reform in Ireland' (Routledge & Kegan Paul, London, 1970).

BURNS, DAWSON, 'Temperance History', 2 vols (National Temperance Publication Depot, London, 1880-1891).

'J.W.C', 'The Militia as an Army of Reserve' (Thomas Hatchard, London, 1856).

CAIN, MAUREEN, Police Professionalism: Its Meaning and Consequence, 'Anglo-American Law Review', vol. 1, no. 2 (1972), pp. 217-31.

CAIN, MAUREEN, 'Society and the Policeman's Role' (Routledge & Kegan Paul, London, 1973).

CAIN, MAUREEN, Trends in the Sociology of Police Work, 'International Journal of the Sociology of the Law', vol. 7 (1979), pp. 143-67.

CENTURION, 'A Few Words on the Military Organisation of Great Britain' (James Ridgeway, London, 1860).

CHADWICK, EDWIN, 'On a Preventative Police' (extracted from the 'London Review' and privately printed, London, 1829).

CLARK, ALEXANDER, 'Reminiscences of a Police Officer in the Granite City Thirty Years Since' (Aberdeen, 1873).

CRITCHLEY, T. A., 'A History of Police in England and Wales, 900-1966' (Constable, London, 1967).

CROSSTHWAITE, J. FISHER, 'A Brief Memoir of Major General Sir John George Woodford' (privately printed, London, 1881).

CUNNINGHAM, HUGH, 'The Volunteer Force' (Croom Helm, London, 1975).

DAVIES, W. E. 'Police', 'Encyclopaedia Brittanica' (9th edition, London, 1875-89).

DICKENS, CHARLES, 'The Uncommercial Traveller' (Penguin, Harmondsworth, 1964).

DONZELOT, JACQUES, 'The Policing of Families' (Random House, New York, 1979).

DORSET CONSTABULARY (INSPECTOR J. GRAY) 'The Dorsetshire Constabulary, 1856-1956' (Dorchester (?), 1956).

ELIOT, GEORGE, 'Daniel Deronda' (Penguin, Harmondsworth, 1967).

EVANS, GEORGE EWART, 'Where Beards Wag All' (Faber & Faber, London, 1970).

FINER, S. E., 'The Life and Times of Sir Edwin Chadwick' (Methuen, London, 1952).

FURNESS, JOSEPH M., 'Municipal Affairs in Sheffield' (W. Townsend, Sheffield, 1893).

GOSDEN, P. H. J. H. 'Friendly Societies in England, 1815-1875' (Manchester University Press, Manchester, 1961).

GREENE, GRAHAM, 'The Confidential Agent' (Penguin, Harmondsworth, 1963).

GRICE, J. WATSON, 'National and Local Finance' (P. S. King and Son, London, 1910).

HALL, STUART et al., 'Policing the Crisis' (Macmillan, London, 1978).

HARDY, E. 'How to Repel Invasion: The Rural Police of England and Auxiliary to Rifle Corps' (R. Hardwicke, London, 1859).

HARRISON, BRIAN, 'Drink and the Victorians' (Faber & Faber, London, 1971).

HARRISON, ROYDEN, 'Before the Socialists' (Routledge & Kegan Paul, London, 1965).

HARRISON, WILLIAM, 'The Description of England' (1587) (Cornell University Press, New York, 1968).

HART, J. M., The Reform of the Borough Police, 1835-1856, 'English Historical Review', vol. 70 (1955), p. 411.

HART, J. M., The County and Borough Police Act, 1856, 'Public Administration', vol. 34 (1956), p. 405.

HASBACH, W., 'A History of the English Agricultural Labourer' (P. S. King, London, 1908).

HAWKER, JAMES, 'James Hawker's Journal: A Victorian Poacher' (Oxford University Press, London, 1961).

HEATH, F. G., 'The English Peasantry' (F. Warne & Co., London, 1874).

HENNOCK, E. P., Compositions of Borough Councils, in Urban History Group, 'The Study of Urban History' (Edward Arnold, London, 1968).

JEFFRIES, RICHARD, 'The Toilers of the Field' (Longmans Co., London, 1894).

McCLURE, JAMES, 'Spike Island: Portrait of a British Police Force' (Macmillan, London, 1980).

McKENNA, FRANK, 'The Railway Workers' (Faber, London, 1980).

MacLAREN, J. ANDERSON, The Police Authorities of the United Kingdom: Their Constitution, Revenue and Responsibility at Law, 'Judicial Review', vol. 22 (1910), p. 46.

McNAUGHT, THOMAS P. 'The Recollections of a Glasgow Detective Officer' (Simpkin & Marshall, London, 1887).

A MAGISTRATE (R. ASPLAND), 'Public Instruction and Moral Improve-
    ment' (privately printed, London, 1846).
MAITLAND, F. W. 'Justice and Police' (Macmillan & Co., London,
    1885).
MANGING, INSPECTOR, 'The First Hundred Years of the North Riding
    Constabulary' (Northallerton, 1956).
MARK, SIR ROBERT, 'Policing a Perplexed Society' (George Allen &
    Unwin, London, 1977).
MATHER, F. C., 'Public Order in the Age of the Chartists' (Man-
    chester University Press, Manchester, 1959).
MIDWINTER, ERIC, 'Social Administration in Lancashire, 1830-1860'
    (Manchester University Press, Manchester, 1969).
'Militia: The Proper Field Force' (T. & W. Boone, London, 1859).
OSBORN, NEIL, 'The Story of the Hertfordshire Police' (Letchworth,
    1969).
PARRIS, HENRY, The Home Office and the Provincial Police, 1856-
    1870, 'Public Law' (1961), p. 230.
PARRIS, HENRY, 'Constitutional Bureaucracy' (George Allen & Unwin,
    London, 1969).
PEARSON, S., 'The Lincolnshire Constabulary' (Lincoln, 1957).
PHILIPS, DAVID, 'Crime and Authority in Victorian England' (Croom
    Helm, London, 1977).
PLOMER, WILLIAM (ed.), 'Kilvert's Diaries, 1870-1879', 3 vols
    (Jonathan Cape, London, 1938-42).
'Policeman! A Tract' (William MacIntosh, London, 1868).
'POLICEMAN Y', 'His Songs and Ballads of War and the Military'
    (London, 1872).
'Police Tyranny' (G. Osborne, London, 1885).
POLLARD, SYDNEY, 'The Sheffield Outrages' (Adams & Dart, Bath,
    1971).
PULLING, CHRISTOPHER, 'Mr Punch and the Police' (Butterworth,
    London, 1964).
QUINLIVAN, PATRICK and ROSE, PAUL, 'The Fenians in England 1865-
    1872' (John Calder, London, 1982).
READE, CHARLES, 'Put Yourself in His Place' (Smith Elder & Co.,
    London, 1870).
REDLICH J. and HIRST F. W., 'Local Government in England', 2 vols
    (Macmillan & Co., London, 1903).
REINER, ROBERT, 'The Blue Coated Worker: A Sociological Study of
    Police Unionism' (Cambrdige University Press, Cambridge,
    1978).
REINER, ROBERT, The Police, Class and Politics, 'Marxism Today,
    vol. 22, no. 3 (March 1978), pp. 69-80.
REINER, ROBERT, The Police in the Class Structure, 'British Journal
    of Law and Society', vol. 5, no. 2 (Winter, 1978), pp. 166-84.
REITH, CHARLES, 'The Police Idea' (Oxford University Press, London,
    1938).
REITH, CHARLES, 'Police Principles and the Problem of War' (Oxford
    University Press, London, 1940).
REITH, CHARLES, 'The British Police and the Democratic Ideal'
    (Oxford University Press, London, 1943).
REITH, CHARLES, 'A Short History of the British Police' (Oxford
    University Press, London, 1948).
REITH, CHARLES, 'The Blind Eye of History' (Faber & Faber, London,
    1952).

REITH, CHARLES, 'A New Study of Police History' (Oliver & Boyd, Edinburgh, 1956).

'The Revolution in the Police and the Coming Revolution in the Army' (London, 1872).

ROBERTS, ROBERT, 'The Classic Slum' (Manchester Universtiy Press, Manchester, 1971).

ROBINSON, CYRIL D., The De-Radicalisation of the Policeman: A Historical Analysis, 'Crime and Delinquency', vol. 24 (April, 1978), pp. 129-51.

ROBINSON, CYRIL D., Ideology as History: A Look at the Way Some English Police Historians Look at the Police, 'Police Studies', vol. 2, no. 2 (Summer 1979), pp. 35-49.

SIMPSON, H. B., The Office of Constable, 'English Historical Review', vol. 10 (1895), pp. 625.

SMELLIE, K. B., 'A History of Local Government' (George Allen & Unwin, London, 1946).

SPEAIGHT, GOERGE, 'Punch and Judy: A History' (Studio Vista, London, 1970).

SPIERS, EDWARD M., 'The Army and Society' (Longmans, London, 1980).

STAINTON, J. H., 'The Making of Sheffield 1865-1914' (E. Weston & Sons, Sheffield, 1924).

STANLEY, C. R., 'The Birth and Early History of the Leicestershire Constabulary' (Leicester, 1954).

STEDMAN JONES, GARETH, 'Outcast London' (Clarendon Press, Oxford, 1971).

STORCH, R. D., The Policeman as Domesdtic Missionary: Urban Discipline and Domestic Culture in Northern England, 1850-1880, 'Journal of Social History', vol. 4 (Summer 1976), pp. 487.

TABRUM, BURNETT, 'A Short History of the Essex Constabulary' (Essex County Chronicle, Chelmsford, 1911).

THOMPSON, FLORA, 'Lark Rise to Candleford' (Oxford University Press, London, 1965).

THOMPSON, S. P., 'Maintaining the Queen's Peace' (Birkenhead, 1958).

VINCENT, J. R., 'The Formation of the Liberal Party' (Constable, London, 1966).

SOMERS VINE, J. R., 'English Municipal Institutions' (Waterlow & Sons, London, 1879).

WALLER, STANLEY, 'Cuffs and Handcuffs' (Rochdale, 1957).

WATT, IAN A., 'A History of the Hampshire and Isle of White Constabulary, 1839-1966' (Winchester, 1967).

WEBB, S. and B., 'The Parish and the County' (Longmans Green & Co., London, 1906).

WEBB, SIDNEY, 'Grants in Aid' (Longmans Green & Co., London, 1920).

WILLIAMS, RAYMOND, 'The Country and the City' (Paladin, St Albans, 1975).

WOODFORD, SIR JOHN GEORGE, 'Remarks on Military Flogging' (Keswick, 1835).

WINSKILL, P. T., 'The Temperance Movement and Its Workers', 4 vols (Blackie & Sons, London, 1892).

'White Rose: Journal of the West Riding Constabulary', vol. 16 (1956).

INDEX

Adulterated Food Act (1875), 54
'Alpha', 138
army, 3, 4, 80, 138; used in local disturbance, 23, 32; during Murphy riots, 37

Birmingham, 108
Blackburn, 23
Bolckow & Vaughan (Middlesbrough), 46
borough town councils, 45, 150
Brackley Poor Law Union (Northamptonshire), 57
Brayshaw, Richard (detective officer, Sheffield), 123, 144
Brighton, 86
Broadhead, William, 67
Bruce, H. A., 29
Burton-on-Trent: maltings, 88

Caistor (Lincolnshire), 18
Carrington, Lord, 49
Carter, Captain (chief constable, Buckinghamshire), 49
Cartwright, Major General Sir William (HMIC), 38-9, 56-9, 142
Chadwick, Edwin, 8, 22
Chambers, James (constable, Hertfordshire), 123, 146, 147
Cheetham, Harold (ex-policeman, Stockport), 4
Cheshire, 51
Children's Employment Commission (1862), 45
City of London Police, 102, 117, 134
Cobbe, Colonel (HMIC), 41, 150
Cockeridge, Superintendent (Hertfordshire), 70
constables, 65; additional constables, 45-6; appointed under local act, 14; parish constables, 13-15, 158; special constables: used in Murphy Riots, 34
'contamination': policemen's social theory, 140-1
Convocation of Canterbury, 152
county chief constables, 43, 46-7, 137, 150; and Home Office, 29; social background, 47-8; and Volunteer movement, 29
County Rate Expenditure Bills (1850s), 25
Coventry Ribbon Strike (1860), 33
Crimean War, 3, 23, 25, 57, 163
Criminal Justice Act (1855), 20
Chandos, Marquis of, 39
'Cromwell', 142, 161
Curtis, Sergeant (Sheffield), 125

Davies, J. E., 158
'D.C.C.', 137
deputy chief constables, 137
detection, detectives, 158; see also Brayshaw, Richard
Devonshire, 85
Dickens, Charles, 7
Disraeli, Benjamin, 39
Dublin Metropolitan Police strike (1873), 136
Dundee City police strike (1873), 136
Durham, County, 112

Essex constabulary, 21-2, 23, 39
East Coker (Somerset), 87
East Riding of Yorkshire, 31

Eton, 118
Excise: as licencing authority, 151
Explosives Act (1875), 54, 55

Fenian Disturbances, 32-3
'42Z' (Religious Tract Society), 145
'Fourth Class Constable', 127
'Freedom', 128

Game Laws, 6, 30-1, 51, 63; see also Night Poaching Prevention Act
Girdlestone, Canon, 85
Glossop, Mr (head constable, Birmingham), 135
Goodchild, Constable (Metropolitan Police), 136
Great Marlow (Buckinghamshire), 112
Green, Constable (Birmingham), 114, 143
Grey, Sir George, 25, 27, 28, 31, 62, 131

Hampshire constabulary, 126
Harrison, William: 'A Description of England', 65
head constables, 28, 43; of Cambridge, 31; of Sheffield, 159; of Wolverhampton, 120
Her Majesty's Inspectors of Constabulary, 26, 38-41, 54, 139, 152
Home Office, 27-32; circular on county pay, 131; Home Secretaries, 29-30; Instructions to police (1840), 31; Parliamentary Staff, 30; Permanent Under Secretary, 28, 29, 32, 33; relationship with provinces, 3; use of police in local administration, 54
Huddersfield, 162; Improvement Commission, 114
Hull police strike (1853), 134
Humphries, Superintendent (Warwickshire), 141

invasion fears, 90

'Justice', 161

Kilvert, Francis, 7, 118, 143
Kirkland, Constable (Sheffield), 162

Lancashire, 85
legal commentators, 158
Leicester, 145
Leicestershire, 51, 52
Lewis, Mrs, 118
Licencing Act (1872), 153, 154; licencing laws, 44, 150
Lighting and Watching Act (1833), 15
Lincoln: election riot, 33
Little Milton (Oxfordshire), 88
Liverpool, 153, 155
Local Government Act (1858) 15, 16; Local Government, County Councils Act (1888), 55
lords lieutenant, 19, 49
Ludlam, Superintendent (Lancashire), 35
Lynn, John (head constable of Devonport), 145

MacHardy, John Bunch Bonnemaison (chief constable of Essex), 22
magistrates: rural, 18-19, 47, 50, 52, 147
Malmesbury (Wiltshire), 88
Manchester police strike (1853), 132-4
Metropolitan police, 57, 87, 134, 145; Metropolitan police acts, 6, 149; Commissioners, 5; Instructions to: 6; as model for provincial forces, 5, 9, 17-8, 22; 'principle of prevention', 17-8
Middlesbrough, 42, 46, 89, 132
militarism in police forces, 137-8
militia, 161; see also police: defensive force; Militia Acts (1850s), 24; militia, local connections, 24; used in Murphy Riots, 34
militiamen, 3
Millbank prison, 87
Moore, Sir John ('Military Training'; 'Moral Training'), 4, 38
Municipal Corporations Act, 6, 60 see also police legislation;

police clauses: 14, 27, 42
Murphy, William, 33-4, 120
Murphy Riots (1866-71), 3, 14,
    32-8; in Ashton, 35, 38; in
    Bacup, 35; in Blackburn, 37,
    38; in Bradford, 34; in
    Birmingham, 35, 37; in Dukin-
    field, 35; in Manchester, 36;
    in Oldham, 35; in Staly-
    bridge, 34, 35

National Association for the
    Promotion of Social Science, 29
New Model Army, 4
Newcastle-upon-Tyne police
    strike (1871), 135
Nicholls, Constable (Sheffield),
    103
Night Poaching Prevention Act
    (1862), 147, 149, 150
Northampton, 81, 85, 87
Norwich, 155
Nottingham, 81

Offlow Hundred (Stafford-
    shire), 86
Ontario, Canada, 85
Orange Order, 121

Palmerston: police bill of
    1854, 26, 27
Parochial Assessment Act
    (1836), 61
Parris, Henry, 28, 32
Pearman, John (inspector,
    Buckinghamshire), 80, 112,
    114, 117, 118, 140-1, 142,
    158, 160
Penal Servitude Acts (1853,
    1864, 1871), 25, 63; see
    also transportation
Peninsula War, 4, 38
petty sessional division, 2;
    a basis for police distribution,
    47, 50; relationship with
    quarter sessions, 19
Philips, David, 70
police (see also boroughs, chief
    constables, constables, head
    constables, Royal Irish Con-
    stabulary, superintending
    constables, watch committees)
    accountability, 31;
    assault on, 154-5, 162;

as basis for defensive forces,
    19-20, 22, 23-4; see also
    militia; Volunteers;
    burial funds, 125;
    committees of quarter sessions,
    47, 49;
    conference (1872), 129;
    'Police and Constabulary Al-
    manac and Guide', 51;
    'discretion', 6, 146, 155;
    distribution: counties, 2,
    51-2; hierarchy based on
    division, 105; ratio police to
    population in divisions, 39,
    50; see also petty sessional
    division; police officers;
    and drink, 107, 108, 144, 151,
    162; see also licencing laws;
    education, 103-4, 138;
    families, 115-6, 161;
    'Police Guardian', 9;
    history, 1;
    journals, 103, 122;
    legislation, 18-9, 62; con-
    solidation, 26, 29; grant-in-
    aid, 27, 55, 62; objections
    to, 59; and vagrancy, 57;
    County and Borough Police Act
    (1856), 2, 6, 16, 24, 25-7,
    32, 41, 42, 49, 53, 69, 114,
    124; Inspectors of Constabul-
    ary, 38; impact on boroughs,
    42; County and Borough Police
    Act (1859), 124; Police and
    Constabulary Act (1840), 45,
    124; Rural Police Act (1839),
    47, 60; Special Constables
    Acts (1842; 1850), 18; Super-
    intending Constables Acts
    (1842; 1850), 14, 18; see also
    Municipal Corporations Act,
    Lighting and Watching Act,
    Local Government Act, Public
    Health Act;
    literacy, 103, 107, 110, 138;
    living accommodation, 117-18;
    rent: 112-3;
    used in local administration,
    8, 15-6, 39, 42-3, 53-5, 113,
    138, 149; as assistant poor
    law relieving officers, 53-4;
    as inspectors of weights and
    measures, 53;
    marital status, 81;

mortality, 121;
Police Mutual Assurance Association, 40, 126, 127, 129,
142;
neutrality, 5-6;
'Police News', 7;
officers, 105, 119;
officer mobility, 17; sergeants, 40;
orphanage, 40, 120;
pay, 108-10, 111, 113-4;
allowances, 113;
method of payment, 108;
sick pay, 108;
poetry, 146;
promotion, 40, 96, 97,
105-8, 113, 115; 'merit
class', 107;
recruits: age, 80; back-
ground, 69-79; Irish
background, 70, 78-9; 85;
previous trades, 73, 76;
rural and industrial, 89;
religion, 120, 121;
rule books, 5, 138;
seen as servants, 7, 31, 37,
130, 160;
'Police Service Advertiser',
9, 125-6, 128, 132;
superannuation, 38, 40, 41,
124-5; system of gratuities,
125; bills, 128;
trade unionism, 129; strike
action, 130, 131, 132-6;
turnover, 92-6, 161;
working hours, 122
policing, 8, 14
policemen: legal definition, 32
Preston, 155
Prevention of Crimes Acts, 146;
see also Penal Servitude
Acts
Public Health Act (1848), 15, 55
'Punch', 162

rates: poor rates, police rates,
61; rate law, 159; rate-
payers, 59-63; county rate-
payers, 25, 47; ratepayers
and the Home Office, 25,
28; urban ratepayers and
the Murphy Riots, 37-38;
ratepaying politics, 42-4
Raynor, Constable (Cambridge),
108
Reading, 87
Reith, Charles, 4, 5; on police
and public relations, 17
Riot Damages Act (1882), 37-8
Robinson, Cyril D., 141
Rochdale, 44
Rose Inn, Thurgoland (Lancashire), 162
Rowan, Charles, 5, 18
Royal Irish Constabulary,
21, 22-3, 24
Ruxton, Captain (chief constable of Kent), 29, 90
Sadler, Mr (head constable of
Stockport), 140
Select Committee on the Police
(1853), 18, 21, 22, 23;
(1875), 129-30
Sheffield, 43, 68, 103, 105,
132, 139; Sheffield watch
committee, 67
social discipline, 52, 96-7,
119, 150, 161
Stafford: boot and shoe
trade, 87
statistical surveillance, 27,
42, 45, 139, 140; col-
lection of criminal statistics, 27
Stoke Mandevill (Buckinghamshire), 88
Stratford-upon-Avon, 55, 122
Summary Jurisdiction Act
(1879), 159-60
Sunderland, 125
superintending constable system, 14-5, 19-21, 47;
origins in Kent, 19-20;
see also constables; police
officers
Swing, 163

Teignsham (Devon), 88
temperance organisations, 144
Thompson, Flora, 118
town councils, see boroughs
Town Police Clauses Act (1847),
15
Turrell, Gilbert (head constable, Cambridge), 31,
105
Turrell, Mrs, 118
trade dispute, 105

transportation, 25; ticket-of-leave system, 25, 63; see also Penal Servitude Act and Prevention of Crimes Acts

vagrancy, 25-6, 56-9; in Northamptonshire, 56-8; ticket-of-way system, 57-8; Vagrancy Act (1824), 56; vagrancy laws, 147; 'vagrant crime', 40, 53, 62
'Verdad', 126, 127, 128
Volunteer movement, 29, 32
Volunteers: plans to use police as volunteers, 20, 40; used in Murphy Riots, 34

Waddington, Horatio, 32
watch committees, 43-5, 81, 125, 130, 155; attitudes to police, 114-5; and head constables, 31, 46-7; and Home Office, 28; judicial role, 31, 43-4; legal status, 21; see also borough town councils
West Riding of Yorkshire, 43, 85
Widows and Orphans Fund of the Wiltshire Constabulary, 125
Wigan, 23, 120
Wild, Superintendent (Warwickshire), 141
Williamson, George (inspector, Northamptonshire), 120, 122, 147
Willis, Captain (HMIC), 39
Wilson, Constable (Lancashire), 162
Wiltshire, 50
Wine and Beerhouses Act (1869), 153
Woodford, Captain (HMIC), 39
Wrenn, Mr (superintendent, Merthyr Tydfil), 137
Wycombe (Buckinghamshire): furniture manufacturies, 85

'X', 131

yeomanry, 33, 38; used in Murphy Riots, 34
Young, William (superintendent, Bedfordshire), 127, 142